Life from Scratch

Life from Scratch

a memoir of food,
family, and forgiveness

SASHA MARTIN

NATIONAL GEOGRAPHIC

Washington, D.C.

Published by the National Geographic Society
1145 17th Street N.W., Washington, D.C. 20036

Library of Congress Cataloging-in-Publication Data
Martin, Sasha.
  Life from scratch : a memoir of food, family, and forgiveness / Sasha Martin.
    pages cm
  Includes index.
  ISBN 978-1-4262-1374-8 (hardback)
  1. Martin, Sasha. 2. Cooks--United States--Biography. 3. Cooks--United States--Family relationships. I. Title.
  TX140.M37A3 2015
  641.5092--dc23
  [B]

                    2014033548

The National Geographic Society is one of the world's largest nonprofit scientific and educational organizations. Its mission is to inspire people to care about the planet. Founded in 1888, the Society is member supported and offers a community for members to get closer to explorers, connect with other members, and help make a difference. The Society reaches more than 450 million people worldwide each month through *National Geographic* and other magazines; National Geographic Channel; television documentaries; music; radio; films; books; DVDs; maps; exhibitions; live events; school publishing programs; interactive media; and merchandise. National Geographic has funded more than 10,000 scientific research, conservation, and exploration projects and supports an education program promoting geographic literacy. For more information, visit www.nationalgeographic.com.

National Geographic Society
1145 17th Street N.W.
Washington, D.C. 20036-4688 U.S.A.

For information about special discounts for bulk purchases, please contact National Geographic Books Special Sales: ngspecsales@ngs.org

For rights or permissions inquiries, please contact National Geographic Books Subsidiary Rights: ngbookrights@ngs.org

Interior design: Melissa Farris

Printed in the United States of America

15/QGF-CML/1

For my brother, that shooting star, still blazing in my heart.

We shall not cease from exploration,
and the end of all our exploring
will be to arrive where we started
and know the place for the first time.

T. S. Eliot

CONTENTS

Author's Note

MEMORY IS AN IMPERFECT COMPANION AT BEST, and so these pages portray the events of my life only as I remember them. Still, I've done my best to be objective. I've made sacrifices for narrative flow: Certain minor characters are composites, and the occasional scene has been reordered or collapsed. Names and certain identifying attributes of characters have been changed; the notable exceptions are my husband and daughter.

Prologue

THIS IS NOT THE BOOK I MEANT TO WRITE.

This was supposed to be a spirited book about the four years I spent cooking my way around the world from my tiny kitchen in Tulsa, Oklahoma. The pages were going to be filled with sweet stories about overcoming pickiness and teaching my husband and daughter to love the world cuisine I featured on my blog, Global Table Adventure. It was going to be an easy book to write—one that wouldn't make me cry, or make my relatives so nervous that I'd be obliged to employ pseudonyms.

But try as I might, I couldn't stay within the parameters of such a narrative; the easy truth is as much a lie as any. What drove me to obsessively cook a meal from each of the world's 195 countries cannot be explained by a simple passion for cooking alone.

Most people who have had a rough background will admit there's something unsettling about finding happiness after difficulty—that even after we unwrap this gift, we don't know how to stop searching,

13

rummaging, pilfering for something else. We walk haltingly through life, ready for the other shoe to drop. The question is not if, but when.

There is a hunger for peace so deeply rooted in me that I cannot trace the origins to any one moment in my life. So I had to start at the beginning, from the foods of my wayward childhood, to those that shored up my teenage years overseas, to those I discovered in my blog. Together, they helped me learn to love my world as I cooked my way around it.

Everything depends on the moment the spice hits a hot pan: whether it sizzles with a mouthwatering fragrance or turns to ash. Once, I thought happiness was the sizzle in the pan. But it's not. Happiness is the spice—that fragile speck, beholden to the heat, always and forever tempered by our environment.

This is the story I share with you.

PART ONE

Conflict of Heritage

"Good kitchens are not about size."
—Nigel Slater

CHAPTER I

Living Room Kitchen

I AM MISSING TWO FINGERPRINTS on my right hand. The neat spiral of lines on my ring and middle fingers suddenly flatten out, melted into circles that fan outward like the tail of a peacock. I first noticed the marks in fourth grade, when my school started filing fingerprints for the police. I wondered why mine looked so different from those of my classmates.

After school, I asked Mom about it. But she was driving. She couldn't inspect my fingers. Decades later I found out the truth: At age one I'd toddled over to an open broiler while Mom was making hamburgers. Her back was turned for a second to grab a pot holder. When she came back from the hospital, where they treated my third-degree burns and blasted her for child abuse, she found the shrunken pucks of meat on the still open grate. Cold. Congealed.

She never made hamburgers again.

My older brother Michael and I spent much of our early childhood under the kitchen table, dancing wooden animals across the linoleum. We pretended the old trestle was a cave while Mom stitched odd jobs above us to make ends meet. Our father had vanished long ago: Mom was the only parent we knew. Sometimes Michael would inspect my scarred fingertips. "Maybe you're an alien!" he'd exclaim over the hum of Mom's ancient Singer. I can still see those laughing blue eyes; even in the shadows they sparkled.

I loved to watch Michael laugh. His wiry body wound up from the effort, tears filled his eyes, and his dimpled cheeks puffed out like sails. When he teased me, I'd sulk, lowering my face until my straight-browed, four-story forehead was all anyone could see, my tiny chin and owl eyes buried in my chest. But with the wisdom that came from being 21 months my senior, Michael knew just where to poke my sides until a giggle escaped.

Decades later, whenever I sat alone looking at my marred fingerprints, regret would overwhelm me, as though the rough and tumble course of our childhood had been set in motion by my careless curiosity as an infant. My injury instigated our initial visit from the Department of Social Services; though the judge dismissed the case, there was no wiping the slate clean once our names were in the system. Over the years, the kitchens I grew up in and around continued to draw me in, like a moth to a flame, as though I might recapture whatever innocence I'd lost in that warm, fragrant space.

There are mysteries buried in the recesses of every kitchen—every crumb kicked under the floorboard is a hidden memory. But some kitchens are made of more. Some kitchens are *everything*.

A few years after I burned myself, when I was four and Michael was six, Mom moved us to a streetcar suburb of Boston called Jamaica Plain (though whatever plains had been in those parts had long since been covered by concrete). Our one-bedroom apartment was on the first floor of a skinny triple-decker house with cream siding and evergreen trim. In those days, gangs roamed the parks, and shifty figures lurked by the towering railway known as the "Elevator Train" at the end of our street. But the meager rent was all Mom could afford.

I still remember our first night there—how the empty rooms echoed, how the December air made the tip of my nose cold, and how Mom turned on the oven to warm the rooms more quickly. Michael and I sat on the bare mattress—the only item in the apartment, borrowed from a friend. It felt like midnight, but we were too wide-eyed to sleep.

Mom stood, hands on her broad, bony hips, scanning the inky windows and the snow beyond. She was short; barely five foot two, with a petite, oval face that made her cocoa-bean eyes and frizzy curls more prominent. But Mom could fill any room she walked into with one of her signature looks: dark angled brows knit tightly together in what appeared to be a scowl.

A car screeched by as she stood in front of the windows. Or maybe it was a truck. All I remember is the loud bass rattling the windowpane and Mom's capsized eyebrows.

"Why are you always mad, Mom?" I whispered, peering up at her.

She turned to me, her Peruvian knit skirt catching a puff of air.

"Don't be silly," she said, her brow smoothing. "That's just how my face is shaped." She rummaged through her bag. "What this apartment needs are some curtains." She left the room, returning moments later with a sheet that she draped over the window nearest our heads. For about a week the three of us slept huddled together on the mattress under a scratchy wool blanket.

The final sleeping arrangements soon became clear: Mom in the bread-box bedroom on the other side of the kitchen, Michael and I each against our own wall in the living room. Since he was half a head taller, he got a huge, twin-size mattress, while I slept on a smaller bed cobbled together out of reclaimed two-by-fours. Mom sewed curtains for the windows and then another, from an old lace tablecloth, to drape along the posts that rose up at regular intervals across the length of my bed. She called it my castle.

In the morning, we'd shuffle into the kitchen to pick out our clothes for the day. The room felt enormous, despite the meager floor plan, lack of counter space, and awkward, freestanding stove. But the deeper we explored the space, the more the room offered. It was not just for cooking and eating; it was also a closet, Mom's sewing room, and with nowhere else to convene, our living room.

Since our beds took up most of the actual living room, the kitchen was the only place to put our dresser. Never one to let a perfectly good surface go to waste, Mom found a piece of scrap laminate and placed it on top to create a makeshift prep area. She screwed hooks into the side to hang her cast-iron pans and bolted an old, hand-cranked mill to the edge, showing us how to grind our own flour. Shaking clouds of flour out of my socks became an inevitable part of our morning routine, despite Mom's constant reminders that I should close my drawers all the way.

As time went by, Mom added more and more inventive details to our new home. One day while exploring the Bunker Hill Monument, she found an old railroad tie. Impervious to the stares and whispers of strangers, she lugged it home in the trunk of her car and bolted the enormous timber to the wall above the dresser. Here she stored a jumble of brown glass spice jars. "Spices do better when kept in the dark," she explained. "It keeps them potent." The finishing touch was a few silvery branches of eucalyptus suspended from the railroad tie. They filled the air with their honeyed, woodsy scent.

Every morning after breakfast, Mom would take out her old Singer and begin her freelance work as a seamstress, hemming the wool trousers and silk skirts of lawyers and bourgeois homemakers while Michael and I played at her feet. She found the work from ads tacked to billboards around town. When things were slow, she made our dress clothes too, converting a 25-cent pair of XXL pants from the thrift store into a Christmas dress for me or a blazer for Michael. With the scraps she made my doll's clothes. My job was to collect the fabric from the linoleum floor and thread the needle.

Through the years, Mom approached food the same way she approached sewing: Not a scrap should be wasted. "Beggars can't be choosers," she'd always say, promising to ship our leftovers to China if we didn't eat up. So we choked down what we were given: heaping mounds of spinach tossed with nutmeg and green onion, fried liver, rice-stuffed cabbage rolls, corn chowder, and the dreaded block of "welfare cheese," as long as my forearm and as thick as my thigh. The processed bites tasted like wax, but Mom said we needed the calcium.

Mom practiced what she preached. When our molasses sandwiches were flanked by slices of suspiciously fuzzy bread, she would shrug off our complaints, saying a little mold never hurt anyone. If we had browning bananas, she'd whip up a batch of her Hungarian crepes—a recipe she learned from her father—and let Michael and I roll them up together with some yogurt and maple syrup. The result, endlessly drippy and sweet, was one of our favorite childhood treats— one that made us believe that our lives were as ordinary as any other.

🍴 Overnight Crepes

Even though she's half Hungarian, Mom calls these thin pancakes crepes instead of "palacsinta." And perhaps they are crepes;

most *palacsinta* are prepared with carbonated water to lighten the batter. Mom omits this trick, instead relying on an overnight rest to make a silkier batter. Like magic, all the lumps are gone in the morning.

Still, like any good Hungarian, Mom makes an art of rolling up the crepes with a wide range of sweet and savory fillings. Her simplest preparations are smeared with apricot jam, sprinkled with crushed walnuts, and stacked under a dusting of powdered sugar. Sometimes, they're rolled around leftover chicken paprika and reheated in a warm oven. My favorite is a Hungarian-American hybrid: sliced fruit (whatever is on hand), a spoon of yogurt, and a drizzling of maple syrup. Speaking of syrup—traditionalists will say to keep the batter fluid; it should pour like cold maple syrup. Thin as needed with extra milk.

- 2 large eggs
- 1 cup milk
- 1 cup flour
- 1½ teaspoons almond or vanilla extract
- Pinch of salt
- Butter, for cooking

Finishing touches:
Seasonal fruit (bananas, pears, apples, peaches, berries), apricot jam, maple syrup, yogurt, powdered sugar

In a medium bowl, whisk together the eggs, milk, flour, extract, and salt. Cover and refrigerate overnight.

In the morning, whisk the batter smooth. Preheat a 10-inch nonstick skillet over medium heat with a little butter. When it sizzles, ladle in ¼ cup batter. I lift the pan a few inches and slowly twist my wrist until the batter spreads evenly over the surface to fill the entire pan. Return to the burner and cook until the top of the crepe changes from shiny to dull, then flip. Cook a few more seconds, or until done. The first one is always a mess. Eat it, and carry on with the rest. Store cooked crepes in a warm oven until they are all cooked.

Finishing touch: Roll each crepe with desired fillings.

Makes 8 crepes

Though she could easily have plunked Michael and me down in front of a TV as she worked, Mom felt that this particular appliance should be used with caution. If we complained of boredom, she'd sit us down to write letters, design our own paper dolls, or read from her extensive children's book collection, which included Leo Tolstoy's *Fables for Children*. She kept "the boob tube" in her bedroom closet. No matter how many seams she had to stitch, she'd only bring out the two-dial black-and-white set once a week, for what she called "educational shows," like *Mister Rogers' Neighborhood, Leave It to Beaver*, or Julia Child reruns. Sometimes Michael got to watch an old Western or a cop show called *CHiPs*.

Though I'm not sure how it qualified as educational, I was allowed to watch *The Addams Family*, starring apparent witches, a disembodied hand, and a big ball of walking, talking hair in sunglasses. Part of the fascination was that strangers liked to tell me I looked eerily like Wednesday Addams, the small black-haired girl with too-big eyes and straight-lipped face. Like her, my quiet stares seemed to unsettle the adults around me.

But it went deeper than that: These oddball TV characters made sense to me. Like Mom, they found the habits of conventional society ridiculous, and were genuinely surprised when neighbors abhorred their eccentric lifestyle. These misfits stood their ground, triumphing over their neighbors' judgment and criticism.

I also loved watching Julia Child bumble and laugh her way through the kitchen. I must have been five when I told Mom that I wanted to make the roast lamb I'd seen Julia make on TV.

"OK," she said, "Write down what we need to do."

"But I don't know how to write—"

"Nonsense," she said and handed me a slip of paper and a pencil.

I filled the small sheet with graphite waves—my first recipe. Mom sat behind me and jotted down the basic instructions. To pay for the ingredients, we collected change in an old jelly jar, Michael helping me scour the sidewalk for pennies. A few months later, once we had enough, we bought the lamb and a one-ounce jar of mint jelly just in time for Easter.

I don't remember Julia's recipe any more, or if what we ultimately cooked even was her recipe—and perhaps that was never the point. The point was to get creative in the kitchen, and that's what Julia Child inspired—what she *always* inspired. With Mom's guidance we rubbed butter and fresh rosemary over a rack of lamb, pressed fat knobs of garlic into slits throughout the flesh, and blasted it in a 500-degree oven. We didn't have white paper caps to keep the exposed bones from burning, or a fancy roasting pan like what Julia might have used, but we shaped the rack into a crown and the rosemary-encrusted meat came out tender and juicy all the same.

"Great work," Mom said with a serious nod as she drew her knife between the bones through the buttery flesh, releasing a puff of gamy steam. Her words made me grin, showing the gap in between my two front teeth.

The three of us devoured the feast at the living room kitchen table silently, alternating between the soft meat and bright bursts of mint jelly. We hadn't trimmed the thick, white fat from our roast; Mom said it was the best part. She showed us how to chew it and drink the blood pooled up on our plates. As she tipped the porcelain to her mouth, we watched in rapt horror as the swirling, red juices slid between her lips. The brine tasted faintly of metal.

"Waste not, want not. It'll help you grow," she winked.

After that Mom let me cook at her side whenever I wanted. She sewed me an apron from a scrap of bright orange fabric, and I paraded through the kitchen in that simple cloth with regal swagger, a wooden spoon for a scepter. And with Mom as my royal counsel, I learned that food never had to be pedestrian.

Instead of serving up plain hard-boiled eggs, Mom tucked whole raw eggs in a braided nest of challah dough; after it finished baking, Michael and I clamored to excavate and peel our edible treasures. And instead of feeding us uninspired bowls of Jell-O, she drilled into raw eggs and taught us how to blow out the insides. After we washed the shells, Michael and I took turns pouring Jell-O through a funnel, into the cavity. Peeling back the cold shell to find a quivering raspberry egg was magic we could create.

Fueled by Mom's inventiveness, my imagination grew unchecked. No meal was beyond the realm of possibility. As time went on and I learned to write, I'd record recipes for such unlikely delicacies as Julia Child's *pâté en croute*. If we lacked the time or the means to make a dish, Mom would hand me a pencil and butcher paper.

"No reason to go without," she'd smile. "Draw it—make me hungry!"

When I was done, she'd feast her eyes on my crude illustrations as though the graphite lines formed an edible banquet. Her inevitable approval always came with one word, exclaimed loud enough to make me jump: "*Yum!*"

CHAPTER 2

A Lifetime Past

OVER THE YEARS, Michael would occasionally ask about our father. "Oh, what do you want to know about him for?" Mom would say, ruffling his chestnut mop. "That was a lifetime ago."

But the two of us spent many afternoons swinging side by side at the park across the street, trying to imagine what our father might look like. Michael said he was probably a firefighter or cop, like Ponch on *CHiPs*. I secretly hoped he *was* Mr. Rogers.

In the absence of a flesh-and-blood father, Michael became my de facto protector. If someone suspicious wandered too close to us while we played, Michael would whack a stick, *rat-tat-tat,* along the underside of the swinging bridge until the offender wandered off. And if the neighborhood kids teased me during a game of kick ball, he'd give them what for, even if it meant he got kicked out of the game.

Though Mom continued to be tight-lipped about her early life, children absorb more than adults might like to admit. This much we knew: Our mother had once had it all—the American dream. And our father was the con artist who ruined everything.

Of course, I now realize that life is never so simple. There are many dreams in a lifetime—dreams that flourish or flounder for reasons much more complex than can be pinned down to any one person or situation. Such is the case with my mother.

Mom was raised in a Catholic immigrant home in Boston, with three generations and several branches of the family tree under one roof. She speaks of her Italian Grammie's bubbling, sweet-sauced kitchen with the sort of giddy admiration some scholars have for the Roman Empire: Through her young eyes, that kitchen arena was as wildly entertaining as any amphitheater and filled with equally staggering feats of acoustical engineering.

On Sundays, Mom and her best friend, Patricia—a tall, red-headed cheerleader from the tenement apartments down the road—often convened around the kitchen table to watch Grammie make the kitchen sing. With a *"click-click-click,"* the stove would start the show, followed by hiccuping pots, a humming refrigerator, and the bombastic babble of a language the girls would never learn.

The ingredients were the true stars, wheeled home from the market in Mom's old wicker baby carriage. Every time Grammie unloaded bagged fowl or severed artichoke heads from that unlikely chariot, my mother was thrilled. Not to be outdone, Grampie brought home the daily catch, wrapped in brown paper parcels from his tavern on Atlantic Ave.—fish so fresh it seemed to leap into the pan on its own. By lunch, the table would be a cornucopia: stuffed artichokes; a batch of "zucchini pie," a crustless slapdashery of eggs, thinly sliced zucchini, Parmesan, and parsley; Grammie's homemade ravioli; spinach with a wisp of nutmeg; or soft nubs of boiled potatoes tucked in nests of spaghetti. (This last was made by Mom's magpie aunt Fina, who'd eaten the dish in Genoa as a young girl.)

And then there was the *torta di riso*.

I like to imagine the scene: Grammie frying onions in lard, dancing around the grease until the onions mellowed and she could beat them into day-old rice, eggs, Parmesan, and a ragged handful of parsley. Then she'd knock hunks of carrots and potatoes into a sputtering pot of fowl. Every few minutes when she'd push the bird's bony feet back into the pot, Patricia would ask, "Does anyone actually eat those?"

Mom responded in her thick Boston accent: "No, but they're good for flay-vah."

Grammie always gave the girls three squares each of torta di riso and a few plucks of the once stringy bird. "*Mangia, mangia!*" she'd sing. "Eat, eat—too SKINNY!" Even as Patricia grew curvy, the savory rice squares never filled out Mom's beanpole limbs.

For Mom, this was a spectacle of heritage; for Patricia, curiosity. The Italian food adventures were so different from those of her Irish upbringing. With her mother regularly resting her nerves, Patricia found comfort in her friend's loudmouthed, hot-blooded brood.

⁓

By age 15, the girls discovered a different sort of attraction: dating. On Saturday nights, they went down to the local church hall to dance the bug with boys in letter jackets and slim-jim ties. The boys lined one wall, the girls the other. It always took forever for the first guy to muster the courage to cross the invisible divide. One night, too eager for formalities, Mom flounced across the room and asked if anyone wanted to dance. A boy named James, the only one with a sensible haircut in a sea of ducktails, stepped forward. After that he always took her to the Saturday night dance.

Five years later, Mom and James were married.

Mom went on to earn her B.S. Ed., double majoring in math and science, with credits toward a master's degree in the psychology of adolescents from Boston State College. She worked as a math teacher at a nearby school, he as an architect.

By the time she turned 25, in the mid-sixties, they had three children—Connor, and the twins Tim and Grace. Mom quit her job after the twins were born. I've seen pictures from that era—little Connor with a trim vest and a balloon of black curls, Tim's ear-to-ear grin, and Grace, a blond angel in pink seersucker. But it's Mom who makes me look twice. With her neatly styled curls tamed beneath pillbox hats, she resembled Jackie Kennedy.

Though Connor, Tim, and Grace were more than a decade older than Michael and me, I still remember how Mom would gasp if we deigned to call them our half siblings. "That doesn't make any sense," she'd scoff. "There's no such thing as *half* family. Just call them what they are—your brothers and sister. Anything else is splitting hairs!"

～⁀)

Mom's friendship with Patricia was a rudder in those early days. The women knit matching sweaters, received matching full scholarships to the Museum of Fine Arts certificate program, and were each other's bridesmaids. After Patricia and her new husband, Pierre, had three daughters, the two took turns hosting playdates and potlucks.

In the beginning, the food was easy—maybe a quick noodle casserole, a garden salad, a pitcher of lemonade. But when Patricia moved to the suburbs, their gatherings evolved into sit-down dinners with cloth napkins and etched stemware. As she learned the exacting recipes of her new husband's French family, Patricia began dabbling in velvety salmon mousselines and cheese soufflés. Mom once told me that, though the food was excellent, after a while, there was too much white porcelain. "Either Patricia's plates were growing," she said, "or the portions were shrinking."

It wasn't long before Patricia and her girls followed Pierre's career out of the state—and, by the end of the sixties, out of the country. The women wrote letters, but the distance made visits few and far between.

Drawn in by the culture of the times, Mom transformed into a wild child, her knit sweaters and pillbox hats replaced with belted tunics and hair so big that it looked like an Afro.

Some might say they married too young. Some might say they should have lived a little before having a family. But by 1970, James and Mom were headed for divorce. When it finally went through, Mom was 29; the kids were 7 and 4. She successfully fought to get an annulment, to the bewilderment of her navy-man father: "How can you get an annulment? You have three kids!" he exclaimed.

Mom stood her ground: She and James had been too immature when they made their vows for the marriage to count. She wanted to be free to remarry, not just in the eyes of the state, but also in the eyes of God.

Although Mom was awarded custody of the kids, she agreed to transfer custody to James, since he was a good father and had a secure career. She knew it was better for the kids to have that stability. In the bitter turmoil of their split, James decided to move to New Jersey, so he could raise the children near his mother, sister, and her four children. Mom still gets mad when she talks about it. She says the six-hour drive might as well have put them on the other side of the world. From then on, she only saw them a week or two out of every year.

⁓

As Mom likes to say, "When it rains it pours." By 1973, her brother and mother had both died, months apart: he, murdered by his drug-addict tenant, and she after succumbing to cancer. With the kind of blind, mechanical resolve that can only be mustered in the face of extreme grief, Mom opened a leather shop on Cape Cod with her new boyfriend, Ed. She used her savings and borrowed a couple thousand dollars from Ed's brother, which she repaid in two months. Mom's true talent and passion was sewing, learned at her Grammie's side. It allowed her to express her creativity without the rigid rules that had come with working in the school system. But she still made good use of her math degree, setting the prices, tracking overhead, and keeping the books.

With modest pricing and creative designs, business boomed almost immediately. Within months, Mom and Ed had eight employees. Give Mom five minutes to reminisce and she'll recount the time John Lennon ordered a custom leather suit from her. Dig a little deeper, though, and she'll admit that the summer help turned Lennon away because he wanted the suit made the next day, a Sunday. The 16-year-old cashier informed Lennon they were closed on Sundays, explaining that it takes more than a day to make a custom leather suit.

Mom shouted, "You don't say 'no' to *John Lennon!* You close the store for a man like that." But when she ran down the street hoping to bring him back, he had disappeared.

Mom saved her profits to buy a few rental properties. In the summer, tourists filled the apartments and provided enough security that she could travel in the winters. Together, she and Ed explored Machu Picchu, the Amazon rain forest, Ecuador, Columbia, and the Galápagos Islands. They even stayed a few days with Patricia and Pierre, who were then living in Venezuela—their first reunion since Mom's good friends had left the States a year earlier.

While abroad, my mother watched how the locals ate. South America never left her. Inspired by *agua fresca,* the blended fruit drinks made throughout Central and South America, she concocted smoothies well before the leotard- and leg warmer–clad ladies of the eighties. She kept avocados in a bowl and made fish a weekly affair. And there was always a piece of chocolate hidden somewhere in the recesses of her kitchen.

Three years later, on a blinding spring morning in the mid-seventies, a man named Oliver walked into the shop and introduced himself as an artist and an inventor. He wanted Mom to make wineskins for him out of her finest leather. He showed her his drawings and said they'd make millions.

For weeks Oliver's lanky silhouette moved, barefoot and shirtless, through warrior poses on the private lawn directly across from the shop. Soon, Mom was bringing her famous smoothies out to him, basking in his crooked smile.

Ed didn't like all the attention Mom showered on Oliver, but found himself outmaneuvered in the face of his rival's charisma. Three months later, Ed and Mom ended their relationship. Their business became a casualty of the breakup.

Once Ed moved out, Oliver offered to help Mom convert the garage of one of her rental units into an apartment, lining the walls with cedar planks scavenged from a construction site. Soon, they settled in together. Since Oliver didn't believe in working for the man, they scraped by with Mom's tenants' payments.

Michael was born a year later.

Mom repeatedly asked Oliver to marry her, but there was no pinning this tumbleweed down. He was temperamental, prone to disappearing for days, even weeks or months at a time. One day he took their Volkswagen bus down to the five-and-dime for milk and ended up 1,200 miles away in Florida. Another time he vanished for three months, reappearing to explain he felt like camping in the mountain mists awhile. Mom used to say he probably had kids all over the country. Their relationship was explosive and, like a postcard of the seventies, riddled with drugs and chaos.

By 1979, Mom was pregnant with me, and had taken Oliver back several times. Eventually he convinced her to sell off her rental properties for cash. When he disappeared with the money, she grabbed Michael and the emergency funds she'd secretly stashed behind the kitchen stove and ran halfway around the world to Samoa.

Years later, I asked Mom why she went abroad while seven months pregnant instead of selecting cribs, stocking up on diapers, and knitting booties. She paused, then gave three explanations. The first was that she wanted to put flowers on Robert Louis Stevenson's grave. The second was that she wanted to see the setting for cultural anthropologist Margaret Mead's research on teenagers in Samoa. And the third was that she wanted a break from winter on the Cape. I soon intuited that the silence between her answers had everything to do with my father and their on-again, off-again relationship.

During this capricious adventure, my mother astonished locals. Not only was she unmarried and pregnant, with a small child, but she also immersed herself in the culture by renting a *fale* for six weeks. Fales are houses without walls, where crickets and spiders and cockroaches are free to wander in and out. At night, gauzy, white netting was her only protection from the giant mosquitoes.

Still, Mom says a life without walls is the most efficient and harmonious way to live. And it's also the only way to live in Samoa, where the sun smolders so deeply that it settles into a person's very marrow. Without walls, the slightest breeze can work its way into the fale and bring a whisper of relief.

Whenever Mom walked through the village, the women along her path would ask her the same questions over and over: "Where are you going?" and, in the same breath, "Where is your husband?" Before she could answer, they'd scoop up little Michael, whose baby blond hair entranced them, and walk a ways with Mom. They soon learned there was no father, no husband.

The women fawned over Mom's widening belly, bringing her roasted pork, breadfruit, taro, coconut crème in taro leaves—all cooked on brick and wood fires. They made Mom part of their community. Michael and Mom washed these gifts down with Samoan cocoa while I grew strong from within.

Mom planned to stay on those islands forever, wrapped in nothing but the traditional lavalava dress. But as my due date drew closer, reality set in. I was born back on the Cape, where Mom found a small apartment to rent with government assistance. She wrote to my great aunt: "I've been paying into the system all these years. Once this baby is born, I'll need to be a full-time mom." She certainly couldn't count on Oliver, and she wasn't about to put us kids in child care to work as a teacher. "There'll be time enough for a career," she added, "*after* I raise Michael and this baby." It almost seemed as if she was trying to make up for the time she'd missed with her first three children.

Once she'd settled in, Oliver started hanging around again, only to vanish three weeks before the birth. When she went into labor, Mom sent all her friends searching for him. A buddy finally brought him back to their apartment. While she labored through the night, Michael played with blocks on an old mattress nearby while Oliver led a raucous game of cards with a friend on the other side of the bedroom door. The closest my mother got to him was the smell of his cigarette smoke trailing into the bedroom where she lay or the pop of his laughter through the papery walls. Sometimes his voice crackled accusingly when his friend would drop a beer bottle. Other times, he'd call out "Cheater!" when a questionable hand was played.

It was just Mom, one of her friends from the shop, and a midwife in that darkened room when I arrived around midnight. After they left, Mom remembers showing a sleepy Michael his new baby sister. In the still of the night, he leaned over and gave me a kiss on the cheek. Mom waited for Oliver to fawn over me, but he never came. When she registered my birth a few days later, he was long gone. There is no father listed on my birth certificate—just a blank spot underscored.

Mom named me Musashi. The most famous Japanese samurai of all time, Musashi was a fearless and calculated warrior whose skill with the sword is said to have been so great that he never lost a duel (including his very first, which he fought at the age of 13). These fights were always to the death: Losing one would have cost Musashi his life.

When I asked Mom why she chose such an ancient and macho name for a newborn baby girl, she simply rolled her eyes and said, "I thought your father would like it."

A woman can leave a man several times, but still not muster the resolve to cleave through the stubborn tendons of attachment. Mom could navigate the emotional tightrope of Oliver's drug use, drinking, and stealing; she could manage his moods and frequent disappearing acts. But in the end, her concern for Michael and me forced her to sever all ties. She couldn't bear our disappointment when he'd vanish, and she couldn't help us understand his temper.

The winter before my second birthday, Mom uprooted us from the Cape, abandoning a life and the friendships she'd meticulously built over eight years to give us a fresh start in Boston. She took only what she could cram into an old leather carryall from the shop. "At some point you just have to face the facts," she said of her departure, "Nothing was going to change. It's like math: Two plus two is four, and it always will be. The realization just hit me: We had to move on."

In the years ahead, Mom rarely spoke of Oliver. If we wondered aloud about him, her eyes would flash, the corners of her mouth turned down. She tried to hide her emotions by looking away or changing the subject, but Michael and I could read her. They had been together five messy years—enough to leave more than one scar.

Mom never dated again and made sure we never knew our father, trashing photos and erasing all connections to that era. Sometimes, when we were out and about in the city, she'd pull Michael and me into a doorway, muttering, "Why won't he go *away?*" If we asked, "Who?" she'd shake her head a little too quickly.

I wouldn't learn my father's name (or that I was once named Musashi) until I was 21, and wouldn't see a photo of Oliver until I was 29. I only knew him as Mom described him: "a charismatic con artist."

For a long time, it never occurred to me that my father could be out there somewhere. Father's Day came and went uncelebrated, a holiday for other people, like Chinese New Year or Rosh Hashanah. Mom was the only father I ever knew. I even considered myself Italian Hungarian, like she was, never really considering that in truth I was likely only a quarter of each.

Years later, when Michael added "a father" to the top of his Christmas list right above "world peace," the ache that bubbled up in me felt as alien as the words.

CHAPTER 3

Lean Years

WHEN WE ARRIVED IN BOSTON, Mom waited in line with the rest of the city's lost souls to secure the last two spots in an overcrowded homeless shelter. Even as everyone shuffled, Mom stood tall, frizzy mop clipped back, while three-year-old Michael ran circles around her with his baby doll.

I suppose she could have asked my grandfather or someone else in the family for help, but her chaotic relationship with my father made favors hard to come by. She'd left in such a rush that there'd been no time to secure work or accommodations.

Though the thin soups and stale bread at the shelter were miserable, my brother and I ate with gusto. Because we were still scrawny little tots, we were able to sleep on either end of one cot, while Mom slept on the other. We lasted there three days.

After Mom made a few collect calls, we ended up at a friend of a friend's place on the cracked side of Boston's suburbs. We crammed ourselves into the corners of Barbara's tall, blue gingerbread town house. Mom paid her way by doing laundry and cooking. Little by little, she saved enough of her assistance checks of $350 a month so that we could finally move to our own apartment in Jamaica Plain.

Even in Barbara's borrowed home, Mom had to improvise to make ends meet. She never lacked imagination.

In my first memory, I am three, maybe four years old, sitting at a small metal table with a white Formica top, just big enough for two. In front of me is a small white bowl, filled only halfway with Os. Michael sits on the other side of me, hungrily eating his dry cereal, his cheeks puffed up like a chipmunk.

"Where's the milk?" I ask him.

"I don't think there is any," he whispers.

"But I want some," I say, my voice drawn out in a whine.

Before either of us can utter another word, Mom pulls a bottle from the fridge and splashes a tiny bit of red juice into each of our bowls.

"It's cranberry," she says. "Barbara won't mind if we borrow . . ."

"Why are we always eating Barbara's food?" Michael whines.

"Try it," Mom urges. As if to show us how good juice can be with cereal, she bends at the waist, spooning a bit into her own mouth. She makes exaggerated *yum* sounds, smacking her lips and making silly faces. Michael smiles up at her, despite himself.

He takes a bite, then another.

"Whoa, Mom, this is *good*," he says, and starts to airplane the food into his mouth, making loud buzzing sounds.

I sit back in my chair, unsure.

"Milk is boring. This is—" She takes a deep breath and then pats my hand, lifting the corners of her mouth like a curtain. "Not everyone can say they've had juice in their cereal. Not even the Queen of England."

That does the trick. I bring the spoon to my lips, only once pausing to look down at the now pink Os that look like candy. The tart juice squeezes at the inside of my cheeks.

For years after, Michael and I beg Mom to add juice to our cereal instead of milk.

~~~~~

Cranberry juice wasn't what Mom wanted for us—she yearned for that bombastic kitchen of her childhood, that immigrant arena. She wanted to give us a *heritage*. But by the time we had our own place in Jamaica Plain, not only were her mother and brother gone, but her dad and sister had also moved away from Boston.

My own name became the victim in this crisis of identity. Mom changed it multiple times before my tenth birthday. Though I was born Musashi, I became Sashi, then Sashann, then Sasha. Much later at my ninth birthday, I became Alexandra. My last name was my father's, then my mother's. When I was about three, Mom settled on giving me her late mother's maiden name "Lombardi," which rolled off her tongue like an Italian lullaby.

The decision was both sentimental and feminist; Lombardi put the power of my female lineage behind me. From what I observed of my Italian cousins, whose homes we often frequented for Thanksgiving and Christmas, my new name gave me license to yell whether I was sad, happy, or anything in between.

Each time the Boston courts awarded my foiled and stamped name-change documents, Mom sent out calligraphic announcements to everyone she knew in purple marker on scraps of card stock. She treated each reinvention like a festive occasion, taking us on the train into the North End, where we'd eat Italian subs to celebrate. For dessert we'd go to Maria's for cannoli or tiramisu.

When the festivities were over, if I complained about my new fate as "Sasha" or, later, "Alexandra," Mom would look me straight in the eye. "Don't you know?" she'd say with all the certitude of a weatherman, "You need a name for every stage of your life. Butterflies don't go by 'caterpillar' forever. And they certainly don't go by 'pupa' one second longer than they have to. *You*, my dear, are no longer a pupa."

Immediately all sorts of questions about butterflies would occur to me, and I'd completely forget about the name change.

A name alone cannot keep a heritage alive. Mom shuttled Michael and me across town every month to the home of our closest living Italian relative, Great Aunt Fina. She'd boil hefty pots of her famous potatoes and spaghetti, tossing the classic Genovese combination with red sauce while Michael and I played with her rotary phone or ran through her parsley beds.

Mom also brought us to visit the Italian relatives on the fringes of our family tree—ones who wore gold *coronos* (squiggly horn pendants), white patent leather shoes, and pompadours. I never really knew where the bloodlines ran together, but I lapped up the culture eagerly. Nothing was done quietly; there was even drama when washing the dishes. I'd ask Michael: "Are they all mad—or crazy?"

Mom, who couldn't understand the Italian cacophony, would hear us whispering, and offer, "Isn't it great?! I could listen to them all day."

One of our favorite excursions was to Cousin Alfred's place. When we'd ask how we were related to him, Mom would always say, "Who cares? He's family."

Alfred always wore a bow tie. He was impossibly old, with memories from the late 1800s when the ice cream scoop, cotton candy, and stop sign were invented. Tall and lanky, Alfred bent slightly when he walked, as though he were perpetually rolling out dough. But his voice didn't shake, nor did his hands. Mom said cooking kept him young, and she might be right: Alfred lived 104 years.

His signature dish was meat sauce and ravioli. But we knew better than to ask him how it was done. "Waddya mean, how's it done?" he'd say, clucking his teeth. "Watch, watch. That's the only way to learn anything." Alfred's sauce started weeks before he ever picked up a spoon, when he mail-ordered dried porcinis from Italy. The actual cooking took two days: one day to brown, stir, and bubble, and one day to rest. As the wild mushrooms, hamburger, and sweet sausage mingled with the onion and a crush of tomatoes, we all trekked down to the large plank table in his cellar to watch him make the pasta.

After rolling the dough into two thin sheets, Alfred spread one with pork and spinach filling, and then topped it with the other. He used a special rolling pin with a raised grid to crimp dozens of ravioli in one pass. Even though I was just four years old, Alfred let Michael and I drive the ravioli cutter through one of the crimp marks the pin had left behind.

The ravioli was an even more involved recipe than the sauce, taking upwards of three days. But Alfred prepped the filling and dough before our arrival, leaving us to delight in the magic at the end of the journey.

🍴 Cousin Alfred's Meat Sauce

"Meat sauce" doesn't do this recipe justice. It's filled with nearly a dozen sweet Italian sausages, the umami of dried porcinis, and the best tomatoes Italy has to offer. There's a richness that comes from using first-press olive oil and sweet, sweet onion (while any

onions will certainly do, Alfred specified Bermuda because their natural sugar helps balance the sauce).

Although I have a tendency to add garlic to my sauces, in traditional Italian cooking either onion or garlic is used—never both. Alfred pureed the tomatoes with a food mill and ground the meat with a meat grinder. His sauce was an exercise in love, a taste of the Old World. Here is my modernized version, which relies heavily on a wooden spoon and pre-ground meat. But I like to think the flavors remain as hearty as he intended. Although it might seem ambitious to make a gallon of sauce, Alfred taught me to freeze leftovers in 2-cup, freezer-safe containers for future meals; not only is it handy, but it saves effort in the end.

- 1 ounce dried mushrooms (porcinis, if available)
- 2 sweet Bermuda onions, chopped
- ½ cup olive oil
- 1 pound lean ground beef
- Three 28-ounce cans San Marzano whole peeled tomatoes
- Two 6-ounce cans tomato paste
- 2 generous pinches nutmeg
- Generous pinch allspice or cloves
- Salt and pepper
- 10 sweet Italian sausages

Soak the dried mushrooms in one cup recently boiled water. Cover and set aside.

In a large Dutch oven or heavy-duty pot over medium-high heat, fry the onions in olive oil until soft, sweet, and golden brown. Add the beef and continue browning.

Next, pile on the canned tomatoes and their juices, the tomato paste, nutmeg, and allspice or cloves, salt, and pepper. Finally, chop the mushrooms and add them and their cup of liquid to the pot. Give everything a stir and bring to a simmer.

Top with raw sausages—just plunk them in whole (Alfred said so). Cover and keep the mixture at a gentle bubble for about 4 hours.

Remove the sausages and, when cool enough to handle, slice into half-moons. With a wooden spoon, break up the tomato chunks, if there are any, and stir the sausage back into the sauce.

At this point Alfred covered the sauce and left it on the counter overnight. Times have changed, so I must recommend refrigerating the sauce for 8 hours—more if you have the time. During this rest, the flavors will mingle and deepen.

Though the sauce keeps for about a week in the fridge, I like to freeze it in 2-cup portions so I can enjoy the bounty over several meals. Frozen, it will last at least 6 months.

It is simply wonderful on top of hearty pasta, like spaghetti or rigatoni, with a liberal heaping of freshly grated Parmesan. Alfred liked it best over ravioli. I find it delightful in lasagna, too, though Alfred never did this himself.

Makes about 1 gallon

CHAPTER 4

—●

Just Desserts

IN THE FACE OF OUR NOISY ITALIAN HERITAGE, the living room kitchen in our new apartment in Jamaica Plain felt too quiet. There should have been a grandmother bustling among us, chiding in Italian, bumping elbows, laughing too loud. The only times Mom managed to capture the energy of Grammie's kitchen was when Connor and the twins, Tim and Grace, came to visit.

Mom made a big fuss before each of our siblings' yearly weeklong visits, especially when it came to planning what we'd eat. One autumn she ushered Michael and me into an orchard on the outskirts of Boston to pluck fallen apples for Michael's birthday pie. He always requested it, since Mom wouldn't let us get those "slabs of poison-soaked garbage" we eyed at the supermarket. I must have been about five years old, Michael almost seven.

"They're bruised," we'd cried in dismay when we saw the misshapen fruit around us. But Mom reminded us that soft apples make the best pie. I asked if we had to pay for them. "Not if they've been on the ground," she said. "What if animals had scavenged them? Who knows what damage they'd do? Tell you the truth, we're doing the farmers a favor keeping pests off their land."

I figured she was probably right—and anyway, I liked having the orchard all to ourselves. When Connor, Tim, and Grace arrived, we had a bowl of apples and a box of candles ready for the pie.

As with all our visits, we took a while to get settled. Our siblings would load their backpacks and sleeping bags into Mom's small bedroom; she'd sleep on the living room floor near Michael and me. Though Michael was happy to see his older brothers and sister, he often acted out to sustain Mom's attention. He didn't just cry; he wailed. He could kick up a full-blown scene in a matter of seconds, without regard to where we were. Once on the other side, though, he lit up with an expansive, dimpled grin, ready to roughhouse.

Though Michael and I were skinny, our half siblings had the added height of freshly sprouted teenagers. The boys had Mom's earthen hair, while Grace's bloomed goldenrod. As soon as they put down their bags, the tiny apartment resounded with the ruckus of five kids with a license to run, play, and do as we liked. Not only could we get our clothes muddy, but we could also track the dirt in. "That's what baths and mops are for," Mom reasoned, "so live a little."

I'm not sure if Connor, Tim, and Grace found our lifestyle a relief or disconcerting. I know they hated to be so far from us. The feeling was mutual; we were always trying to figure out a way to get our households in the same city, or even state. In the end, we gave ourselves up to the little time we had together.

The cramped kitchen was the only place we could all fit; we'd congregate around the mismatched chairs, elbows on the counters, sometimes sitting cross-legged on milk crates. While the older kids shaped the piecrust and squeezed lemon juice over the apples, Mom handed out scraps of dough and a few slices of apple for Michael and me, allowing us to put whatever we wanted into our "inventions." Everything was fair game, but I always went straight to Mom's spice rack, that hodgepodge collection situated on the railroad tie shelf above my clothes dresser. In addition to the spices she used in her pie—nutmeg, allspice, and cinnamon (which mom called "sin")—I dusted on some hot paprika and a handful of raisins.

I loved it when we crammed together around that old wooden table. In those days food was never just sustenance; the very act of cooking knit our disparate lives together.

After the pie was done, Mom plopped the glass dish on the table and shooed us outside for an hour or two. She knew she could never keep us from cutting into it unless we were far enough away that we could no longer sniff that intoxicating whiff of cinnamon and apples.

When we finally sat down to eat, Mom stuck a candle in the pie's center and said with a smile: "Happy Birthday, cutie pie!" We all sang to Michael, ate two slices each, and licked our plates until they gleamed. Any leftovers were served for breakfast with a big dollop of vanilla yogurt.

Even as the dishes were washed, we'd beg Mom to make the pie again. But there was never time. Inevitably Connor, Tim, and Grace had to go back to their dad, three states away. When our visits ended, all of us cried, especially Grace and me. To make the separation easier, she slipped me elaborate, handwritten notes adorned with bubbly hearts and flowers. When I was too little to read them, Mom or Michael helped me, indulging me dozens of times until I knew the words by heart.

Day after day I shut myself away in my castle bed, staring at the drawings until I could almost see Grace sitting next to me. Without her and her brothers, the house was too still. When the last crumb from our meal was swept up, often Mom disappeared into her room for hours at a time. She said she was napping.

There's a difference between poverty of resources and poverty of spirit. For a long time, Michael and I were oblivious to hardship because of Mom's determined efforts. But in the end she couldn't erase the reality of our situation. Nowhere was our poverty more apparent than when we went out into the community, which seemed to operate under a constantly shifting set of rules. Even figuring out where we could buy our groceries was to risk humiliation.

A year after we moved to Jamaica Plain, a new health food store opened two miles from the apartment. When we got the notice in the mail, Mom decided we'd go immediately.

Mom had tied my babushka on extra tight when we'd left the apartment, tucking my long brown hair into the neck of my woolen poncho. She'd pointed to the trees, whose leaves stood silver against the charcoal sky, and said we needed to hurry; there was rain on the way. But she'd said it with a smile since we were going to make a German Tree Cake.

Broiling 21 crepe-like layers of batter into a cake, Mom decided, would be the perfect rainy-day activity. She got the recipe from a German woman at a folk dance. Mom made a habit of asking foreigners what they like to eat, pressing them until they shared something she could add to our patchwork of recipes.

Michael and I wandered into the dry goods section, where I reached into a large barrel.

"This cereal tastes funny," I said.

Michael stood on tiptoe, his corduroys rising a couple of inches above his loafers, and peered inside the barrel. His hair fell into his eyes. Already in second grade, he could read. "That's *dog food*, Sash." He giggled, but took a handful, too.

The egg-shaped man behind the counter was talking to Mom in a low grumble. She looked upset as she waved her hand over her selections: chocolate, eggs, almonds from the bulk bin, and a tin of almond paste. There was also an avocado. Mom promised we could split it for lunch. But our car had broken down again, and we had walked two miles from our apartment to the health food store. I was hungry *now*.

The man's voice grew loud. "I'm sorry, ma'am. I can't change the rules. We don't take food stamps."

Mom glanced over at Michael and me, straightened her small shoulders and knit her eyebrows together.

Michael marched to her side. "Come on, Mom, we don't need his stupid food," he said taking her hand, and scowling up at the clerk.

Mom tucked the food stamps back into a fold of her coat. She counted out a few coins from her change purse, looked the man squarely in the eyes, and placed them on the counter with a sharp *click*.

She managed our avocado lunch, but it would be another few weeks before she could hem enough trousers to buy the ingredients for the German Tree Cake. We begged her to go to a different grocery store, one of the many chains near our apartment where she could use her food stamps. But she said we deserved to shop at the health food store just like anyone else.

Mom saved her money, and when we left the store the second time, we had what we needed. After a painstaking morning spent broiling the 21 almond layers and another afternoon glazing it, the first bite was nowhere as good as I expected.

It was better.

🥄🍴 German Tree Cake | Baumtorte/Baumkuchen

....

This is the kind of cake that pulls family together around the stove, incites gasps when sliced, and tastes like escape. The stacked almond cake looks like the rings of an ancient tree, whose secrets hide under chocolate and crushed almond bark. Golden apricot jam drips like sap.

There's no denying it—this cake is a lot of work. German bakeries resort to a rotating spit to "paint on" nearly two dozen layers. Mom knew the best way to tackle it is over two days: one for baking, another for decorating. While the layers broil, I set a timer and make a game of cleaning in bursts. By the time the last layer browns, the kitchen sparkles.

For the batter:
14 ounces almond paste (a tightly packed 1⅓ cups)
6 tablespoons half-and-half
12 tablespoons (1½ sticks) unsalted butter, softened, plus
    more for cake pan
1 cup sugar
10 large eggs, separated (put the whites in a large bowl)
1½ teaspoons vanilla extract
1 cup cake flour
¾ cup cornstarch
¼ teaspoon salt

For assembly:
Apricot jam (about a 10-ounce jar)
Slivered almonds (1 cup or so, coarsely ground)

For the chocolate glaze:

52

6 tablespoons butter
1 tablespoon dark rum
1½ teaspoons vanilla extract
2 tablespoons light corn syrup
6 ounces semisweet chocolate chips (1 cup)

Grease and line a 9-inch springform pan with a round of parchment paper.

For the batter:
In the bowl of a standing mixer fitted with the paddle attachment, beat the almond paste with half-and-half, one tablespoon at a time. Start the mixer on low, then increase to medium until smooth. Beat in the softened butter until the mixture is fluffy, then beat in the sugar. Scrape the bowl as needed. Incorporate the egg yolks—one at a time—and the vanilla extract. (At this point, I dab a little vanilla extract on my wrists, just like mom.)

In a medium bowl, whisk together the cake flour, cornstarch, and salt. Beat it into the batter in thirds on lowest speed, scraping the bowl as needed. Finally, use a hand mixer to beat the egg whites in a large bowl until they form medium peaks. Fold the egg whites into the batter in thirds, until it looks like an almond paste cloud.

To bake the cake:
Preheat the broiler for a few minutes.

To make the layers, use a ⅓ cup measuring spoon to scoop a heaping mound of batter into the prepared springform pan. Use a pastry brush to spread the batter all over the bottom of the pan, right up to the edges. Place under the broiler and cook until browned. The key is to get the batter deeply browned so that the layers show when the cake is sliced; this takes about a minute per layer for me. As the cake gets taller (and closer to the broiler), the layers cook quicker so adjust accordingly.

Every few layers, brush on 1 tablespoon of apricot jam (save half the jar for later). Continue in this way until all the batter is used up. Let the cake cool to room temperature in the pan, then wrap in plastic and refrigerate overnight.

To decorate the cake:

For the glaze, melt the butter, rum, vanilla extract, and corn syrup together in a small pot. Simmer for one minute, then remove from heat and add the chocolate. Cover and let sit a few minutes. Meanwhile, run a knife around the edge of the cake and release from the springform pan. Spread top and sides with remaining apricot jam to seal the crumbs.

Whisk the chocolate glaze until smooth and glossy. Working over a cooling rack set over a baking pan, pour the glaze on top of the cake and spread evenly over the sides. Decorate with ground almonds by pressing a palmful onto the sides of the cake. Alternatively, sprinkle them over the entire cake.

Chill to set the glaze. Serve slices with hot tea or coffee. A bit of whipped cream is a nice touch.

Enough for 10 to 12

CHAPTER 5

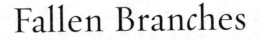

Fallen Branches

ICHAEL AND I MIGHT HAVE PLODDED along relatively unscathed through childhood; certainly Mom's inventiveness kept things upbeat. But my mother tends not to hold her tongue when convention defies her notion of logic. And she will not sit silently on the sidelines, despite the repercussions.

Mom made a point to question even the most conventional wisdom. Gingerbread cookies weren't just for the winter; in July and August, she'd make them into ice cream sandwiches that we'd enjoy after a run through a spraying fire hydrant.

She insisted that no child of hers was going to wear a seat belt. "If we're in an accident, we need to be free to jump out of the car to protect ourselves. An uncle of mine did that, and lived. The person wearing a seat belt didn't. I won't have you living with a false sense of security," she declared. If Mom got a parking ticket for taking the only open spot by our apartment, thereby blocking a handicap ramp, she scoffed at the court clerks: "I *am* handicapped, I have *kids!*"

Nothing was sacred. Everything could and should be questioned.

~~~

Mom kept me away from kindergarten, saying it was much too soon to take a child from her mother. She'd tried it with Michael and hated how they'd forced him to lie down when he'd refused to take naps years earlier. "There's no humanity in the system," she'd say. "Why can't they just let the energetic kids out to play instead of treating them like mummies?"

But by the mid-eighties there was no more putting off school; I was six years old. It should have been a wonderful experience: Great Aunt Fina helped pay for Michael and me to attend the small Catholic school around the corner, Our Lady of Lourdes. This was a luxury Mom could never have afforded on her own, and one that her father would not have offered (being of the very Hungarian mind-set that now she was in her 40s, she should pull herself up by the bootstraps).

Even in this homogeneous environment, where uniforms and French braids bobbed in neat rows along the waxed hallways, I stood out as different. For first grade, Mom lowered and fringed the hem on my pinafore until it fell clear down to my calves, asserting that anything above the knee was for "hussies." She didn't let us buy the school lunches, either; they were, she explained, charity for people who didn't know how to cook.

At every turn Mom challenged the school principal, Sister Margaret, a tight-lipped, round-bottomed schoolmarm who spent most of her days holed up in a shuttered office. At the end of the year, when Mom challenged her for allowing sex education videos into elementary school, the resulting hollering match echoed through the halls. Mom said she didn't want her six- and eight-year-old learning about sex at school; that was family business.

Word traveled fast: When Mom showed up to the next PTA meeting, she was met with whispers and sidelong glares. One of my classmates told me that *her* mother said *my* mother was a troublemaker.

Mom couldn't catch a break. Her unconventional way of seeing the world was misunderstood by our neighbors and the authorities; the same went for her tone, Italian and insolent. As though to exact vengeance on my mother for her apparent transgressions, Sister Margaret called the Department of Social Services during the last week of school and slapped Mom with a 51A, reporting her for child endangerment as an unstable mother. A trim social worker in a tweed suit plucked Michael and me from our classrooms right in the middle of final exams. She said she was taking us to see Mom, and then drove in the opposite direction.

Michael detected the lie first. He unfastened his seat belt, twisted in his seat, and kicked at the car door. I held my breath, wondering if it would swing open or the glass would shatter, but nothing happened. Without slowing the car, the social worker reached back and refastened Michael's seat belt. Michael slumped in defiance, fighting the tears that spilled down his cheeks. "You're a liar!" he yelled.

When I realized what was happening, I pressed my face and hands against the window and began to cry, watching as strange houses flickered by. I blubbered that I didn't want to go; I wanted my mom. She was going to wonder where we were; she needed us. The lady just pursed her lips and kept on driving.

We ended up a mile away at a turquoise town house with plastic-covered sofas. Our room was in the attic. There were four beds with sagging middles, two of which were already claimed by other foster children.

Before the social worker left, I asked how Mom would know not to pick us up from school. The woman assured me that someone would call her from the courthouse. She put her hands on my shoulders and added that everyone really did have our best interests at heart.

We lived there six weeks. One of the other foster kids was moved almost immediately, leaving us to bunk with a 14-year-old boy who'd just been released from a mental institution. "He's in transition," the social worker told us, "so be nice to him."

At night I'd wake to the boy pressed against me, muttering. One time I saw him climb in Michael's bed. I didn't sleep much after that.

During the day Michael and I took to playing stickball with fallen tree branches and rocks. One day Michael's rock landed square in the center of our roommate's forehead. Michael said it was an accident. The boy left for stitches and never came back. For punishment, the man of the house, José, handed Michael a bar of soap and told us that from now on, if we wanted a bath, we should run through the fire hydrant. Michael didn't talk back; he'd seen a gun on the man's mantel.

We were always hungry. One afternoon Michael and I wandered into the kitchen and asked José for a snack. His enormous back was to us, his fat pressed into the crevices of a small vinyl chair. At the sound of my voice, he ran his hand through his black hair, narrowed his eyes, and started yelling in Spanish. He reached into the basket on the table and began throwing apples at me.

Though he didn't stand much taller than me, Michael didn't run. He puffed up his little chest and half-rushed the man, who stood up, dwarfing Michael. When José came at him, Michael grabbed an apple off the floor, took my hand, and pulled me outside.

When she heard about the incident during visitation, Mom turned the tables and filed a 51A on the foster home. She won.

It was almost unheard of for a parent to fight the system, let alone successfully. In light of Mom's determination to hold the foster home accountable, accusations that she was unfit no longer held water; the judge agreed to move us in with one of our Italian cousins as a stopgap measure until justice could be served. In late fall, four months after Sister Margaret had us pulled out of school, the court finally allowed Mom to bring us home—but not without assigning a court-ordered therapist to our family.

Mom requested that Michael's therapy be supplemented by weekly sessions with a priest at our local church. "The boy needs all the fatherly influences he can get," she said. "I want his spirit to be tended, not just his mind." But shortly after the sessions began, Michael warned me to stay away from open confession with "that priest." When I asked him why, his eyes were stormy. "Just *don't* Sash." He was in tears when I ignored him. I couldn't understand why—the priest had me in and out of his office in a few quick minutes before ushering in the next boy.

That year we attended a large public school on the other side of Jamaica Plain, but the challenges continued. One night in March, Michael and Mom had a big blowup over some stupid no-big-deal thing, as kids and their parents are wont to do. Michael stormed out of the house in his pajamas and plunked himself down on the icy curb, arms crossed, fuming. He had no socks or shoes on. Mom wasn't bothered. She said he needed to cool off, and that he'd come back in when he realized it was 30 degrees out. A few minutes later a social worker drove by on his way home from work.

The man asked my brother why he was outside. "My mom's mad at me," he huffed, leading the social worker to believe Mom had sent Michael outside with malicious intent. In a moment that Mom later told the court was tantamount to kidnapping, the man sped off with Michael, called the authorities, and filed another 51A. The operator instructed him to bring Michael back to the house, though, and we went to bed assuming all had blown over.

In the meantime, the Department of Social Services must have pulled up our history. Later that night, we woke to three bangs on the door. Two police officers and two social workers rushed in. One officer hoisted me from bed and grabbed Michael with his other hand. "Emergency removal," the officer said, "for the children's safety."

Michael yelled and Mom hollered at the officer until her voice cracked, but she was fighting in quicksand; her outburst all but guaranteed a longer placement and more thorough inquisition.

Over the next seven months, we would be placed in three different homes because of this one incident. Each foster home was worse than the last. Mom—who by now had traded her flowing tunics for stiff blazers and calf-length pleated skirts—proved this in court, successfully filing 51As on the last two.

When I asked Mom during one of our weekly supervised visitations why it was taking so long for us to come home, she said, "They've got it all backward. They make the parents guilty until proven innocent. Plus they're dragging their feet, setting the court dates two months apart. But I'm going to get you kids home."

Even after we came home, Mom still had to update the courts. Long days were spent on wooden benches outside massive courtrooms, waiting for the heavy gavel of judgments. The eyes of the state were everywhere, monitoring our every move. We couldn't even play in the rain without having paperwork filed.

At night I'd fall asleep to the hum of Mom's sewing machine while she rushed through odd jobs to keep the little money we had flowing. In the middle of the night, I'd wake to the tap of her thrift shop typewriter. I'd see her at the kitchen table, surrounded by papers, crafting arguments for the next morning's court sessions. She used her courses in childhood psychology to argue our case in 50-page documents. "If they think I'm not working for welfare, they've got another thing coming," she once declared. "I'm earning it!"

One time, Michael and I crept into the last row of the marble-paved courtroom to watch one of the cases unfold. I held my breath, afraid that the echo of our steps might upset the wrong person and destroy our chances of staying with her. But no one noticed us. Amid a lot of mumbling and paper shuffling, Mom talked about my good grades and Michael's creativity.

The judge looked over the materials, took off her glasses, shook her head, and finally said, "Someone's doing a good job with these kids."

Mom scoffed, looked around, and raised her hands, as if to say "I'm a single mom—who else do you think there is?"

The rougher things got, the tighter I gripped onto Michael. He and my giant white teddy bear were my only constants as our notion of home was subsumed in the chaos.

⁓

Eventually Michael grew quiet. By age 10 or 11, he'd stopped kicking, and stopped fighting back. Occasionally he'd get in fistfights or steal something, like candy. Though he'd been assessed as above average in standardized testing, he struggled with his emotions and eventually, his grades. In one psychological test, the examiner noted:

"Michael was cooperative and friendly throughout the testing session. He also seemed downcast at times, and at one point began to cry for no reason that seemed attributable to the testing material. He cried for a time, then regained his composure and continued. He said he did not know why he had started to cry. This underlying sense of loss causes periodic bouts of sadness. He put forth good effort on all various tasks, and his rapport with the examiner was good. In sum, Michael is a bright, sensitive boy who at times feels quite sad, and as a result has difficulty mobilizing his considerable cognitive and emotional resources."

True to the psychologist's assessment, Michael fell behind in school, leaving us just one grade apart in school. By the age of nine, I felt like a plant, constantly being repotted without enough time for my roots to recover, ever weakening. With each placement, I retreated deeper into my shell. I made myself small and did as I was told, whether the directive came from my mother or the courts.

After four years of this, our family therapist said that a stable home would be less disruptive to our emotional well-being than the constant court battles. When I was 10 and Michael was 12, Mom relented. She pulled out the typewriter one last time to draft a letter, begging family and friends to take us in—for good.

Mom's court-assigned lawyer took her words and made them official, sending the letter to everyone she could think of. My 80-year-old great aunt was too elderly to take us in. My grandfather was in the same boat. In their 20s, Connor, Tim, and Grace were barely adults themselves, and would never have been approved by the courts. Mom's ex-husband James had his own commitments, as did her sister and cousins. Mom even had the lawyer send a letter to the Lombardi vineyards in California on the off chance that the owners would consider us family and take us in. They respectfully declined.

Finally, Mom's old friends Patricia and Pierre Dumont agreed to become our legal guardians. Though the women had been each other's bridesmaids in the sixties, they hadn't seen each other since Mom had visited Venezuela a decade or so before—shortly before her life became complicated by Oliver and later by the day-to-day grind of making ends meet.

Time hadn't thawed the Dumonts' warmth or devotion to their friend. Patricia and Pierre had been considering adopting children, and with three mostly grown daughters, they wanted a boy. Two more children would give them a full house again. Bringing us to their Rhode Island home would be the perfect arrangement.

Mom says that once the Dumonts made their decision, there was no turning back. Patricia and Pierre marched into the courtroom to inform the judge of their intentions. They were a sight for sore eyes, decked out in bright colors, rippling scarves, clicking shoes, and beaming smiles. They floated through the sea of scruffy souls in line for traffic violations, DUIs, and nonpayment of child support. Any and all concerns the judge brought up were quickly dismissed by the Dumonts: They had the means, the love, and the time to take us in.

The day Mom broke the news, she pulled a Sara Lee pound cake from the freezer and set it on the counter to thaw. This was a special treat, something not in our food stamp budget. Because it was store-bought, it somehow seemed even more glorious, coveted the same way I coveted Wonder Bread over Mom's homemade version or bottled Italian dressing over her simple splashes of olive oil and vinegar.

Mom let me lick the cake that stuck to the cardboard lid, but when I asked her for a slice, she told me to get Michael, who was playing across the street. As I exited the kitchen, I heard a whisk against metal. *There'll be whipped cream, too,* I thought, grinning, and ran the whole way to the playground. Michael let out a gleeful whoop at the mention of the treat.

While we sat at the table, Mom sliced a pint of fresh strawberries and spooned them over thick slices of cake. She dipped a giant metal spoon into the stainless-steel bowl and topped each plate with a cloud of whipped cream.

The strawberries were Michael's favorite, the pound cake was mine, but we loved the whipped cream in equal measure. While we spooned the cake in big, heaping bites, Mom told us for the first time that we would be moving in with another family, the Dumonts. She said they were old friends, but we'd never heard their names before.

Suddenly the cake tasted like foam and clung to the corners of my mouth. I swallowed hard. Even the cool glass of milk couldn't wash the tightness away. I put down my fork and asked Mom when we could come home again, thinking that this was just another foster home drop-off. A few days? A week? A month?

Mom said we couldn't come home again: This time it was forever. Though Michael and I wouldn't be adopted, per se, we also wouldn't be foster kids. The Dumonts were to become our legal guardians. I looked over at Michael, sitting there blankly. I wanted him to say something, make Mom change her mind. But he didn't move.

"What about saying goodbye to Connor, Tim, and Grace?" I asked. Mom reminded me that they were all the way in New Jersey. Michael and I would be leaving in a few days for Rhode Island, where the Dumonts had a large house.

When I searched Mom's quiet face, I saw that she spoke the truth: Michael and I were leaving for good. I can still remember the haunted look in her eyes, how her spirit slumped, even while she held her chin straight for the benefit of our questioning eyes. This wasn't abandonment. This was defeat.

But instead of taking us down with her, she thrust us bravely into the arms of two dear friends, hoping and praying our lives could be better.

🍴 Winter Pound Cake

I went two decades without so much as a slice of pound cake. Too many memories were attached to those rich crumbs. But one chilly day in my 30s—months after the last worthwhile strawberry had been plucked—I decided to dust off an old recipe from Cook's Illustrated *and try to make the cake my* own. *Instead of fresh sliced strawberries on top—which even in summer often need tossing with sugar to coax out their natural sweetness—I folded featherlight, freeze-dried morsels into the batter. Frozen with summertime still clinging to their bloodred, dimpled skin, these berries pack in bold flavor without making the crumb sodden.*

With the added glow of lemon or orange zest and a couple splashes of cream, this cake is a comfort beside any frosty window. It's true: A slice of pound cake does wonders to thaw the coldest of days.

NOTE: Best baked in a shiny aluminum pan. If using a glass baking pan, drop oven temperature by 25 degrees, or the cake will not cook properly.

½ pound (2 sticks) unsalted butter, softened, plus more for loaf pan

Zest of a lemon or orange

1¼ cups granulated sugar

1½ teaspoons vanilla extract

4 large eggs, plus 1 yolk, at room temperature

3 tablespoons heavy cream

¼ teaspoon salt

1¾ cups all-purpose flour, lightly whisked to remove lumps

1 ounce freeze-dried strawberries, broken into ¼- to ½-inch morsels (a scant 1½ cups)

Preheat oven to 325°F. Grease a 5 × 9-inch loaf pan.

In the bowl of a standing mixer, cream the butter with the lemon or orange zest, then stream in the sugar, beating on medium speed until fluffy and white—a good 5 minutes.

In a medium bowl with spout, whisk together the vanilla, eggs, yolk, cream, and salt. Dribble very slowly into the butter mixture so as to not curdle the mix, beating until just combined. If it does curdle, a tablespoon of flour will restore the emulsion. Scrape as needed.

Add the flour, a bit at a time, mixing on low to incorporate. Fold in the dried strawberries with a spatula. Spoon the batter into a prepared loaf pan, and smooth the top with a spatula. Bake on the center rack for about 70 minutes, or until a knife inserted into the center of the cake comes out with just a few crumbs on it. Cover with a foil tent if it seems to be browning too quickly. Let rest about 30 minutes, then run a butter knife around the edge and turn it onto a rack to continue cooling.

Serve at room temperature with whipped cream and hot tea. To store: Wrap in plastic, then foil. Keeps a handful of days—though I imagine it'll be long gone before then.

Enough for 8 to 10

CHAPTER 6

The New Order

I HAVE NO RECOLLECTION of saying goodbye to Mom. I don't know if they had to tear us out of her arms or if we obediently wheeled our canvas suitcases toward our new lives with only a sideways glance over our shoulders. Our first moments with the Dumonts in the spring of 1990 are almost as elusive. We met them in an office building, likely the Department of Social Services, where someone had set out a giant cheese pizza and a plastic clamshell of cupcakes from Stop & Shop. I couldn't help but wonder what Mom would say about that.

A tall crane of a woman in a white pantsuit took a group photo. She must have been the social worker. Patricia and Pierre flanked the edges with their three daughters, Lauren, Heather, and Antoinette, sandwiched between them. The oldest, Lauren, was already grown and out of the house, working on her doctorate in Boston; Heather, 21, was wrapping up her senior year at Duke University; and Antoinette (or Toni as they called her), was 16 and the only one still living at home.

Michael and I were in the front row, short, skinny, and conspicuously Italian. Our new family towered around us like a grove of trees. Pierre topped out the group with his chestnut, "Leave It to Beaver" locks and dimpled chin, in a wool sweater with elbow patches. Like their father, the girls were unusually tall, with long, rustling masses of strawberry blond and auburn hair. Though Patricia was the shortest, she was still a full head taller than Michael and me—her high-waisted slacks emphasizing the canopy of her hips.

Taking a family photo with strangers was uncomfortable enough, but then the crane suggested Patricia put her hand on my shoulder— my only distinct memory of this day.

"Come together now," she said.

Patricia considered, her plump hand hovering awkwardly near my shirtsleeve. In that brief pause, Michael threw his arm around me. He seemed so grown-up all of a sudden, so much older than his 12 years. I slumped toward him in relief.

They were so kind to take us in, filled with the best of intentions. And yet, I don't think anyone could have prepared them for the challenges that come with taking on two half-grown kids that psychologists had once assessed as "overly identified with their mother." We came with all kinds of "baggage," and almost none of it fit in our suitcases.

***

Our new home was a giant white farmhouse on Rhode Island's coast, several hours away. While we unpacked, Michael discovered that Mom had tucked a folded sheet of butcher's paper into his suitcase. She'd traced her hands on one side of the paper, doing it twice—once for Michael and once for me. On the other side she encouraged us to trace our hands, as though our palms were touching, so we could "always be close." But pressing our hands against the outline of her hands somehow made the distance greater.

Though there was room enough for Michael and me to have our own bedrooms, Patricia set up two twin beds in an east-facing bedroom with rose-embossed wallpaper, echoing the arrangement we'd had in the living room at Mom's. I was glad she did; the thought of sleeping in a different room than Michael secretly terrified me.

Even with our beds so close that we could hold hands if we wanted to, I began to have vivid, reoccurring nightmares of not being able to find Michael or Mom.

Those first few weeks I woke up several times a night in a cold sweat, instinctively looking for Mom's silhouette at our old kitchen table. I could only fall asleep once I saw Michael's sleeping form faintly outlined in the moonlight. The steady draw of his breath always soothed me.

The Dumonts' house was scattered with cardboard boxes— some crammed full, others open and waiting. There were mounds of Bubble Wrap in the halls and rolls of packing tape scattered along every open surface. Patricia and Pierre explained that they were mid-shuffle, preparing for a move to Atlanta, Georgia. As soon as school got out, we'd be leaving again. Moving wasn't a big deal for my new family; they were regular globe-trotters, having raised their children in other exotic locales like Morocco, Jamaica, and, of course, Venezuela.

Pierre typically changed jobs every two to three years. Companies hired him to consult on the finances of large projects; when the projects ended, so did his contract. He'd worked in nearly every industry on nearly every continent. Moving and exploring was simply a way of life, a conscious effort to absorb the best the world had to offer.

Patricia and her three daughters were accustomed to the nomadic lifestyle that accompanied Pierre's constant career shifts. Toni said they never settled anywhere long enough to throw out their moving boxes. She also said I should be glad we were just moving to Atlanta, and not halfway around the world.

But it might as well have been.

Living in a household of half-packed boxes made the arrangement feel temporary, more like purgatory than a permanent home. I imagined that if I prayed really hard, Michael and I might be released for good behavior and permitted to fly northward to our *real* home.

Though the Dumonts were nice enough, I missed my curtained castle and Mom's bear hugs. I missed the steady purr of her sewing machine on the dining table, and wondered how she'd thread her needle without my younger eyes. More than anything, I missed cooking with her. And so I begged the universe to send the Dumonts to Georgia without us when the last box was packed.

Michael said prayers weren't going to solve anything. He called Mom every day, ignoring her advice to focus on our new lives, and demanded to come home. He'd memorized her number, and dialed her on an old rotary phone after the house was asleep, huddled over it to muffle the noise. I was always too scared to talk, but I'd listen, my ear pressed next to his, hungry for the sound of Mom's voice. Every time Michael reached out, Mom told him the same thing: "You shouldn't be calling. You need to focus on your new life."

Turns out this response was nothing more than the advice of Mom's lawyer: Years later, I discovered that he'd advised her to cut off communications with us to ease our transition. Though we couldn't quite see the puppet strings, we could tell her words didn't ring quite true. She was tender and loving, and always asked how we were.

But if we listened carefully, we could hear that something was broken. She always got off the phone a little too quickly.

I stayed out of Michael's way after those calls.

Ultimately, Michael was right; no amount of prayers kept moving day away. One dewy morning in late May, a fleet of burly men pulled up to the house with two of the longest trucks I'd ever seen. By noon they'd loaded our entire lives into those yawning vessels, one box at a time. Early the next morning, while stars still pierced the darkness, Patricia, Pierre, Antoinette, Michael, and I piled into their Volvo station wagon and began the drive to Atlanta.

As the car bobbed and weaved from state to state, from hotel room to hotel room, I felt Mom slipping farther and farther away. I held my large white teddy bear close, imagining what she was doing. Had she donated my dolls that I couldn't fit in my suitcase? Was she baking a pie and, if so, who would she give the scraps to?

The miles piled up, sweeping me along until I finally fell asleep. Before I knew it, we'd washed ashore, right up to the foot of our new home.

⁓

The two-story brick colonial sat at the top of a steep, ivy-flanked driveway, more castle than house. Michael and I exchanged glances when we saw it. I was certain our entire apartment in Boston could have fit in the garage alone. On the first floor, there were two living rooms: a formal one that would be used to entertain the odd guest and a less formal one, reserved for Christmas morning. Both rooms were laid out with curvy couches and plush chairs, Tunisian coffee tables, and woven Oriental rugs.

Outside I caught a glimpse of the terraced backyard, which contained a basketball hoop and a large wooden swing set. The Dumonts didn't eat their meals in the kitchen the way Mom did. There was a dining room *and* a breakfast room, decorated with clay pottery from Venezuela, fleur-de-lis tablecloths, and Moroccan paintings depicting colorful, dirt-lined markets.

Two stairways led to the second floor. The back staircase connected two playrooms—one long, the other square, filled with giant baskets of Legos, a coloring station, and oversized couches. Down the hall, Michael and I each had our own bedroom.

My room was a vision of lavender and lace. Under a large, sunny window I had a white table and my very own sewing machine. I held my breath when I first stepped into the room for fear the vision might vanish. I soon discovered another tiny room that Toni called a "walk-in closet." It was the most wonderful thing I'd ever seen: a secret world made just for me.

Clothes—thick, gauzy, and soft—lined the walls. I'd never seen so many clothes in my life. The way they draped reminded me of the curtain Mom had sewn around my old bed. Many nights I'd bring my pillow and blanket into the closet and curl up on the floor. If I closed my eyes, I could almost believe I was home again.

That fall I entered sixth grade in a large public school. Haircuts were the first order of business. Michael's shaggy locks became a new crew cut that made his ears stick out. I went through an overhaul as well. My hair once danced across my lower back; now it barely flitted across my shoulders. We both got braces; month by month, the gap between my front teeth closed.

The calendar soon swelled with after-school activities. I signed up for Girl Scouts and horseback riding; Michael joined Little League and took karate classes. For the first time in my life, I felt like I could do anything, *be* anything. Sure, Mom had told me I could do whatever I wanted in life, but Patricia and Pierre had the means to make it possible.

We spent what free time we had with Toni, who was a junior in high school. Though we both looked up to her, she and Michael quickly grew close.

TV was off-limits at the Dumonts', so Michael, Toni, and I spent our evenings building Lego worlds and rewriting classic fairy tales. On the pages of our notebooks—complete with doodles—Rapunzel became a flatulent recluse. These antics, which often sent us into hysterics, were just what we kids needed to grow close. Moreover, Pierre and Patricia giggled at them, too. I missed Connor, Tim, and Grace terribly, but goofing off with Toni kept my mind off the aching, hollow feeling in the center of my chest.

At school, the slick, popular kids called me "Sushi" instead of "Sasha." I didn't know what the name meant and decided not to look it up. I made friends with a willowy girl from Russia called Alyona, one of the first people I'd met who grew up in another country. Kids mocked her thick accent and tittered when she began wearing a training bra before anyone else. I couldn't understand why they teased her; I thought she was beautiful and that her halting speech was musical. We drew together during lunch, ignoring our sad trays littered with greasy pizza, corn dogs, or sloppy joes.

Now in seventh grade, Michael had an easier time making friends. Mom used to say Michael's charisma was the one good thing he got from our father. If I was "by the book," Michael was the sort to tear the pages out to make paper airplanes. With his dimples and slate-blue eyes, and at 13 going on 20, his boyish body was starting to betray hard lines of lean muscle. Girls didn't stand a chance. Not long after we settled into the neighborhood, Michael had a girlfriend and a small band of friends he phoned at all hours of the night.

I knew he'd really settled in when he stopped calling Mom. Sometime before Christmas, it occurred to me that I hadn't heard her voice in a while.

"Do you think we should call Mom again?" I asked hesitantly.

His eyes flashed darkly, and his right hand clenched. He looked at me a moment, then gave me a big push. I fell back against the wall. Tears filled both our eyes, but before any slipped down his face, he turned on his heel and shut himself in his bedroom.

Though I didn't dare bring up Mom again, I still wanted to hear her voice. After Michael finally left for karate class, I slipped over to the phone in the hallway outside his room. Though I hadn't memorized her number, I tried a few times to punch the right ones into the phone. Each time I was wrong. I called 411, but her number was unlisted. There was nothing else to do.

That was the end of it.

Increasingly, Michael locked up his pain inside his room. Toni once told me she used to hear him crying in there. When she asked him what was wrong, he simply said he missed Mom. I've learned over the years that a closed bedroom door can reveal a broken heart as easily as it hides one. By then it seemed Michael had resigned himself to our new lot, in which clothes didn't come from the thrift store and we had our own rooms for the first time in our lives.

Where we had a *father*.

As we found out, having a father meant leaving muddy shoes at the back door, cleaning our rooms, and playing a pickup game of ball in the backyard. It meant stern scoldings, but it also meant belly laughs and high fives. We called Pierre "Papa," just as his daughters did. The name felt easy, new. Michael soaked up every word he said and was desperate to impress him. On Saturday afternoons, Michael followed Pierre around the house, giving him mock karate chops to the back of his knee and telling him knock-knock jokes. On Sundays, he liked to slip Bibles on the pew behind Pierre when we stood in church. Michael laughed until he cried when Pierre sat on them, honking like a distressed goose.

Pierre worked long hours and went on lots of business trips, so having a father also meant missing him for days or weeks at a time.

Patricia was a fixture in her enormous kitchen. When I tried to call her Mama, the name stuck like glue in the back of my throat. Michael couldn't do it, either. For a while, we just avoided calling her anything at all: It was "excuse me," and "um . . ." and "hey." When she picked up on our avoidance, she suggested we try calling her "Aunt Patricia," but I scrunched up my face trying to say it. In a wounded huff, she said, "Just call me Patricia."

From then on, they were Papa and Patricia, though no one seemed particularly happy about the arrangement.

When Patricia wasn't shuttling us from activity to activity, she stood alone at the kitchen counter, head down, chopping, stirring, kneading, and pounding. Then she'd slide over to the stove and simmer, stew, braise, and roast. *A Prairie Home Companion* ping-ponged through the enormous house, along with a cacophony of clattering cupboards, jingling silverware, and rattling dishes. Patricia's laugh was big and shrill, like a rogue church bell, and rang out in time with the jokes on the radio show.

On any given day, breakfast could be a scramble of eggs, lacy-edged French toast, or bottomless bowls of cereal. Cartons of milk and juice stood at attention each morning. Even weeknight dinners were three-course affairs. Patricia prepared feasts with garlic-roasted chicken, Brussels sprouts blistered with thyme and rosemary, a giant salmon fillet in an overcoat of hollandaise, and béchamel-layered lasagna. Sometimes Patricia made more exotic fare, too, like stewed rabbit or braised endives, and she wasn't above adding several tendrils of bitter frisée to her salads. But it was her hefty ratatouilles that I couldn't get enough of. Each bite was at once sweet and savory, nutritious and indulgent. Even seconds weren't enough; I always took thirds.

🍴 Ratatouille

The key to ratatouille is the layering of flavor. A proper French cook browns each ingredient until the skin darkens agreeably, tasting of fire, garlic, and salty olive oil. Most popular in the south of France, around Nice, ratatouille *actually means "to toss food together." In this recipe, as with so many, don't get hung up on cooking times. Just cook until the food is sweet and the appetite whets—an hour or so from start to finish.*

3 tablespoons olive oil, plus ¼ cup
1 large onion, chopped
1 red pepper, cut in 1-inch pieces
1 yellow pepper, cut in 1-inch pieces
1 teaspoon fresh thyme, chopped
Generous pinch fresh rosemary needles, chopped
6 cloves garlic, sliced
4 Roma tomatoes, chopped
1 pound zucchini, sliced into half-moons
1 smallish eggplant (1 to 1½ pounds), cubed
Salt and pepper

Heat a large Dutch oven or pot over medium heat. Add 3 tablespoons olive oil. Cook onions until deep golden and the home smells sweet. Add the peppers and continue cooking until softened. Add herbs, garlic, and tomatoes. Reduce heat and let bubble gently.

In a large skillet over medium-high heat, fry eggplant in remaining oil. Stir into the onion mixture when brown. Do the same for the zucchini. Once everything is in the large pot, season with salt and pepper, cover and bubble 15 more minutes, until all the ingredients are tender. Serve hot or room temperature with crusty bread.

Enough for 4

Though she was American, Patricia's cooking style showed an in-depth knowledge of French cookery that she absorbed from Pierre's family. In many ways she reminded me of Julia Child, both in what she made and how removed she seemed from the rest of us. It was as though a screen separated her world from ours. Whenever I'd wander into the kitchen to see what she was up to, she ushered me back out with a cheery refrain: "The kitchen's no place for a child! Go find something *fun* to do!"

I heard from Toni that Patricia's mother had died after falling off the roof of their tenement when Patricia was still in high school. So Patricia cared for her little brother and kept house to help her father. Other than the certificate course she took with my mother at Boston's Museum of Fine Arts, Patricia didn't go on to higher education. In the 1980s, even as women flooded the workforce, looking down on those who stayed home with their children, Patricia resolved that her job would be the cooking and cleaning, so that we kids could focus on our studies and get an education. Though her daughters would go on to have careers in medicine, linguistics, and neuroscience, none cook much.

But I wanted to cook. I *needed* to cook. Mom had raised me with the implicit understanding that cooking is the answer to all life's vicissitudes—not just the antidote to boredom, but also a way to ward off the darker realities of grief, separation, and loneliness. If I could just get my hands on a ball of dough or a pot to stir, I could work my way through this new life and be OK. And like a grieving spouse who sleeps in the shirt of a lost loved one, I thought that by cooking—handling ingredients again, breathing in their aroma as they bubbled—I could somehow be reunited with my mother again.

It would take two more decades to admit to myself that there was another reason I wanted to cook in Atlanta: I was desperate to connect with Patricia. Whether or not I could call her "Mama," for all intents and purposes, she was my mother now. I needed her.

Patricia reached out in her own way, taking me clothes shopping or organizing elaborate birthday parties for me, but nothing I could say would convince her to let me help in the kitchen, and I didn't know how to tell her why it mattered so much. Sometimes I'd wander into that giant room while the rest of the house slept and run my fingers along the oak cabinets, wondering what treasures laid inside. I missed the feeling of shaping the dough into whatever I wanted—that feeling of creativity, control, and, above all, closeness with my mother—*any* mother.

***

About a year after we moved in with the Dumonts, when I was 11 and Michael was 13, I had a fit of inspiration and convinced Michael and Toni that we should make Patricia and Pierre breakfast in bed. It'd be the perfect way to thank them for all they'd done for us, and I'd be able to get into the kitchen without being in Patricia's way.

There was just one problem: Patricia and Pierre were always awake before us kids. Since we had no idea when they woke up, we felt we had to stay up all night. It was the only way to be sure we could serve them before they made their own breakfast.

During dinner, Toni winked at Michael and me when Patricia asked us what we'd like for breakfast. The plan was to wait in our own rooms until we heard them go to sleep. When Toni sent out two owl hoots, we were to head downstairs.

I waited and waited; each minute crept by more slowly than the last. Eventually I nodded off. At 2 a.m. I awoke to several low, haunting hoots. When I opened the door, Michael and Toni were already tiptoeing down the hallway, their shadowy forms softly lit by a night-light.

I hurried behind them. Michael flipped on the light switch. Thrilled, I peeled back the cabinet doors for the first time and saw neat stacks of pots and pans, orderly rows of biscuits and jellies, and dozens upon dozens of spices. The three of us set to work.

Because Toni was the oldest, she baked the tube of refrigerator croissants, while Michael sliced up an orange and I poured two glasses of apple juice. I used the fanciest glasses I could find, skinny tumblers with delicate etched roses and gold rims. As an afterthought, I dusted the rims with cinnamon.

We set the treats onto a shiny black tray, along with two kinds of jam, blueberry and raspberry. Michael folded a napkin to look like a fan, and Toni filled a small, blue vase with three white daisies plucked from the back flower bed. By 2:34 a.m. we were finished.

The croissants were still warm, steam swirling into the air. The house smelled like a bakery. "Why don't we wait a bit longer before we bring the tray to them," said Toni, "We don't want to wake them too soon."

We decided to eat the warm croissants while we waited. By 3:15 a.m., when the second batch was ready, our eyes were drooping. We would fall asleep right there on the kitchen floor if we waited another second.

As Toni carried the tray upstairs, Michael flashed me a dimpled smile. I glanced nervously out the window: The sky was still inky, and there was no sign of sun. Toni knocked on Patricia and Pierre's door with Michael close behind her. I hung back several feet, waiting.

After they disappeared into the room, there was a moment of silence: I held my breath. I couldn't wait to hear Patricia and Pierre's reaction to our labors. Suddenly, a jumble of words slapped through the air, too indistinct to comprehend.

Seconds later, Toni and Michael emerged ashen faced. Toni still held the tray, untouched. She set it on the floor outside of the room and mumbled, "We better get to bed. They're pretty mad."

Michael had tears in his eyes. When I opened my mouth to speak, he brushed past me and disappeared into his room. Toni slipped into hers. I stood there a moment and stared down at the breakfast tray before retreating with my blanket and teddy bear into my closet.

In the morning, I woke certain that Patricia and Pierre would see we'd meant well. I waited for them to tell us how good the breakfast was, or to thank us for thinking of them, or to hug us and say it'd be OK. No such luck. Patricia was stony faced, and Pierre was already at the office.

No one ever mentioned it again.

⁂

Michael's best grades were D's. One fall day as we walked home from the bus stop, he confided that he didn't want to show Patricia and Pierre his report card. He was 14, in eighth grade. I was 12, in seventh grade.

"You're lucky," he said, kicking a few stones into the gutter, "Yours is probably covered with A's and B's."

It usually was. I slid my card farther into my coat pocket, not wanting him to find out that this time I'd managed straight A's.

Gingerly, I reached for his card and looked over the markings, the red ink laid out like hundreds of small knife cuts.

"But you got a C in English class," I said, smiling up at him. "That's way better than last—"

"It's not going to matter. You'll see."

"They'll see it—they will," I assured him, even as a sick feeling lurched in my stomach. The Dumonts had high expectations. "You have to make the most of your education," Pierre often said. "No one's going to do it for you."

Michael slowed his walk to a near crawl, dragging out the inevitable as long as possible. By the time we climbed the steep drive, he was primed for a fight. Pierre came from around the side of the house and asked about our report cards. I looked up in time to see Michael take a real swing at Pierre, then a high kick, the kind he'd learned in karate. The scuffle ended up in the dirt, Michael's balled-up report card blowing down the drive.

Michael didn't come out of his room for dinner. The tension boiled over again at bedtime. Michael was right: Going from a D to a C wasn't good enough. After all, Patricia and Pierre had raised a Ph.D. and a soon-to-be doctor.

I thought about sneaking over to Michael's room after bedtime, but when he retreated, he'd slammed his door so hard it shook the walls in my room.

After his 14th birthday, Michael's physical outbursts and quick-trigger temper increased. It was a perfect storm, fed as much by his raging hormones as by our unique family situation. He got in fights at home, at school, with me. He was a volcano, molten emotion always trembling below the surface.

Things went from bad to worse when Michael started stealing again. Instead of swiping morsels of candy, as he had in Jamaica Plain, he went on bigger heists, taking department store jewelry for his girlfriend or bags of chips he'd later sell out of his locker. He even sneaked out at night, despite my desperate pleas for him to stay home.

In the spring, he brought a cemented-up gun to school, got suspended, and was scheduled for his first trial in juvenile court. He hardly looked me in the eye anymore. His once boyish humor became scathing. Looking back, I can see that the split from our old life wasn't as clean as he'd made it look. The girlfriends, the bands of buddies—they weren't enough. A shadow floated over the peace this new life offered. We never spoke about his sadness: Whenever I tried, he shut me out.

I knew he was hurting, but I never guessed how much.

CHAPTER 7

White Flag of Surrender

O NE FRIDAY MORNING IN APRIL, almost two years to the day after we moved in with the Dumonts, my brother succumbed. He was 14.

Pierre was on a business trip in Paris. The only other people at home were me, Patricia, and Heather, who was still living at home as a first-year medical student. It was time for school, but Michael didn't come down for breakfast. We waited in the car, the engine idling. After checking the clock on the dash for the third time, Patricia sent me up to his room, where I knocked and knocked without an answer. My heart was in my mouth when I told Patricia.

"Did you try his door?" she asked.

"Yes," I whispered, my eyes staring down at a crease in my sneakers, "It was locked."

She went into the kitchen and fished a paper clip out of the junk drawer. "Here, wiggle this around until the lock pops out."

As the door peeled back, I saw my brother leaning awkwardly up against the top rail of his bunk bed, legs curled and feet pointed behind him. A line of spit had bubbled out of his mouth and down his chin. I couldn't comprehend what I was seeing, but I knew it wasn't right.

I ran to the stair railing and shouted down, "There's something wrong with my brother."

Patricia came running. After a horrified "Oh, my God," I heard, "Sasha, get some scissors."

I didn't yet understand why she needed scissors, but my gut told me I'd better do exactly as she said. The kitchen was so far away compared to the one in Mom's little apartment, where it had been just a half step from Michael's bed to the stove. I banged open drawer after drawer, finding towels, knives, forks, and tinfoil—but no scissors. By this time, Heather had heard the commotion from her basement apartment and came running.

"Where are the scissors?" I asked.

Without a word, she pulled open the junk drawer that held the paper clips and pointed. I followed as she sprinted up the stairs.

When I gave Patricia the scissors, she was propping up Michael's body. I thought I saw something threading between his neck and the bunk bed. Patricia took the scissors without turning around. "Call 911," she said, her voice high and thin.

There was a phone on a little wooden table in the hall right outside Michael's room. I dialed the number, but when the operator asked, "What's your emergency?" I didn't know what to say. When the question was repeated, I hung up.

As though in a trance, I hovered near Michael's doorway just as Patricia pressed the scissors together and his body fell to the floor. His face and neck were ash-gray. A deep red line divided the grayness from the rest of his body. His skin was dull and waxy, like one of my dolls. Heather tried mouth-to-mouth. Patricia knelt on the floor and pounded Michael's chest. It sounded hollow. I stood there staring at the cut edges of the thick, hay-colored rope on the floor. It looked like a dead snake.

That's when I realized he'd hanged himself. I hadn't been able to tell at first because he was too tall for the bunk bed. His back had been arched in a failed swan dive, face pressed against the bed, feet stretched behind him toward the wall, still touching the floor. His head had hidden the rope.

Patricia yelled again, "Where's 911?"

Silently I pressed myself closer to the wall. Someone must have called them back, because a few minutes later, lights and sirens clamored up the steep drive. EMTs swarmed around Michael with plastic tubes and beeping devices. They were able to get him breathing again, but he'd clearly spent a significant time without oxygen.

The police wanted to know why there was a woman's shoe next to Michael. As it happened, Patricia's had come off as she cut him down. Eventually the misunderstanding was cleared up; Patricia was assured that the questions were just standard procedure. But for hours after the inquisition, her face was redder than her hair.

We stood in the dingy hospital waiting room while the doctor gave us the news: Michael was trapped in a coma. He was brain-dead.

Brain-dead. Brain-dead. Brain-dead: The words clattered around in my head.

"What does that mean?" I finally managed. There was a pause while the doctor looked from me to Patricia. In the silence, my heartbeat hammered in my ears. Patricia stared blankly at the doctor.

It turned out that Michael had been deprived of oxygen too long, which had starved his brain. The doctor said Michael wouldn't be able to think or even walk again. When he compared him to a vegetable, I pictured a giant carrot in a hospital bed. It would have been funny if I weren't so hopping mad.

When the doctor walked away, I asked Heather for her professional opinion as a first-year medical student.

"Do you think he'll wake up?"

Heather opened her mouth to speak, but crinkled up like a paper bag, dropping her head onto my shoulder. Even as she squeezed me tight, her shoulders started to shake. I wondered if maybe I should cry, too; it seemed strange that I hadn't since finding him. But I felt empty, all dried up. The only thing I *could* feel was a twisty sort of feeling in the pit of my stomach, as if I'd swallowed an octopus.

I ran to the bathroom and threw up.

Though Pierre cut his work trip short, it still took him another day to get a flight home from Paris. The first person Patricia contacted was Mom. Mom later told me that Patricia was crying so hard Mom could hardly understand her.

Over and over again Patricia apologized: "I'm so, so sorry. Michael had a terrible accident."

The more she apologized, the more alarmed Mom grew. Before Patricia could tell her what happened, Mom hung up. She was about to leave for her new job at the Boston Trial Court, where she did data entry. She could tell that the news, whatever it was, was going to be bad—really bad. She says now that she couldn't face hearing it because once she did, she could never unhear it.

Patricia didn't call her back.

When Pierre got home from his trip, he called Mom a second time and told her she had to come to Atlanta to see Michael. He was matter-of-fact. Still, he wanted to wait until she arrived to reveal the details of what had happened—until they could speak face-to-face. But when Mom insisted he tell her right away, he gave in. She made flight arrangements immediately.

Pierre was good at handling tough situations. But as the day unfolded, his presence failed to calm Patricia, who continued to walk through the house in a fog. Though she fulfilled her parental obligations, something wild settled into her green eyes.

Although the neighbors brought casseroles over, Patricia continued to cook, almost out of nervous habit. She turned the radio on louder, laughed harder, and made more food than ever before. Sometimes she piled dozens of boiled potatoes on the table. Other times she made a five-eggplant ratatouille so big that we had to hold our plates on our laps to make room for the casserole. No one had much of an appetite, so most of her creations were left untouched. Still, she cooked.

I split those first shattered days between home, school, and the hospital. Every time I passed Michael's room, I held my breath, straining as if I might hear his footsteps again. School days started late: Patricia brought me in later after homeroom. She never explained why, but my friend Alyona confided that the principal was giving updates about Michael over the intercom during morning announcements.

Anger bubbled under my skin. If they were going to be talking about my brother, I wanted to be there. I wanted to know what they were saying. But I never protested the late arrivals; it was getting harder and harder to talk to anyone. Patricia and Pierre argued all the time. But if anyone was still crying, they were now doing so behind closed doors.

After school, Patricia would pick me up and drive me to the hospital. Michael's home was now behind those stale, sanitized walls.

Tubes and wires threaded into his limbs like slack puppet strings. Every day, he looked the same: Eyes shut. Thin gown. Thinner sheets. Thinning body.

After a quick therapy session (which usually involved playing a few hands of "Go Fish" while the therapist made one-sided small talk), I'd ride the steel box up to Michael's room, where I'd pick through my cafeteria dinner in silent vigil, waiting for the slightest flicker of movement in his face or a twitch of his hand. I'd offer him my Jell-O, and when he didn't take it, I'd tell him about my day.

After a while, I'd run out of things to say. Then I'd lay my head on his shoulder, take his oddly cool hand in mine, and play him a cassette tape of Billy Joel's "Piano Man." His girlfriend, also 14, had recorded herself playing it for him. The song gave me goose bumps (and still does) because it so perfectly captures the two sides of my brother.

> *He's quick with a joke or to light up your smoke*
> *But there's someplace that he'd rather be*
> *He says, "Bill, I believe this is killing me."*
> *As the smile ran away from his face*
> *"Well I'm sure that I could be a movie star*
> *If I could get out of this place."*

Michael never so much as fluttered an eyelid. Sometimes I wanted to pinch him or dig my nail under his skin, just to see if that would get a reaction, but I never did. I was irrationally afraid he'd pop up and get me back.

⁓

By the end of the first week, visitors trickled in from Boston: my cousins, aunt, and great aunt. Tim was stuck at work, and Grace had just had a baby. But Connor came two different times. Even with all the visitors, the only time Michael stirred was when Mom flew in to visit.

Two years is such a long time to a young heart. I could hardly believe I was in the same space as her again. When she'd left us with the Dumonts, Mom had said it was "forever." Oh, but I was happy when she walked into that bleached hospital room. She was skinnier than ever, her worn clothes gaping at the waist and neck. Her eyes looked a bit beaten down, but her hair was just as big as before.

After exchanging a knowing look with me, Mom walked up to Michael's side and said, "Hello, cutie pie," as she had when he was little.

I could hardly believe my eyes. For the first time since he'd been admitted, Michael *moved*. His entire body started trembling, and his breathing became shallow and quickened, as if he were having an asthma attack. It was her voice that did it. His eyes even opened for a bit. But he was somewhere else, looking past the ceiling, to something much farther away. He never woke up, not even when she cradled his hand in hers.

Still, Mom stayed by his side. Every day she read him the same creased letter, around 15 pages long. In it she asked him what caused his "accident," each possible explanation taking up one or two lines. She asked him if he was trying to get attention or if someone bullied him at school. Perhaps he was sad? Or was he seeking out some misguided thrill, as some of his friends had done?

I sat in the corner while she read, guilty at feeling content that we were a threesome again. Michael lay there with his eyes open. One day he began chewing his tongue until it bled and the nurse had to put a block in his mouth to keep him from hurting himself.

After that nothing much changed.

Between letter readings, Mom asked how I was doing. I told her about school, about missing her, about nothing and everything. I asked if she wanted to go to dinner, but she thought it best to keep our meetings at the hospital. She didn't want to upset the Dumonts; after all, they were my family now. I pleaded to come home with her, but each time she quietly reminded me that the Dumonts could give me so much more than she ever could.

There were lots of meetings about what to do with Michael. His hospital bill was $4,000 a day. And though the doctors said he might come out of the coma eventually, he'd never be self-aware. He'd never eat again except through an IV connected to his arm. They said any eye movement was pure reflex. I wondered about Michael's breathing when Mom had walked into the room: Surely that meant he was still in there somewhere. But no one else agreed.

Patricia and Pierre offered to put Michael in a home for invalids. Pierre even offered to set up a hospital bed in one of their many living rooms. But Mom shut them down, saying what only the doctors could admit: My brother was already gone.

She said it was inhumane to drag out the inevitable. The doctors took Michael off life support and moved him out of intensive care into a narrow room. The waiting game began.

By now Mom had used up all her vacation time. She flew back to Boston, but promised to come back the next weekend to visit. Before she left, she gave me a bear hug and whispered, "Just keep saying, 'All is well. All is well.'"

Michael's heart gave out a few days later, before Mom could make that next trip out. He'd been in a coma for a month. Out of confusion or perhaps fear, no one told Mom for three days that Michael had died. Patricia must have been gun-shy from their conversation earlier in the month; but secretly I wondered if anger was the real culprit. Most everyone blamed Mom for giving us up. But they didn't know what we'd lived through all those ugly, tattered years.

Mom may not have always made the right choices, but she did her very best. She fought like hell for us. I had witnessed her fierce love. Felt it. Lived it. Sending us with the Dumonts was just one small part of her war—our war. It was a white flag of surrender, reluctantly raised for hope's sake, for a shot at the peace we all so desperately craved.

Now 27, my oldest half brother, Connor, finally stepped up and gave Mom the news. He'd been the last person to see Michael before he died. Finding out after everyone else, Mom responded with all the fury of a cornered mama bear who's lost a cub. She was snarling and crazed and confused, and under it all, just so . . . sad.

Michael still had to be buried. Patricia and Pierre wanted Mom to make that decision, but she couldn't think straight, couldn't decide what to do with him. Finally, she resigned herself to letting the Dumonts bury him in Atlanta. But as my great aunt told Mom, that would never do. My brother needed to come home—*all* the way home. After she offered to cover the expense to fly him back to Boston, Mom signed the papers. Her lost little boy finally made the journey back to where he'd wanted to be all along.

I expected to be on that plane with Michael—or at least, not far behind. I couldn't wait to see my family at the funeral, to sink into their arms while I cried. But Pierre said I'd missed enough school while Michael was in the hospital. In the end, none of us went: not Pierre, not Patricia, not Lauren, Heather, or Toni. They held a small memorial service in Atlanta instead.

Mom wrote me a four-page letter describing the funeral. It was at the Holy Name Church, a few neighborhoods over from our old apartment in Jamaica Plain, where she still lived. Mom hired a harpist who plucked notes as delicate as dewdrops. It was spring, and the lilacs would have been blooming, fragrant and unapologetic. Connor, Tim, Grace, aunts, uncles, cousins—they were all there. Grace's young daughter, Daisy, toddled and made noises all through the mass ("Michael would have liked that"). His old principal was even there ("and says hello!").

Mom added that Michael's baseball hat and karate belt were tucked in his casket with him. She laid a long-stemmed red rose, a small white rose, and a sprig of baby's breath across his chest.

Mom ended the letter, "Patricia and Pierre gave Michael the best two years of his life. He got to do and try everything he ever wanted to do and try. They were very good to Michael. We all tried to help that boy—he had so much potential to be great. Don't look back too much—just enough to figure it out. Look ahead. You have a future. Remember, you can write to me. There is nothing I want more than for you to have a real family and home and good life and be happy because—you may not believe this—I LOVE YOU. And that's the whole truth, and nothing but the truth—so help me God!"

Then she cut her letter short: "But I don't want to dwell on that now. Someday, maybe in 100 years, we can talk about it again."

No one ever explained why we didn't go to the funeral, but I later learned that Pierre had opted not to attend his own brother's funeral years earlier. I suppose some people don't need or want that sort of closure.

But missing Michael's funeral made me feel that part of me was being amputated without my consent. He was gone, and there was nothing for me to do but stand in his sun-drenched room, watch the dust fairies swirl around me, and wonder at the impossible emptiness. The smell of life—his life—stuck to the room like a thumbtack; the little boy in wet slacks, mud-caked shoes tracked in carelessly, grass stains on every elbow and knee.

That's when the tears finally came. I cried out of anger and out of deep, churning loneliness. I cried when his clothes were stripped off their hangers and heaped into bloated, black trash bags for a local boys' home. I cried when his sneakers were thrown in the trash because they were too grimy to donate. I cried because I needed my mom. I cried because I didn't know how to stop crying. And the more I cried, the more hollow I felt.

PART TWO

Another Menu

"*Life is bitter when there is no sugar at the bottom.*"
—Boris Vian

CHAPTER 8

———

Innocent Abroad

About a week after Michael's death, Toni, Patricia, Pierre, and I sat around the breakfast table for the first time in weeks. It was 1992. President Bush had vomited on the prime minister of Japan, Mike Tyson pleaded guilty to rape, and at age 16, Tiger Woods had just become the youngest PGA golfer in 35 years. The spring air felt thick with Michael's absence, yet the sun slid up to the windowpanes and spilled down onto the table, sparkling with the promise of a normal day.

Oh, I still sneaked into the girl's bathroom at school to unload my tears, but this was to be a day without hospital visits or the staggering weight of impossible hope. My brother was gone; nothing could change that.

No longer a rock against the current, I tumbled back into the rhythm of normal life. I returned to school in time for homeroom and fell back into my studies. But now, the "pity stares" cast in my direction by the popular kids ended. For weeks their eyes had followed me through the halls, my very presence silencing their chatter. If they would just start teasing me again, I knew I'd be OK, that I could get through this. And then maybe I could start breathing again.

But first I had to get through breakfast. Fresh-squeezed orange juice, rolls, peach jam, and thick blocks of Irish butter dotted our large white plates. I slumped into the routine of the meal with relief, letting it prop me up and carry me through another day without Michael. But as I placed a soft, shiny roll onto my plate, everything changed.

"Pierre has a new job opportunity in Paris," Patricia said. "We'll be moving in August." The words were exhaled, more confession than revelation. She looked at Toni and me weakly, the corners of her mouth briefly drawn up into a half smile, as though she wanted to comfort us, but didn't have the emotional strength to pull it off. She shook her head, too—almost as if she were saying sorry.

Her words rattled me. We'd barely been in Atlanta two years. I felt a crumpling, a balling up; I held my breath, willing my eyes to stay dry. Like Patricia and Pierre, I was learning to wait until I was alone in my room to unfasten the harnesses of polite composure.

Pierre looked from Patricia to me, then added, "I—I got the offer a month ago, right when . . ." he trailed off, looking at his untouched roll. "I was going to tell you when I came home, but the timing wasn't ri—"

"You mean Paris, *France?*" I asked, feeling the words drop from my mouth like marbles. France sounded far away and dreamy, like a fairy tale . . . or an idea, nothing more than the Mona Lisa or the Eiffel Tower, firmly fixed to the pages of history and geography class. *Not* real life.

Pierre nodded.

"You're going to learn to speak French. You'll go to a French school." He looked at Toni. "Toni will finish her last semester of high school there."

Toni sat back in her chair. "Why can't I just finish school here?" she cried. Her hand played with the necklace her boyfriend had given her on Valentine's Day.

Patricia stared down at the brocade tablecloth, an intricate swirl of rust, mustard, and plum ornamentation that recalled Aladdin's carpet. "Can you please pass the rolls, Sasha?" She didn't look up, slowly tracing her finger along the designs.

"Sure." My words felt louder than usual. I sat taller. "No problem," I added, a new edge to my voice.

"Don't worry, you'll be able to spend your 13th birthday here. We won't leave until August. You'll have a month and a half to say goodbye, Sashita," Pierre added, using the Spanish nickname they often called me, meaning "Little Sasha." "Even though we're going to be in Europe, we decided to let you spend your summers with Connor, Tim, and Grace in New Jersey." He looked over at Patricia, then back to me. "We'll make sure of it. You can keep up your horseback riding, too . . . or maybe you'll find something else you'd like to do once you get there."

Since Michael's hospitalization, the Dumonts had made a considerable effort to make sure I spoke more regularly with my half siblings. As I considered spending several weeks in a row with them, I wondered why I couldn't just *live* with them. But I knew the truth. At 24 years old, Grace had her own budding family. Finances were incredibly tight. Tim was in film school; when he wasn't studying, he was working. Connor was about to get married, wrapped up in his own new beginning.

Who the hell moves to France at a time like this? I thought, shocked by the violence with which the words spun in my head. Feeling like an ingrate, my cheeks flushed with shame. Why couldn't I just be happy for the opportunity to see the world? I looked up the stairs, past the landing, toward Michael's bedroom.

"What about my mom?" I spoke up, working to flatten the tremor in my voice. "Will I see her?"

I felt the air leave the room. Patricia pressed her lips together. No one had heard from Mom since her last letter, not even Connor, Tim, or Grace. It was as if the emotional vortex of Michael's death had finally battered my mother's spirit past the point of no return. She was gone, physically and emotionally.

"Here, have some juice," Pierre said. He splashed a little into my glass, his eyes fixed on the rush of orange swirling up to the top. "You can always write her any time you want."

There was a pause.

"Finish up your breakfast, Sasha; it's almost time for school," Patricia said quietly.

I stared down at the roll on my plate, contemplating the stillness between goodbye and hello. It no longer mattered if the popular kids teased me. My life would never be the same. My hand floated over to my glass. I brought it to my lips slowly, on autopilot. As I chewed the cold pulp, my mom's words skated through my mind:

All is well.
All is well.
All is well.

Up until that moment, I'd taken all the turmoil of my childhood with the buttoned-up obedience of an innocent schoolgirl. Though I'd cried and prayed for different outcomes, at the end of the day I always did as I was told, no matter how sad it made me. But moving two months after losing Michael felt wrong.

Feeling different does not guarantee a different result; one has to *act* to invite change. I had neither the power nor the will to speak out. Perhaps it was a bit of fatalism taking over; nothing I could do would stop the move. I certainly couldn't call Mom or hope to return to her. She'd told me more than once during her visit that my best chance at a good life was with the Dumonts.

And I couldn't talk to Patricia and Pierre. The mere mention of Michael's name was met with averted eyes, as though I'd uttered a curse word. I knew that if no one wanted to talk about him, there was certainly no talking about Paris.

As the move approached, I didn't bargain with the universe as I had in Rhode Island. I didn't pray. In fact, I didn't even pack my boxes, except to make sure my big white teddy bear made the trip. The movers took care of the rest. Instead of bracing myself for the inevitable tremors that would come with a cross-continent move, I simply laid myself open and waited for the earth to swallow me up and spit me out wherever it would.

Before I knew it, I was carrying my suitcase through the glittering glass tunnels of Charles de Gaulle Airport and out into the pulsing heart of Paris. That night, I wrote Mom a postcard, squinting through the jet lag.

September 7, 1992
Hi Mom,
I made it to France! I'm tired, so I drank a coffee on the plane to stay awake. (Ew, I know.) Paris is beautiful. But there are so many buildings all around me.
I miss you and Michael so much.
I love you.

The chipper tone was purely for Mom's benefit. Without the comforting embrace of the familiar, I'd lost all my bearings, like a ship traveling through a moonless night. I washed up in Paris a hollow vessel. I could feel only one thing: complete, all-consuming emptiness.

When Mom didn't write back, there was nothing to do but hole up in my room in our new, suburban town house and cry for hours.

Eventually Paris called to me, luring me out of my room and away from my self-pity. Trains, whistling along the track, delivered me from our quiet *banlieue* (suburb) into its bristling heart, near the Arc de Triomphe, the Tour Eiffel, and the Trocadéro. After the thick heat of Atlanta, the city's foggy coolness slid over me, pulling me along damp sidewalks into cheery boulangeries loaded with macaroons, croissants, thick slabs of flan, and velvety chocolate truffles.

My first encounter with a baguette, torn still warm from its paper sheathing, shattered and sighed on contact. The sound stopped me in my tracks, the way a crackling branch gives deer pause; that's what good crust does. Once I began to chew, the flavor unfolded, deep with yeast and salt, the warm humidity of the tender crumb almost breathing against my lips.

I inhaled entire baguettes while walking along those wide, tree-lined avenues, in awe that a country had developed bread so divine out of nothing more than flour, yeast, water, and salt. The key, I would learn, was giving the dough time to develop. After a slow, cool ferment, it was blasted with an inferno of heat and steam, giving the crumb chew and the crust crackle. This is why, if I were to believe my eyes, no French person deigned to muddle it up with a careless smear of butter.

Hundreds of baguettes later, I cannot understand how the French limit themselves to one trim slice with dinner (though perhaps that was unique to the families I dined with). I suppose it's the result of having eaten good bread for an entire lifetime. In those early days I could never be so moderate; I ate as though the bread held some secret I could only uncover by obsessive consumption. Inevitably, I gained 15 pounds.

⑪ Artisan French Bread

It is possible to make very good French bread at home. Slow and cool yeast development is the secret to big flavor (no warmer than 65°F). I do this by mixing the yeast with a little flour and water ahead of time into a "poolish" starter. For a soft interior and thin, shattering crust, the French use steam-injected ovens. At home, a spray bottle and baking stone are the best tools for the job. This recipe—based on techniques learned at King Arthur Flour—takes three days, though there's barely 30 minutes active work. (It's certainly easier than packing a few bags and hopping on a flight to Paris!) Start on Thursday, and Saturday's dinner will be magnifique.

For the poolish:
2 cups flour
1 cup cold water
⅛ teaspoon active dry yeast

For the dough:
3 cups all-purpose flour
1 teaspoon yeast
2¼ teaspoons salt
Cold water (about ¾ cup)

Day 1 (5 minutes active): Make the poolish around bedtime. In a large bowl, stir together 2 cups flour, 1 cup cold water, and ⅛ teaspoon yeast into a pasty mass. Cover with plastic wrap and set in a cool spot (60° to 65°F) for 16 to 24 hours. Try on a shelf in the basement, by a drafty window, or—if it happens to be summer—over a bowl of ice.

Day 2 (10 minutes active): The next afternoon or evening, when the poolish is full of bubbles, knead in the remaining flour, yeast, salt, and water. The dough should be very wet and sticky.

Use the "slap-and-fold method" to form a dough ball: Stretch the mass up with the hands, then slap it with vigor onto a clean counter, and fold over itself. After 20 such folds, I like to wash and dry my hands, then pat the dough. The surface should be tacky and soft, but not leave gunk on the hand. A dusting of flour might be needed if it's rainy or humid, but I prefer not to add any—wet dough makes bread with bigger air pockets. Cover with plastic wrap. Return to the cool spot for another 16 to 24 hours.

Day 3 (15 minutes active): The next afternoon or evening, the dough will be full of large air bubbles. Slap and fold the dough a few times. The gluten will have developed quite a bit since the previous day; the dough will be smooth and elastic. Divide in thirds. Gently shape into 2-inch-wide logs taking care not to disturb the air bubbles. Nestle them between the folds of a floured cotton dish towel. Cover and let rest in a warm spot 20 to 30 minutes.

Preheat oven to 450°F (with baking stone, if using). Immediately before popping the baguettes into the oven, slash each one three times with a razor (or sharp knife) and spray with water. Cook on a sheet pan or directly on a baking stone until the baguettes are golden brown and the inside is cooked through, 20 to 25 minutes. Cool a few minutes before slicing to keep the crumb from mashing down. Enjoy, without so much as a trace of butter.

Makes 3 baguettes

CHAPTER 9

———●———

The Better Part
of a Minute

THE BAGUETTES WERE the amuse-bouche to Paris's living banquet. I consumed every morsel of that city, sniffing out the
creamiest Camemberts, the fluffiest omelets—even the great
citrus squeeze of a bubbling Orangina. I found myself stopping more
than once to inhale the Nutella-slathered crepes sizzling on every
street corner, filling the air with the scent of chocolate. So much of the
food was a teenager's dream, though much of it challenged me as well.

When I was too afraid to indulge in more exotic dishes, I simply
ate with my eyes. I'd watch as fleets of trim women in black pants
and colorful scarves carried home their daily parcels, trailing sharp
scents in their wake (possibly from an especially stout blue cheese
or gamy duck liver pâté). I'd stand agape in front of butchers' windows, taking in the sight of long, wet cow tongues or embarrassingly
elongated sausages. I'd hold my breath while admiring voluptuous

rounds of stinky cheese, which unapologetically buttressed thick pâtés and quivering gelatins.

If the food of Paris was heady and salacious, so, too was the noise. Every few minutes the pop and whine of mopeds and scooters challenged car bumpers at every turn. When outside got to be too much, I slipped inside or away, into dark, candlelit cathedrals that had taken half a millennia to build, or onto stately bridges carved with the heads of long-lost kings. This city was both alive and ancient in a way I'd never seen, never touched, never felt before. I was small in her embrace—safe.

I disappeared into Paris's unquestioning rhythm, lulled by the babble around me, letting the confusion wash over me. I couldn't communicate with anyone, and I didn't want to. It was the perfect vacuum.

The week before school began, Patricia and Pierre bought Toni and me bicycles, giving us the freedom to continue exploring Paris in our own way. I clung to Toni—her laughter, her smiles, and the unspoken solace that she'd lost a brother that spring morning, too.

As Paris's boulangeries and landmarks became our everyday vistas, the urgent call to explore them was quelled. We settled into our neighborhood, pedaling for hours through the farmland that quilted right up to our small town house on the outskirts of Paris, where we'd pluck snacks right off the land: a few leaves of lettuce, a spicy crimson radish, or the aptly named horse carrot. If I was really lucky, I'd forget about Michael for the better part of a minute.

Then school began, and with it the requirement to communicate. I could no longer play the perpetual tourist. French schools are organized around ability. By segregating the students, teachers were better able to target the learning needs of each group without anyone getting bored or restless.

Since I didn't speak a word of French, I was placed in the bottom tier of eighth grade with the "difficult students"—those who didn't care, or who simply weren't capable of earning the highest marks.

We were called the "C" students. The only level below ours was the special-needs class and, if I were to believe my classmates, I'd end up there if I didn't learn the language quickly enough.

On day one, our immersion class chanted *"Bonjour"* in unison. By the end of the week, I could stumble my way through several sentences. The words piled into my brain, faster and faster. Science was in French. Math. Language. Social Studies. Music. While the rest of my classmates took notes with silver-tipped fountain pens, I poured over the photos and charts in the textbooks to decipher the day's lessons. Sometimes it helped, but usually it didn't.

For the first time in my life I was failing, not just one subject, but every one. Teachers' comments were always the same: *"Travail insuff-isant*. Poor effort." My grades were consistent: 0/20, or the even more infuriating 0.5/20. But I *was* trying. It's just that my grief interrupted my studies, and my studies interrupted my grief. I was a girl divided.

In an attempt to create some sort of cultural familiarity, I'd gravitated toward the handful of Americans at my school. We commiserated about how difficult French immersion was—but I was still doing more poorly than any of them.

After seeing my grades, Patricia and Pierre encouraged me to make friends with some French kids. "They can help you learn the language more quickly," Pierre said, "Your grades will improve."

So against my shyer inclinations, I brought my tray of *steak hache, pommes frites*, and *fromage blanc* to the only open spot at a table of French kids. Their impossibly skinny hips dripped into vintage bell bottoms, baby doll dresses, and tuxedo "tail" shirts that reached the back of their knees. Doc Martens' fireproof soles and steel toes finished off their grunge ensembles and signaled that we were entering the mid-nineties.

No sooner had I sat down than everyone turned to me. One of the girls finally spoke up. "Can I have your fromage blanc?"

Fromage blanc is a mild form of cultured milk, like yogurt in texture but sweeter. The school typically served it with a dollop of raspberry preserves. Every day I'd scan the cafeteria, hoping to see it on the buffet line. Though it was my favorite dessert, I passed it to her without hesitation.

From that moment on I was one of them. They taught me "argot" (French slang) by the wrought-iron fence after school as quickly as I learned proper French in the classroom. I could rarely distinguish between the two types of speech, and often offered crass comments to my teachers, only realizing my mistake when the class erupted with giggles and the teacher flushed.

At recess my new crowd, the Doc Martens, clamored around me to gawk at the things I'd said. They slapped me on the back and taught me new words with knowing smirks, promising they were clean. Though this didn't do much for my grades (which had now been eked up to 9/20), I liked being the "funny" friend.

Before Toni left for college, she came in to my room and sat on the rumpled edge of my bed.

"Sasha, I know you miss him. But be careful not to fall into the same trap he did. You can get through this."

"What do you mean?" I asked.

"You just remind me so much of him, sometimes."

"That's a good thing, right?"

I watched her eyes, looking for a telltale wince. But before I could read her, she pulled me into a hug and tickled me until I laughed.

"Of course, Sash."

In Toni's absence the house fell silent. Instead of coming together in our grief, Patricia, Pierre, and I drifted apart. Pierre worked longer and longer hours, often not coming home until after 10 p.m. Business trips whisked him away for weeks at a time.

When Pierre *was* home, Patricia would pack picnics and we'd eat in the car, juggling china plates, real silverware, and cloth napkins while rumbling along to some famed site, like Mont Saint-Michel—a good four-hour drive. The contortions of the gargoyles were the only therapy we had.

But when Pierre left again, Patricia drifted through the kitchen, anchoring herself with French recipes. French cooking suited her. I think it's how she mourned Michael and processed the fact that her youngest had left the nest. The grimmer her mood and the longer Pierre's trips lasted, the more elaborately she cooked. Soon she was torching oblong ramekins of crème brûlée until their razor-thin sugar crusts all but shattered on sight.

I'd find reasons to walk through the kitchen into the back garden just to catch a glimpse of her artistry. After my fifth appearance, she'd huff, "You're letting the flies in!" or "Inside or outside, which is it, Sasha?" I'd tiptoe to my room or the fields beyond.

Increasingly unsure of how to connect with the Dumonts, I sought out other ways to feel—something, anything. I took my first drink of whiskey at 13 in the girls' bathroom with my new friend Monique. Being a little girl was no barrier to buying booze directly from French liquor stores.

It wasn't long before I was spending afternoons pouring bottles into myself at the local park with the Doc Martens. We'd lie in the grass, make daisy crowns, and watch the clouds spin. We interpreted our world through the lyrics of The Doors, The Cure, and Tom Petty. We called it science class.

For "*quatres-heures,*" French snack time, we stumbled back to Monique's house where she served up *tartines au chocolat,* her brilliant invention. To make the sweet towers, she toasted thick slices of brioche bread until the golden crumb swirled like henna art. Then she used a fat, paddle-shaped knife to slather them with Nutella.

In those days, the chocolate hazelnut spread was not sold stateside so I goaded her to use more, and then more still, until half the jar was gone and each slice looked like frosted cake. Triple stacked, the heat made the Nutella slump into the crevices and drip over the crisp edges.

Sometimes we ate the oozing morsels standing in Monique's kitchen, before the toaster had a chance to cool off. Other times we'd carry the tartines to a park bench surrounded by white wildflowers. No matter where we were, we had to lick the hazelnut chocolate spread from the corners of our lips and fingers.

By the end of eighth grade, I'd forged notes for twelve doctor appointments, eight eye doctor appointments, and seven dentist appointments. On weekends I smeared black lipstick across my lips and disappeared into the few thudding, sexy, vapid nightclubs that let minors in. I pressed myself close to the wrong sort of boys, mistaking their lust for love.

Eventually the noise around me was so loud that I actually *felt* something again. I grew addicted to this whisper of emotion as I moved and danced and *lived*. The poet Shane Koyczan once said, "Addiction isn't so much about pain as it is sanity." Truer words have never been spoken.

This time in my life will always be best represented by the night I sat on the steps of the Parc du Château de Saint-Germain-en-Laye. Its angular pathways overlook the twinkling city and the even more dazzling Eiffel Tower. The metal structure stretched more than a thousand feet into the sky, lit from head to toe like a Christmas tree.

Though we'd long since lost track of the time, I knew it was after midnight. I was drunk, holding a bottle of tequila, leaning on Monique to stay upright. The stone beneath us was cold. The bitter snap of winter radiated through my corduroys until my teeth chattered.

"What now, Sasha? It's getting late," she said. She always spoke English when drunk—the only time she did.

"Watch this," I said, smiling mischievously. I looked up at the Eiffel Tower, raised my right hand, and snapped. Before I could blink, the lights extinguished; first the top row of the tower, then the middle, and finally the bottom. Monique drew her breath in sharply.

"Did you see that?" I stared into the darkness. "I . . . I *did* that!" I pointed my trembling hand toward the spot where the Eiffel Tower should have been, tears filling my eyes while the most pure form of laughter rang out from beneath the liquid armor of intoxication. Deep down I knew that lights on the Eiffel Tower were automated, but in that moment I needed to believe I'd turned them off.

The drinking, the skipping school—all of it—was about regaining some sort of control. That night, I felt that there might be just enough magic in the world to help me through constant upheaval and loss. What I didn't realize was that the more I drank, the less in control I was.

I did my best to hide my new interest from Patricia and Pierre—not because I was ashamed, but because like any true addict, I wanted to protect my habit. But my transgressions caught up with me.

"Have you been skipping school?" Pierre asked one afternoon after I stumbled home from a full day of drinking beer at the park.

"No."

"Are you sure?"

"Of course," I said, "Aren't you supposed to be at work?"

He looked at me steadily, and then sighed.

"What's this?" He pulled a small white note out of an envelope and placed it on the kitchen table: "Sasha has a doctor's appointment. Please excuse her from class today." It was signed, "Pierre Dumont."

"Well, just the once—" I began.

"And this?" he interrupted, tossing down another slip of paper. "And this?" He tossed down note after note, until 27 were amassed in front of me.

I stared at the pile, unable to speak. A few slid onto the floor, fluttering like leaves in autumn.

"You're not going to do this again, Sasha," he said firmly, "You're too smart to waste your life like this."

I recoiled as though I'd been slapped.

"Like my brother?" I screamed. I stormed up to my room, taking two stairs at a time, and slammed the door behind me.

A few minutes later, Pierre sat on the edge of my bed and stared at the floor. "Sasha, we just want the best for you. Patricia and I talked this over. Clearly you have too much time on your hands. We're going to take you to the library every Sunday, and we'll stay there as long as it takes to get your grades in order. And there'll be no more bike riding to school."

The next school day Patricia and I had a standoff in the backyard when I tried to sneak my bike out of the shed. She grabbed my wrist. "There's going to be no bike until we can trust you'll actually go to school," she said firmly. And she didn't back down. We stood like that a good 20 minutes, until finally I wrenched my arm away and stormed off cussing.

"Save that language for your friends," Patricia called after me.

"I don't talk like that to *friends*."

We both flushed. Not only was she not my "Mama," but now I'd shot down the most basic of connections. Still, she picked up her car keys and followed me. "Come on, let's go. I'll drive you."

But I slammed my bedroom door in her face. I wasn't even sure why I was so angry. After all, I'd brought this on myself. I *knew* better than to skip school. But in the moment, it felt like that bike was all I had.

On Sunday, Patricia, Pierre, and I took the RER train into the heart of Paris to the American Library. Like a caged animal, I paced the stacks for hours, sniffing through art, poetry, and recipe books before I reluctantly settled down and began my homework. Library days usually lasted no less than five hours. Slowly, my grades improved.

⁓

By ninth grade, just when it seemed the Dumonts were getting a handle on me, a card from Mom came in the mail—her first communication since Michael's funeral two years earlier. I tore open the envelope in front of Patricia and Pierre, hands trembling in anticipation. As the gold-trimmed card slid out from the ivory linen, I saw a glossy photo of Michael, laid out in his casket, hands clasped across his chest.

Patricia and Pierre sucked in their breath in unison. Patricia said, "Oh, I'm so sorry, Sashita."

I ran out of the house, tearing as fast as I could through the farmland at the end of our suburban street. My lungs burned, my legs shook, but I didn't stop. Soon, I stumbled on some tall cave-like openings cut into the surrounding hills—an old quarry by the looks of it—its wooden gates carelessly left ajar.

I crept past a "No Trespassing" sign. Inside, a maze of limestone tunnels snaked for miles, supported by an occasional rough-hewn pillar. Here and there mushrooms grew on the silt floors, clearly cultivated by local farmers. But for the most part, the great, echoing halls were empty—abandoned. The only light came through grate-covered manholes in the rock above.

I found a corner deep within the tunnels. Taking the card from the envelope, I shut my eyes so that I wouldn't have to see Michael's face again. In the dim light I poured over what Mom had written inside. Though I don't recall her exact words, I know she included a poem I wrote shortly after he died. Now my words felt overly sentimental and trite.

I threw the card among the rubble.

For months afterward, I returned to that dusty space. Sometimes I thought about tasting the mushrooms strewn along my path, but I never did. I told friends I kept going back to find lost treasure, but in truth I was looking for the card. As much as it sickened me, I wanted to find Michael, as well as Mom's lost words. But all I ever found was my growing collection of empty wine bottles.

Patricia and Pierre never knew about my secret place. Though we never discussed Mom's card, they implicitly understood the impact it had on me. In response, they renewed their efforts, catapulting me into as many new places and experiences as possible. By tenth grade, I'd raced with my English class around an ancient Olympic stadium in Greece, snowplowed down the Swiss Alps with the Dumonts, and drunk high tea in England with my history class. In two hours in any direction, I could start anew with different spices, different languages, and different cultures. Summers were split between Connor, Tim, and Grace's and prestigious art camps that Patricia and Pierre sent me to, costing more than a year of state college. All along the way, Patricia continued to send care packages and little notes.

The Dumonts must have figured that by providing so many distractions, I wouldn't have time to feel sorry for myself (or at the very least there'd be no time to drink). In some ways they were right.

But even when my fingers were stained with charcoal and paint, art camp frustrated me—I never could quite capture my dreams. And though I always returned from those trips in high spirits, every idyllic vacation with my siblings' thriving young families (Connor and Grace had both been married by now with multiple children) made the joys of Paris paler, somehow.

~~~

At the end of tenth grade, Patricia invited Grace to visit me in Paris. Though I'd spent every summer since Michael had died with her and my brothers, this was the first time she'd come to see me at the Dumonts', let alone in Europe. I was 16; she was 28. When Grace exited the crowded gate with a quick, sure bounce, I was beside myself with excitement. Finally, I'd be able to share *my* life with *her*.

When Grace smiled, I was surprised to recognize a sliver of my own face in hers. We'd both had long hair when we were younger, but mine was now cropped short and shaggy; hers was styled with the more practical bob and bangs of motherhood. I could hardly believe her daughter Daisy was almost three. I asked Grace if she got the same greeting card from Mom, with the photo of Michael in the casket. She nodded slowly, and then hugged me.

"I don't know what she was thinking," she sighed, "I don't pretend to understand anything she does."

"Is she OK? Have you talked to her?"

She frowned. "No one has. Not since the funeral. But enough about that—let's enjoy this time before it passes us by."

For weeks we stayed up late talking into the night. We giggled about boys. We did each other's hair and nails. We went shopping in Paris's Galeries Lafayette. During the day we hiked to the top of

Montmartre and ate a picnic lunch overlooking the vast city. As Paris wrapped itself around Grace, I was reminded of my first weeks there, before Toni had left and I'd ensnared myself in bad choices.

This could have been me, I thought. And then, *this could be me.*

Toward the end of Grace's visit, after an afternoon of shopping in Saint-Germain-en-Laye, we collapsed into a small bistro for lunch.

"What's good here?" she asked, scanning the bilingual menu.

"It's France. *Everything* is good."

She laughed. "How about this?" she asked, and pointed to the croque monsieur.

I told her any toasted sandwich layered with ham and a smothering of Gruyère cheese, broiled until browned and bubbling, was bound to be a winner. With a little prodding, Grace placed our order in French, blushing when the cute waiter replied in English. (French waiters often speak to patrons in English whenever they detect an American accent.)

As I crunched into half of the buttery, salty, smoky sandwich, I realized—not without a bit of alarm—that no one at school or in a shop or restaurant had spoken to me in English for at least a year. In fact, now that I thought about it, I realized that I was even dreaming in French. Despite my best efforts to remain uninvested in this new life, I'd somehow adapted. I was as close to a native as I could get. *Could this be home?* I wondered.

Sharing Paris with Grace lifted the haze. I saw that though I'd been living there for three years, the alcohol and partying had kept me from the soul of this place.

After Grace went home, it became clear that I had three choices for my future: I could sit in my room and weep for a little boy's life that could never be resurrected; I could drink under the trees until my heart was intoxicated enough to think it was full; or I could move into this world, fully and without hesitation.

For my first few years in Paris, I'd trudged indelicately through the former two options. But I now saw that it was time to see the magnificent grandeur of the place through the simple enjoyment of a croque monsieur—of belonging.

12-Minute Croque Monsieur

The croques monsieurs found in Parisian bistros are gloriously indulgent, dripping with toasted cheese and ham, under a layer of bubbling béchamel. There are many variations on what is essentially a fancy grilled cheese, some made on a panini press, others in the oven. The most popular rendition is made with Gruyère, a sharp cheese known for its fantastic melting qualities.

Though many choose to replicate the croque monsieur at home with homemade béchamel sauce, Monique taught me the simplest method of all, which relies on crème fraîche—a fermented dairy product similar to sour cream—for richness. As the sandwich bakes, the tangy spread melts into the bread, softening the center—a striking contrast to the blackened outer edges. Crème fraîche can be found in the dairy case.

For bread, Monique prefers pain de mie—good quality sandwich bread, often square in shape, though I find the recipe excellent on most anything the bakery has to offer. Though Monique doesn't pre-toast her bread, some might prefer the added crunch this gives the center of the sandwich.

2 slices good quality sandwich bread
2 tablespoons crème fraîche
3 or 4 thin slices Gruyère cheese
1 slice ham cold cuts

Preheat the oven to 425°F.

Toast the bread, if desired. This can be done in the oven during the last few minutes of preheating.

To assemble the sandwich: Spread a slice of bread with a tablespoon of crème fraîche. Add a slice of cheese, a slice of ham, and a second slice of cheese. Add the second slice of bread and spread the top with another tablespoon of crème fraîche. Finish with a final slice of cheese.

Bake for 6 minutes, then transfer under the broiler until the top of the sandwich is bubbling and lightly browned.

Enough for 1 sandwich

CHAPTER 10

Salt of the Land

S HORTLY AFTER GRACE LEFT, Patricia and Pierre announced that we'd be moving to Luxembourg, a pencil tip of a country several hours north of Paris. Pierre had secured a contract at a small manufacturing firm there. As their financial director, he'd be monitoring the money on a special construction project for a Fortune 500 company in parts of eastern Europe. There'd be a lot of travel. He spoke enthusiastically about the project and told Patricia and me how much we'd love pastoral Luxembourg. Patricia didn't say much.

At 16, I received the news with equal parts trepidation and excitement. My fears of starting over again—of building yet another home—were mostly quelled by the prospect of a clean slate, of unhinging the walls I'd so determinedly constructed in Paris. Over the four years since Michael's death, I'd formed an identity there as the wild one, the wounded one, the loose cannon. The exertion had exhausted me.

By nature I am not an extrovert; that had been Michael's role. As much as I'd like to think I reinvented myself in Paris, I was still struggling, mixed up in a fast crowd. I often wondered if Pierre and Patricia realized this, and decided that the only way for me to move forward was to cut me off, once and for all, from the Doc Martens—to give me a fresh point of view, literally.

Three months later, we moved to a three-story cobbled farm-house in a small town on the outskirts of Luxembourg City. Across the street, three goats bleated and two cows bellowed behind a weathered stone wall. My long, skinny bedroom had been converted from the days when attics were reserved for mice and hay.

I slid my bed under an angled skylight, where I could watch Orion's Belt glimmer in the blackness. I wondered if Mom saw the same stars from her bedroom window. Somehow the world felt smaller when I believed that she basked in their brightness, too. Where Paris had consumed me, Luxembourg cradled me; its undulating hills and valleys, thick forests, rolling pastures, and trim town squares were humble and quiet after the gritty grandeur of Paris.

Patricia must have felt it, too. Almost immediately her cooking shifted to the salt of the land: lamb stews, green bean soup, plum tarts, easy roasts. Her new kitchen was smaller than the ones she'd previously had, filled with the narrow darkness typical of a home constructed in the 1800s.

To ensure that I got my grades in order, the Dumonts enrolled me in an American school and had me repeat tenth grade. The school had once been a convent. Vines trailed along the crumbling stone and plaster walls. The windows were long and pointed, like enormous pope hats. A statue of Saint Mary still graced the tiny courtyard.

My entire class was made up of just 18 students, most of whom had known one another their whole lives. Unlike the rough-edged Doc Martens, these kids wore polo shirts, khakis, and Mary Janes. Not only did the girls *not* wear black lipstick, they didn't wear makeup at all (unless sheer lip gloss counts). Social events included basketball games. And from what I could tell, being a good student was *cool.* Only a few juniors and seniors operated on the fringes, sneaking off campus to smoke for ten minutes during lunch, or staying out until midnight on the weekends.

I gravitated toward these relatively tame rebels out of habit. But every time I ran across the street and hid behind a stone wall for a hurried smoke, every time I threw back a beer after class, I tasted disappointment. I couldn't believe how easily I'd settled back into my bad habits.

My failure to reinvent myself ate away at me. Two months into the school year, I sunk into what felt like depression. At first I was listless in the early evening. Then my eyes glazed over during class. Pierre chalked it up to the move. "Take a shower, you'll feel better," he said.

But this was unlike any fatigue I'd ever experienced. Unable to concentrate, I excused myself from classes to sleep on the cool floor of the darkened auditorium until school let out. I crashed when I got home, only waking for dinner, generally eating little more than a crust of bread or thimble of stew. After a couple of weeks, I stopped waking up for dinner. I wondered, in passing, if this is what it felt like to be a bear—to hibernate.

With Pierre's urging (he didn't want me to fall behind), I continued going to school through fever and chills. And because I didn't know how to stop, I also sleepwalked through my social life. One Friday afternoon, I drank half a pint of beer that came back up on the public bus. The next day my skin was yellow, and I couldn't keep water down. Pierre and Patricia took me to the ER for a battery of tests. While the lab processed my blood work, the doctor did an ultrasound. He looked grim.

"We're not sure what's wrong with you. Your symptoms seem to point to hepatitis C, but it could also be a severe case of mononucleosis. Your liver is *very* damaged. I've never seen anything like it."

He pointed to the ultrasound, a wash of incomprehensible black, white, and gray. He put down the image and took off his glasses.

"Miss Lombardi, you might not make it," he finally said, speaking English slowly, trying to make sure I understood. His eyes were clear and blue, soft but unblinking.

I nodded and closed my eyes. The illness had overwhelmed any desire for self-preservation. I wanted to tell him I knew why my liver was damaged, that I was stubborn and stupid and unable to control my drinking. I wanted to tell him I needed help.

Instead I retreated under the paper hospital bedding and slept. When the lab work came back, I learned I had mononucleosis. Though mine was the most severe case they'd ever seen, the doctor said that in time my liver would fully recover. For two weeks, nurses pumped fluids into me, took more ultrasounds, and monitored my white blood cell count. Color gradually returned to my cheeks, and I was moved out of intensive care.

One day a chipper redhead popped into my room.

"Hi, Sasha, how are you feeling?"

I looked at the girl blankly. She seemed familiar, but I couldn't quite place her or her British accent.

"It's me, Annie. Can I come in?"

Before I had a chance to object, she rushed into the room. Her ear-to-ear grin all but caught her freckles on fire. That's when it hit me. This girl was in my class. We hadn't spent time together; she was almost a year and a half younger than me, and didn't smoke or drink. She deposited a tote full of homework and a signed card from classmates on the edge of the bed and then sat down at my side.

"Now onto the important stuff—let's talk boys!"

None of the other kids I'd been hanging out with had come by. In fact, aside from Patricia and Pierre, Annie was my first visitor.

"How come you're being so nice to me? Coming all the way out here, to the hospital?" I asked, overwhelmed.

"Why not?" She shrugged her shoulders.

"It's just that it's really far away—"

"Nonsense. I know what it's like to move, and to be the new kid. Where are you from? Do your parents move a lot?"

"Nowhere, really." I looked down, "Actually, they're not my parents. I'm adopted. That's why I don't have red hair."

I don't know why I lied. I'd always said Patricia and Pierre were my guardians before.

She reached across the bed to pet my hand. "You and I are going to be good friends." She smiled again. Her warmth immediately dissolved my defense mechanisms.

After I got out of the hospital, Annie and I were inseparable. With her friendship, I no longer felt the urge to sneak off campus and smoke. Instead I threw myself into my studies and activities. I joined the basketball and softball teams. I continued theater and choir. I was the yearbook editor. I made the honor society.

This is not to say I didn't rebel anymore. Though I still stayed out late and socialized with some of the older kids in school, they were on a serious curfew. When I pushed the limits, I was only out until 2 a.m.

Patricia and Pierre let me be as long as my grades didn't suffer. And they didn't. For two years, I excelled in every subject and slowly built my confidence.

But Patricia seemed to be sinking under the pressures of yet another move, another language barrier, another world. Though she'd grasped a fair amount of French when we lived in Paris, the shopkeepers of Luxembourg seemed to favor Luxembourgish and German. Whereas the expat community at school insulated me, Patricia kept more and more to herself, only connecting with the other mothers in passing.

She perked up when her girls came home for the holidays. Patricia and Pierre made a point of flying their daughters home every Christmas and Thanksgiving, often extending the invitation to their boyfriends, who'd be put up at a nearby hotel. For two precious weeks

Patricia would bubble over, laughing and cooking the way she'd done when I first arrived in Atlanta: preparing roast chicken with tight, crackling skins, silken gravies, and cheese soufflés that never fell. One year she replaced our Christmas stockings with tights, which stretched to accommodate three times as many gifts.

But after she dropped the girls off at the airport, the gloom resurfaced. Patricia spent an increasing amount of time locked away in her bedroom. Sometimes I wouldn't see her face for weeks, though dinner would be on the table when I got home from school, fresh and steaming.

I wondered if it was my fault that Patricia was so sad.

Every time I called her "Patricia" and Pierre "Papa," I felt a twinge of guilt. But I couldn't undo the past. When an unwitting parishioner at our church looked from me to Patricia and remarked, "Oh, I see the family resemblance!," neither of us knew how to respond.

I hunkered down, head tucked firmly in my shell, waiting for Patricia's smile and big laugh to echo through the house again. When she'd finally emerge from her room—and she always did—I tiptoed around the house in an effort to keep the peace as long as possible.

One day in the winter of 11th grade, I sat at the breakfast table, eating a bowl of cereal before a basketball game. It was 6, maybe 7 a.m. I hadn't seen Patricia for days. Suddenly, in the early morning quiet I heard a rustling upstairs, and then a stomping. Someone was coming downstairs—fast.

Patricia thrust her head into the breakfast room, a scowl contorting her face. She opened her mouth, then thought better of it. When she stomped back upstairs and slammed her bedroom door, the whole house shook. A moment later, she was back. She looked at me, then fled back upstairs and slammed her door again.

Finally she was back. "Michael killed himself because of you," she fumed. "It's *your* fault, not mine. I picked up the phone when he was talking to a friend. He said *you* were driving him crazy."

She turned on her heel and disappeared into her room.

I stared at the empty doorway in shock. Five years had passed since Michael had died. I'd never heard her say anything about his death, let alone whose fault it was. My mind swirled with anger, disbelief, and then doubt. The thought of being responsible for his death was too much. Adrenaline pushed into my veins, fingertips, and toes. A scream rose up inside my chest. But I shut my eyes and silenced my simmering emotions. There was no peace in this forced quiet, only stubborn survival. Slowly, I shouldered my gym bag and left.

Patricia's words consumed me for the next days and weeks while I replayed them over and over: *Could she be right? Was it my fault? Did he give up on life because I was a pain in the neck?* It seemed ridiculous. My friend Annie assured me that it was. But since I hadn't heard the conversation, I couldn't be sure.

Annie said she thought Patricia blamed me because she had her own guilt to unload. "Think about it, Sasha. She took you kids in. He died on her watch. Everyone knows it wasn't her fault, but that doesn't mean she believes it. She *had* to make you the scapegoat, just to make the hurt ease up."

I wasn't sure, but I did know one thing: I didn't want to upset Patricia again. I hollowed out my personality in an attempt to remove any potential source of conflict, real or imagined. Instead of telling her I didn't like the Swiss cheese she put on our hamburgers, I simply said I was vegetarian—except for fish and chicken. I left the house as much as possible, finding solace in my friendships. I never told Pierre what had happened; he watched me come and go with a look of bewildered concern. I kept the conversation with Patricia to the essentials, like what time I had to be at school, or where my sport trips would take me.

On those trips, my friends became my family—Annie more than any other. When she invited me to spend Christmas with her in Spain, we all welcomed the idea. Annie and I spent those two weeks eating paella, a traditional Spanish rice dish made with smoked paprika, saffron, and all manner of fish or meat. We wandered daily through the neat orange groves in the valley below her parents' small villa. One afternoon, I plucked an orange from the branches but found that the center was more pith than pulp. When I asked Annie when the fruit would sweeten, she shook her head and said, "No telling."

One evening in early spring, I came home from school to find Pierre in the kitchen holding a box of spaghetti, reading the label.

"What are you doing?" I asked, surprised to see him there. He was never in the kitchen, unless he was grabbing one of his daily apples from the fruit basket on the counter. "Where's Patricia?"

"Patricia went to the States to take care of her dad for a few months." He turned the box in his hand, tracing his finger along the ingredients label. "Hey, do you have any idea how to make this?"

"What do you mean, she went to the States?"

"She . . . she just had some things she needed to take care of."

I waited for him to elaborate, but he kept staring at the spaghetti box.

"Did I do something wrong?" I asked. "Is she mad at me?"

"No." He shook his head sadly, "She's just mad at the whole world right now. She needs some time. And her father needs her."

I considered Pierre's expression, so tightly controlled, but so clearly brokenhearted. This string bean of a man had no idea what to do without his wife. For the first time, I noticed a few strands of gray in his brown hair.

I took the box from his hand and read the label: "Boil 2 quarts of water. Add pasta. Cook 8 to 10 minutes."

Pierre got out a measuring cup and began to dump 8 cups of water into a pot, one by one.

"You really don't need to do that," I laughed. "Let me help."

I filled the pot with a rush of water, stopping when it was three-quarters full. I cranked the heat to high, dumped a handful of salt in the water, and popped on the lid. Pierre reached for the tomato sauce, but I pried Patricia's *Joy of Cooking* off the shelf and thumbed through the worn pages until I found the entry for home-made Alfredo sauce. I accidentally added the flour after the milk, so it came out lumpy, but a quick taste proved that the mash was still edible.

Next I chopped a salad. Pierre and I enjoyed our makeshift dinner at the breakfast table with mismatched plates and paper napkins. It was nowhere as beautiful as Patricia's meals, but it was seasoned with the luscious sauce of accomplishment. While we ate, I asked Pierre if I could help cook dinner again sometime.

"You don't need to worry about dinner—"

"But I *want* to."

"Well, how about I make dinner during the week, and if you want to play on the weekends, go for it." He looked over to the basket of potatoes. Their knobby eyes were sprouting white, slender roots. "What do you think about starting a garden? We could grow Brussels sprouts. And potatoes."

I clapped my hands. "Let's do it right now!"

So we went outside, beneath the sinking sun, and tilled the overgrown garden patch until the dry crust was replaced with moist, black soil.

The next day at school I rushed to my friends, thrilled with the prospect of cooking again. "Who wants to start a cooking club? We can all take turns hosting at our houses. I can go first!" I wanted to make sure I'd be able to get my night in before Patricia returned.

That Saturday, Annie came to the house with a basket of lettuce, tomato, red onion, feta cheese, and olives. A soft baguette was tucked under her arm, still warm from the bakery. We paraded solemnly into Patricia's long dark kitchen.

"It feels so weird being in here," I confided.

"I wouldn't worry about it. Can't let a perfectly good kitchen go to waste!" she said, flipping on the light switch.

We hunted through the cabinets, rummaging until we uncovered a green stoneware mixing bowl. Carefully I added some flour, four eggs, and a sprinkling of water to make homemade pasta. But the dough was a stiff knot, ravines cracking through the surface even as we tried to knead it together. I remembered how Mom used to say Grammie made hers with the strength of a hundred Italian sailors.

"I don't know, maybe we should rest our arms for a minute," I said.

Annie threw a damp cloth over the dough and we ran down to the liquor store. Ignoring the shop owner's recommendations for a crisp white wine, we filled our arms with sangria mix. Back at the house, we poured it into a pitcher along with sliced oranges, limes, and lemons.

Twenty minutes later, I poked the mound of dough with my finger and was surprised to find that it dimpled softly. I cupped my hands around it and squeezed. The craggy surface yielded, mashing together smoothly. Annie and I laughed. Maybe what appeared to be strength was in truth a question of knowing when to work the dough and when to let it rest.

Pierre came in to see what we were doing. I handed him a half-glass of sangria and shooed him out of the kitchen.

"We're fine. Thank you," I said, smiling.

"OK!" he said, cheerfully.

"Really—thank you." Suddenly tears were in my eyes, "I don't think you'll ever realize what this means to me."

One by one the girls arrived. While Annie greeted them, I made the Alfredo sauce a second time, whisking whole milk and Parmesan into the pale roux until a velvety white sauce formed. This time there were no lumps. I ladled it over the hot pasta.

The seven of us sat around the dining table, candles lit, wine-glasses filled with scarlet-washed fruit. We were only 17 and 18, but we felt like grown-ups. We were so engrossed in conversation that we didn't even finish the sangria.

Our cooking club continued at everyone's house, one each week. We ate Turkish food at Yonca's house and Irish stew at Maeve's house. Annie decided nothing would be better than to host a chocolate feast. It was one of my happiest high school experiences: building friendship while sharing the joy of communal dining and creation.

❚❚ Homemade Pasta Dough

Homemade pasta has a mild, toothsome quality that dried pasta cannot match. Even after a good boil, the slippery noodles seem thirsty, soaking up the sauces and broths in which they swim. I, for one, believe all chicken noodle soups should contain such love.

Though most pasta recipes use semolina and omit water in favor of olive oil, mine is a good beginner recipe—easily workable. But it does need to rest. Twenty minutes in the beginning gives the water time to distribute evenly, smooth out the gluten strands, and soften the mix. If the dough springs back during rolling, two things can be done to relax the gluten further: Occasionally lift and slap it down onto the table—or walk away for a few minutes.

A note on salt: Mom taught me what her Grammie taught her—salt the water, not the dough. She says it keeps the dough from getting tough.

5 cups all-purpose flour
4 large eggs
A little water

Add the flour to a large bowl or mound it onto a clean kitchen counter. Push one of the eggs into the center of the flour and swirl it around to make a crater. Crack the eggs into the crater and beat them into the flour. I like to use my fingertips, but a large fork works well, too.

When the eggs are evenly distributed, stream in the water. I typically use a half cup, but on a dry day, ¾ cup may be necessary. Work the shaggy mass into a rough ball; the dough should be stiff and knotty looking, almost craggy. Cover with a damp cloth and let rest about 20 minutes. This will give the water time to distribute evenly through the flour, making smoother and more pliable dough. Knead for 5 minutes.

From here, the dough can be rolled thinly and sliced with a pizza cutter to make fettuccine. Sheets of dough can also be filled to make several dozen ravioli. While rolling, remember to dust the pasta dough if needed, and slap it down once in a while to get the gluten to relax.

Gently boil until tender, keeping in mind fresh pasta typically cooks twice as fast as dried. Bite to test doneness. If any white remains in the center, keep cooking.

Makes 2¼ pounds

CHAPTER II

On Borrowed Time

W HEN IS SHE COMING HOME?" I asked Pierre as I cut into the tender red skin of a newly harvested potato.

In Patricia's absence, spring had given way to summer. Our potato sprouts had cracked through the dirt and formed leafy plants. For weeks, Pierre and I had piled soil around each tender stem, hilling them for the best yield. When the leaves yellowed and dropped, we'd pulled the tiny potatoes from the dirt and boiled them with a touch of salt. I had no idea if Patricia had called with an update, or if she and Pierre were even talking. But I couldn't take the silence any more.

"I–I'm not sure," Pierre said, staring at the mound of potatoes on his plate. Whenever I asked him about her, he stuttered, clearly heartbroken. So I stifled my questions, and we continued our meal in silence.

Another few months went by. I started my senior year of high school. The green leaves began to lose their vibrant hue, and just when the first few began to fall, Pierre announced that Patricia would be home that weekend.

Though bewildered by the sudden news, I was happy for Pierre that she *was* in fact coming home. And she wasn't coming alone. Patricia had decided to bring her dad back to live with us, converting the dining room into his bedroom, since his health was deteriorating and he needed care. She and her father had become close since her mother's tragic death when Patricia was a young girl.

That night I crept into the kitchen and checked every last corner for crumbs. I scrubbed it down and silently slipped out again.

⁓

That fall, I put my nose down and focused on college applications, applying to a dozen schools all over the United States. Patricia never mentioned her time away, but resumed her duties with weary determination. But she was different. Her eyes glanced off mine. It was as if my very presence tormented her. It grew worse and worse, until Patricia ignored me so completely for two weeks that I began to pinch myself, wondering if I'd become a ghost. I wondered if she knew I'd been cooking in her kitchen, and asked Pierre if he thought that was the reason for her behavior toward me.

"I don't know, Sasha." He looked up the long, narrow stairway to her shuttered room.

"You have to find out. Please," I cried, "I feel . . . invisible."

An hour later, Pierre emerged from her room and motioned me outside into the blue winter light. We sat on a stone bench under an old oak tree by the vegetable patch. No one spoke for a long while. I traced my sneakers through the dirt. Finally, he cleared his throat.

"Did you tell Annie's parents that you were adopted?"

I looked up in surprise. Lately I'd told a lot of people that.

"Well, yes, I—"

He took a deep breath. "You shouldn't have done that."

"I know it's not true, but . . ." I looked down at the potato plants, now blackened from the frost. I wondered if the roots would survive the winter. "It was just easier than saying *guardian*. It sounded nicer . . ."

"Sash, we didn't adopt you on purpose. We want to keep the door open for you to see your mom again. We never thought you'd be with us this long. Your mother led us to believe this was . . . a temporary arrangement."

I'd been with them seven years.

"But she doesn't want me." My lip was trembling. "She's made that clear. I haven't heard from her since Paris—what, almost three years ago?! And even that was . . ."

"We know she's had some difficulties since Michael died. We just . . . we always hoped she'd be able to take you back."

"Is this because of Paris?" I asked, feeling my ears burn. "I've been trying to be better."

"No, it's not that, Sasha." He paused, looking me in the eye for the first time, "We've always felt this way."

I sat back, shell-shocked by the words he hadn't said—the ones that trembled between the lines and whispered, "We don't want you. We never have."

Later, Annie tried to tell me that this couldn't have been what he meant: He was just trying to keep my relationship with my mom a *possibility*. But I'd been a temporary fixture in enough homes, by now conditioned to believe the worst. I didn't question Pierre or my new assumption: This family was borrowed.

Whatever Pierre had said to Patricia worked; the next time I saw her, she was civil, and I tiptoed through life again. But something short-circuited deep inside me as I worked to override my urge to *belong*.

Around Thanksgiving Patricia handed me a large padded envelope from my mother. She told me the contents might help with my term paper for psychology class. I opened it tentatively, half afraid I'd find another photo of Michael in his coffin, as I had a few years earlier. But inside were hundreds of photocopied pages from various books about the psychology of family. Carefully penned annotations marked nearly every page. I studied the familiar blue scrawls, warming when I read: "I suppose I can write more often now that you're a bit more grown up."

I turned the envelope over in my hands and saw that the last line of the return address read "Jamaica Plain, Massachusetts, 02130."

It turned out that Patricia had written to my mother over the last few weeks and asked her to help me with my research: "I realize you must be very busy, but I wish you would give more time to write Sasha. You're missing out on a very special relationship."

A month later, at Christmas, a large cardboard box showed up outside my bedroom door. The return address was Mom's. Inside was a letter, a wooden keepsake box filled with cinnamon sticks and pinecones from the Boston arboretum, a book of traditional Christmas carols, and a half dozen blueberry muffins moldy from the three-week delivery time. Despite the green mold, I contemplated eating the muffins. But when I unwrapped them, the scent bowled me over. They landed in the trash with a thud.

I rummaged through the other treasures, choking back giddy laughter. I spent the afternoon turning the box over in the filtered afternoon light, singing the carols in quiet rapture, and setting each item on my desk, as if a shrine.

I wondered at the timing, but didn't dare ask for fear of another upset. What mattered was that after a three-year drought, Mom had written twice in one month. For the remainder of the school year, she continued to send letters at this pace. I wrote her back in equal measure.

In the spring, college acceptance letters began trickling in. Of the

12 schools I applied to, 11 accepted me. I took Wesleyan University's offer in Middletown, Connecticut. It had a reputation for attracting hippies/conservatives/liberals/rednecks—in other words, everyone. Certainly I could find a place there.

Best of all, the school was only a few hours from Boston. Though I didn't know what the future held with Mom, I wanted to be near her. Pierre helped me fill out the financial aid forms, and assured me he would pay the balance. He said it matter-of-factly, as though it were an understood part of his duty to me.

By the time I graduated from high school, Pierre's work contract in Luxembourg was over. All summer he continent-hopped, going from job interview to job interview. I wondered where we might live next. Perhaps we'd spend Christmas in the Sahara or along the Great Wall of China. But nothing panned out.

Pierre started dying his graying hair before interviews, which only made me wonder why he wasn't retiring. I figured he had to be at least 55, maybe 60. He and Patricia decided that when I went off to Wesleyan, Pierre would continue his hunt stateside so Patricia could care for her dad in the comfort of his hometown, Boston.

The entire house operated on transitional time. Though Patricia and I were civil again, I'd internalized the reasons they'd decided not to adopt me. I believed myself to be broken, fractured, unworthy of their love. Their home came to remind me of who I *wasn't*, and who I could never be.

Weary of walking on eggshells, I spent the summer with Annie and Eliot, my boyfriend du jour, and avoided home as much as possible. Patricia and Pierre loosened their grip on me too. I'd be leaving soon enough.

~～∽

On the morning I left for college, Pierre was a time zone away at yet another interview. The house was uncommonly still, so quiet I thought that I might be the only one home. A few days earlier, Patricia had said that she wouldn't be able to drive me to the airport. I knew better than to ask her why. Annie's parents agreed to take me.

As I waited for their car, the sun clamored over the hills, promising an impressively hot August afternoon by Luxembourg standards. I leaned out of the skylight in my room, angled just two feet above my bed, and let the warm breeze ruffle my hair. I stared out over the undulating hills and wondered what the next decade would hold.

Annie's parents pulled up a few minutes early, and I strained to hoist my giant blue duffel bag onto my shoulder. I'd packed clothing and framed photos as well as the letters from my mom. The weight of my belongings made me stagger, and I was forced to pull the bag down three flights of tile stairs, its belabored *thump, thump, thump* marking my descent. Together, Annie and I hoisted it into the trunk, our small frames disappearing behind the bulging contours.

Just then Patricia opened the back door, her lips pressed into a hard line. She kept her hands tight at the sides of her housecoat. As I approached to hug her goodbye, she took a step back and raised her hands. She struggled for a moment, as though trying to decide what to say to me.

Finally, she managed, "Where's Eliot?" She looked down into the car for my boyfriend, whom she'd taken a liking to.

"He's—"

When she saw Annie's parents, she cut in. "I thought *he* was going to take you."

Before I could respond, she spun on her heel, went back into the house, and slammed the door behind her.

I stared at the door for a moment. The handle never moved, and there were no shadows in the windows. Finally, Annie put her hand on my shoulder and led me to the car. Only when the plane rumbled off the tarmac did I realize that I'd forgotten my white teddy bear.

PART THREE

Cleaving

---

*"You can outdistance that which is running after you,
but not what is running inside of you."*

—Rwandan proverb

CHAPTER 12

School Days

THIRTY-FOUR HUNDRED MILES LATER, my brother Tim picked me up from LaGuardia and drove me to Wesleyan University. He resembles the comedian Jerry Seinfeld in more than just looks, and soon had me laughing. As the miles piled up between us and the airport, I felt as if I were shedding a dry, too-small skin.

Before long, I settled in at school with a full course load, a well-behaved group of friends, and a shaggy-haired, prep school–graduate boyfriend named John. Though most of my freshman class was literally drunk on their freedom, I felt sobered by the responsibilities that came with college life and steered clear of the frat parties that thumped along the sidewalks.

As far as I was concerned, what had happened on that last day in Luxembourg could be water under the bridge if I could just show Patricia and Pierre how well I was doing. In September, when Pierre wrote asking for my new email and phone number, I was relieved. My friends didn't understand my reaction, but without a hug from either of them on the day I left Luxembourg, I genuinely felt that I needed such permission to reach out. Pierre wrote that he and Patricia had donated many of my things, including my roller skates, to a local shelter. He also enclosed money for books and school supplies, and signed off, "We are looking forward to hearing about your experiences and impressions."

Pierre and I emailed a few times after that, but Patricia remained silent. When I called their new house in early November, I was in for a surprise.

"Hello?"

"Hi, Patricia, it's Sasha. I was—"

"Hold on."

A moment later, Pierre picked up the phone.

"Hi! I was wondering what you guys are doing for Thanksgiving?" There was silence. "Hello?" I asked. "Are you there?"

"Yes. Sasha, I . . . we think . . . well. Now that you're 19, there's really no reason . . ." He took a deep breath. "Y–you probably don't need to be staying with us anymore. Of course, we'll continue paying for school, but after that . . ."

I twisted at the phone cord, winding the rubber spiral tightly around my index finger.

"Of course, yes. You don't have to do that. I just thought . . ."

All is well. All is well. All is well.

"No, we want to. It's the right thing to do. Have a happy Thanksgiving, Sasha."

I closed my eyes: "You, too."

I was confused; the letter had indicated a genuine concern for my well-being and future, but if I was to believe Pierre, this was it.

I wondered if his daughters felt the same way. It seemed unlikely: Toni had sent me a boom box and card to perk up my dorm room, and Lauren and Heather had sent occasional updates as well.

As dusk turned to twilight, I thought over my time with them, remembering all the nights I'd stayed out past curfew, the times I'd cursed at Patricia and Pierre out of teenage angst, the times I'd secretly wished I could live anywhere but with them.

Yet they'd given me so much: the best of everything. In the years I spent with them, we lived in the United States, France, and Luxembourg—just 3 of the 12 countries I experienced, including visits to Norway, Tunisia, Greece, and Spain. Though cherished family and friends washed in and out of my life like driftwood, I'd still managed to cultivate a yearning for adventure. I'd seen, lived, tasted the world. I was curious and hungry—because of what they'd given me.

Even after my conversation with Pierre the winter before, I hadn't expected things to end this way. His words felt like a sentence, except that instead of locking me up, I was locked out.

I stared down at the phone.

Nothing, it seemed, was forever. Even as I gave in to the status quo, I felt a wave of homesickness, yet didn't know what or who for.

∼

When I wasn't with my siblings in New Jersey, I disappeared into my boyfriend John's extraordinarily *normal* family on Cape Cod. As I strolled arm in arm with him along the snowy beaches, I didn't have to wonder about Patricia and Pierre or decide if it was time to find my mom (it had been seven years since I'd last seen her in Atlanta). And yet she felt so close; John's parents lived 15 minutes from where I was born. I often caught myself scanning the scattered, faceless tourists, looking for Mom's small shoulders or that mass of curly black hair on the off chance that she still visited the Cape from time to time. I was equally as afraid that I'd spot her as I would not.

When spring break rolled around, John gently suggested that we mix things up by going to see friends in Boston. We were sitting together at the campus cafeteria. "That sounds nice, but..." I stopped, thinking of Mom. I didn't have her number, but if she hadn't moved, I did know her address. "Do you think I could look up my mother while we're there?"

He gave my leg a squeeze and nodded. "I was wondering when you'd ask."

We retraced the winding roads and dusty alleys that led to the old apartment in Jamaica Plain. The shuddering elevator train that once spat pedestrians onto the cracked sidewalk was long gone, but even without it I knew we were close. A curious mix of salsa and rap still spilled out from the Latino market a half mile from our house, where Michael and I once ate ice pops on hot summer afternoons. John turned down a small street lined with enormous oaks, end capped by old warehouse buildings.

My street: There was the fire hydrant I'd splashed in and the handicapped ramp where Mom had once parked, only to get a citation. There, suddenly, was the park where Michael and I had played all those years ago. As I stared at the empty swings drifting ever so slightly in the breeze, I could almost see little Michael run by with a belly laugh, his chestnut hair dancing across his blue eyes. I drew my gray hoodie close around me.

John slowed the car to a crawl.

"Is this the right place?" he asked. I followed his gaze across the street: There it was, with the familiar evergreen trim. Nothing stirred: No neighbors milled about; no engines idled but ours.

"That's the apartment," I said slowly, pointing to the first floor, then to the narrow window next to the doorbell. "That's where my bed was—under that window. Our landlord and some other guy lived in the two apartments above us. It's hard to believe it's been almost nine years since I last crossed that threshold . . ."

I could still see the seashells we'd scattered like mulch around the rose bushes more than ten years ago. They were dusty and cracked, half buried in the dirt. A few stray blades of grass poked through.

I didn't get out of the car right away, but pressed my back against the seat and closed my eyes. I was starting to feel dizzy.

"You don't look so hot, Sash. You wanna come back later?"

"No."

"Do you want me to come with you?" he leaned across the center console and placed his large hand over mine. I pulled away and shook my head.

"No," I whispered.

I peeled myself off the seat, slipped through the squeaking chain-link gate, and climbed the steps, gripping the rail to steady myself. The porch creaked and bowed underfoot. For a moment I thought I was falling. By the time I reached the doorbell, my hand was shaking so hard I could barely ring it. No answer.

I rang it again, pressing my ear against the window to be sure it was working; still no answer. I peered in through the blinds, but a leggy spider plant hung in the way. What I could see of the room was hazy and dark.

"This was a mistake," I said, back at the SUV. "Let's go."

John held out a pen and paper through the window. "Hey. Don't give up."

"She's not home," I said. "Maybe we can come back some other time."

He didn't move. Finally I took the slip of paper and pen and wrote, "Hi Mom, it's Sasha. I'm in town for a few days. If you'd like to get together, you can call me on my boyfriend's cell phone, 555-1818. We're staying with a friend in Arlington. I hope you're doing OK. I love you."

I dropped the paper into her mailbox and shut the lid tightly, my hands lingering on the cool metal for a moment before walking away.

John's phone didn't ring until 3 p.m. the following day.

"I don't know this number, Sash. Do you think it's—"

I grabbed the phone from his hand and walked briskly across the living room.

"Hello?"

"Hi . . ." Her voice was small and unsure. "Is this Alex?" Though the name she gave me at my ninth birthday was on my legal documents, no one else had used it since.

"Yes. But I go by Sasha now."

Only a crackle of static broke the silence.

I waved John out of the room. "Can I come over to the apartment?"

"Oh, no, that wouldn't be . . ." she paused, then brightened, her voice picking up cadence as she thought of a more neutral meeting point: "Why don't we go out? There's a nice Chinese restaurant halfway between us in Cambridge."

John offered to come with me to dinner; what's more, he helped me pick out my outfit—an oversize blue button-down shirt, a skirt, and strappy heels. I wore my hair in a high ponytail.

When we arrived, the parking lot of the Golden Dragon was dark and mostly empty. Yellow streetlights pooled over a few scattered cars. After a quick check inside the restaurant, I realized Mom wasn't there yet, or she'd given up waiting.

I made a beeline for John's SUV, but he reached for my hand and pulled me firmly back onto the sidewalk.

"She'll be here, Bean. Just wait."

"This is ridiculous, John. She's not coming."

But John wasn't listening. I followed his gaze just in time to see a small white car slip quietly into the other end of the parking lot. The driver, invisible in the darkness, made her way slowly around the lot before finally stopping in front of us. When she reached across the seat and swung the passenger-side door open, I caught a glimpse of her small, slender hand; the skin was smooth and distinctly olive, even under the garish streetlights.

The shadowy figure leaned farther toward us, and a mop of salt-and-pepper curls bounced into the light.

"Mom!"

She returned my look with an openmouthed smile. Her brown eyes shone out from behind a pair of spring-green cat-eye glasses.

"Oh, wow . . . Hi!" she said, "You look . . ."

Every time she opened her mouth to speak, her foot floated off the brake pedal and the car lurched forward. Finally John ran around to the driver's side and escorted her to the curb. While he parked the car, Mom and I stood across from each other for the first time since I was 12, at Michael's bedside. We didn't hug; we simply drank each other in like two thirsty wanderers. I felt unshackled in her gaze, as though she was seeing my spirit, reading me, downloading the past several years of my life.

I took in her trim capris, her soft rose lipstick, brown cashmere sweater, short blue crocheted neck scarf, and brown leather handbag, which gleamed under the red, blinking "open" sign that hung crooked in the restaurant window behind us. I'd never seen her with lipstick on before.

"I thought you'd be wearing a babushka," I said, shyly. Without it she almost looked like a different woman.

"A babushka? It's been nearly a decade, Alex. You're not the only one who's changed."

I considered reiterating that I preferred "Sasha," but the thrill of seeing her suddenly made the detail feel unimportant. She glanced at my heels and plunging neckline, which suddenly felt two inches too low. The last time she'd seen me, when Michael was in the hospital, I was prepubescent. Now I was almost 20—a woman. I pulled at the back of my shirt, covering up as best I could.

Once inside, the three of us looked over our menus. Mom and I kept peering over them at each other, grinning foolishly in the dim candlelight. A slip of a waiter walked up and began to share the specials.

Mom glanced sideways, up at him and then back to me.

"Here, Alex," she said, cutting sharply into his recitation, "I want you to have this. Can you use it?" She slid a small, silver camera across the booth to me.

I gave the waiter an apologetic smile, "We need a minute." He retreated with a nod.

Mom sat back and announced, "I hate when they do that. A *real* waiter knows when his customers need him and when they *don't*. Why interrupt our conversation?" She shook her head, then tapped her fingers on the camera. "I can't figure those things out. Can you?"

Digital cameras were all the rage in 1999, but I didn't have one. "Uh, John, will you take our picture?" I asked.

When I put my arm around my mother, she felt papery thin in my embrace. I was half a head taller than her. My thighs looked plump next to hers. The once familiar scent of eucalyptus surrounded her.

"So how have you been, Mom? I can't believe you're still in the same apartment."

"Actually, I'm in transition. I've been living in a hotel for several weeks. My landlord wants to evict me, but I told him that after almost 20 years, he can't do that."

"I guess not," I said faintly. "Speaking of transitions . . . Did you know I'm not staying with the Dumonts anymore?"

"Right! You're in school."

"It's more than that. Things were difficult in Europe. I think they're just tired."

"Nonsense! They're your parents. They love you."

"Yeah, well, you're my mom," I said quietly, looking back down at the menu.

The waiter approached us but none of us looked at him, and he slunk back behind the bar without a word. John got up and followed him.

"I got the invitation you sent for your high school graduation," Mom said brightly. "That was so nice!" She pulled the envelope out of her purse, and handed it to me, indicating the postmark. "But the ceremony was already over when you mailed it?"

"You would have come?" I looked up, genuinely surprised.

"You never know," she shrugged.

"No," I muttered. "I guess not."

John popped back in his seat, his smile fading when he saw our pained expressions. I shifted in my seat and tried to think of something else to say, but came up blank. A few minutes later, the waiter delivered a steaming platter of General Tso's Chicken.

"I didn't know what else to order," John offered meekly. He always ordered General Tso's.

Mom pulled two small plastic bottles out of her purse. One contained olive oil, the other apple cider vinegar. She misted the chicken with a cloud of vinegar. Sharp fumes filled the air, causing John and I to cough violently.

Mom watched us with detached amusement, then handed John the olive oil.

"This is the good stuff. First press," she confided, "You never can tell with these places, so you have to come prepared. The vinegar will kill any germs."

"What's the olive oil for?" John asked.

"Flay-vah."

"Oh," he looked at me briefly, then obliged, drizzling a line of olive oil over the chicken.

He was the only one who ate.

⁓

Back at the car, John didn't start the engine right away. "You look just like her, Sash." He grinned.

"You think? My hair's not quite as big, though . . ." I giggled. "I can't believe it finally happened. I mean, it was a little intense, but . . ." I paused, watching as her car slipped back into the stream of taillights. "I have a mother, John. That was my *mom*."

I'd finally looked into her eyes again, sat next to her, spoken with her, taken a photo. Heck, I even had her *phone number*.

"I know," he said, his voice hushed.

"Do you think she'd let me stay the summer with her?" I asked, the words escaping before I had time to think them through.

"Just so long as I get to see you, too," he said, "I'd miss my Bean if you were with her *all* summer."

He took off his glasses and kissed me. I let myself disappear into his embrace, relaxing as his adoration washed the adrenaline away.

CHAPTER 13

Reunion
and Remembrance

A FEW WEEKS LATER I mustered the courage to ask my mother if I could spend the summer with her. I wanted nothing more than to be around her, learn from her, be her daughter. Sure, there were lingering questions about, well, everything. But I wasn't angry, and the questions weren't burning—not at first. Sitting in the same room as her would be enough. I'd spent nine years wanting nothing more than *her*.

While she didn't refuse outright, Mom insisted on emailing the Dumonts to make sure it was OK with them. I told her that in the nine months since I'd called about seeing them for Thanksgiving, Pierre had only contacted me a handful of times; the only time I *saw* him was when he took me to purchase some school clothes around Christmas. Pierre responded to her email with two simple lines: "Of course. *Sasha needs you.*"

It was as though he was thrusting me into my mother's arms, dutifully, the same way she had thrust me into theirs when I was ten. Thinking back to the Thanksgiving phone call, I wondered if the Dumonts *hadn't* been cutting me off. Perhaps they had been trying to help me spread my wings and find a roost with Mom.

Apparently liberated by Pierre and Patricia's blessing, Mom rented a trendy loft in the heart of Boston's Italian quarter, the North End, and furnished it with a kitchen table, two chairs, and a bed. She said I needed to connect with my Italian roots, so I was surprised when she told me she wouldn't be staying there with me. She kept the apartment in Jamaica Plain, "just in case," but given her shaky situation with the landlord, split her nights between there and a hotel. During the day, she worked as a receptionist at a high-end salon.

When I asked Mom how she could afford two rents on her salary, she stood a little taller and pronounced, "This isn't any old apartment; this loft costs $1,800 a month."

My jaw dropped.

"But it's worth it!" she added. "You'll get to be around your Italian heritage for a change." I pressed her further, but she shrugged me off: "Just *enjoy* it, Alex."

The small, heavy-beamed loft was rimmed with windows that opened right above a flower shop. Orange, red, and pink bouquets spilled onto the sidewalk below. I was on the fifth floor, a few blocks from the main drag, Hanover Street, and 30 yards from the harbor. From the kitchen window, I could watch men perched like lanky Italian roosters crowing at curvy, red-lipped *belle donne* who clacked along the sidewalk. On warm evenings I could smell the old men's cigars.

I got a job within walking distance, at Faneuil Hall Marketplace, where I worked the counter at the Museum of Fine Art's gift shop. In my free time, I roamed the North End with Mom—her idea. Every evening and on the weekends, we systematically worked our way through the best restaurants and shops—none of which were on Hanover Street.

"When lines are that long, you know the food won't be good *and* it'll cost too much. That variety of Italian food," she advised, "is for the *tourists.*"

She walked me over to Polcari's Coffee for sesame candies, to Maria's for dollar slices of Sicilian pizza and cannoli, and to a hole-in-the-wall called Dino's that only kept its door open long enough to sell out of their daily batch of fresh spinach ravioli. Their pasta was delicate, the spinach filling laced with the most tantalizing whisper of nutmeg, the sauce bright with disarming bursts of unadulterated tomatoes. Mom said it was the only pasta in Boston remotely as good as her grandmother's.

With each stop, my mouth remembered what my mind had long forgotten; I had visited these curiosities with Mom and Michael more than a decade earlier. When I talked to Mom about these memories, she'd alight on the joyful ones before promptly flitting back to the food in front of us. I could feel an invisible barrier when it came to talking about the past. If I opened my mouth, I was half afraid I'd shatter the spell.

One day I came home from work to find Mom already there. The apartment was perfumed with the sweet aroma of roasted tomatoes. There was something earthy, too—like cinnamon or nutmeg.

"I'm in here!" she called out from the kitchen cheerily. I rounded the corner just in time to see her pull a baking sheet out from the broiler.

"You cooked?" I asked, peering over her shoulder with a curious smile. This was the first time she'd cooked for me since I was little. On the floor beside her was a large cardboard box, half unpacked. Pots, wooden spoons, and two dozen spice jars were piled up pell-mell on the counters.

"Are you moving in?" I asked.

"I think I might," she grinned, and handed me a toasted square of cinnamon raisin bread topped with tomato sauce and two translucent slices of mozzarella. She swirled thick rivers of olive oil over the top of the cheese until it pooled over onto the plate, finishing it off with a generous dusting of hot paprika. We sat down at the kitchen table.

"Never brown the cheese," she said, as she slid the plate toward me, "that's a sign of a careless cook."

"What exactly is this?" I began, looking down at the curious, steaming concoction that was by now marooned in olive oil.

"Pizza."

Mom watched intently as I pressed my knife through the cheese into the crispy bread and brought the glistening, oozing morsel to my mouth. The sweet raisins coupled with the cinnamon and hot paprika suddenly and unexpectedly brought me back to the kitchen in Jamaica Plain. There was no other taste in the world like this.

I was six years old again, swinging my feet under the kitchen table. Michael and I ate and chanted in equal measure: "Pizza. Pizza. Pizza."

"Wow," I said, and took another, larger bite. I shut my eyes and settled into the memory, a smile tracing vaguely along my lips.

Mom's Curious Cinnamon Raisin Pizza

. . . .

Never one to let lack of ingredients stump creativity, Mom first made this "pizza" when we were out of regular sandwich bread. Whenever I tell someone about it, they inevitably scrunch up their nose. And yet, against all odds, the touch of sweet raisins and cinnamon delightfully punctuates paprika-topped pizza. The combination reminds me of some Middle Eastern and Central Asian cultures, which include cinnamon and raisins in their savory rice dishes.

2 slices cinnamon raisin bread
2 generous spoonfuls marinara
2 slices mozzarella or provolone
1 or 2 glugs olive oil
A couple pinches hot paprika

Toast two slices of cinnamon raisin bread under the broiler. Spread on a heaping spoonful of marinara, and top with a slice of mozzarella or provolone. Return to broiler until hot and bubbling. Mom would say not to brown the cheese, but I prefer the deep nuttiness that comes from an extra minute under the broiler. Drizzle with good quality olive oil, and dust with sharp paprika. Enjoy with a fork, a knife, and a triumphant smile.

Enough for 2

As I closed in on the last quarter of the pizza, Mom made an announcement. "Just so you know," she said, "I got rid of all your bras while you were at work today."

I froze, mid-bite. "Are you serious? Why would you do that?"

"That room was a mess! I thought I'd get it shipshape. And then I find you're wearing . . ." she scrunched her nose. "Push-up bras? You don't need that junk! Does John make you wear them?"

Though John had bought a few for my birthday, I wasn't about to admit it. "Mom! I'm not 12 anymore."

"No. You're not. But I'm your mother. And I'm trying to figure out who you are." She screwed up her eyes and looked at me steadily.

I squirmed in my seat, waiting for her to look away, even for a moment. When she didn't, I stomped up to the loft, yelling over my shoulder, "You're wasting your time! I'm just going to buy them all over again."

At $30 a pop, good bras were beyond the reach of my summer-job minimum wages. Outraged, I lay down as far as I could from the railing, arms crossed, listening to the swish and clatter as Mom cleaned the kitchen below.

At least, that's what I thought she was doing.

In the morning I woke up to find my mother sitting on the side of my bed. "We're moving back to the old apartment. Get packing, Twinkle-Toes."

"I thought you were having trouble with your landlord?"

"Oh, that's all settled," she waved her hand dismissively. "I just didn't think you were ready for all those memories."

I looked at her newly composed face, considering the disarming realization that in all likelihood, there'd never been a disagreement— or if there had been one, it was little more than an excuse to protect me.

Real anger flashed for the first time since I'd contacted her a few months earlier. *Why was everyone so hell-bent on controlling my experience of the past? Why couldn't I be allowed to decide when I was ready?*

"But the box you brought over last night? What was that all about? I thought you were finally moving in?" I asked.

She rolled her eyes. "A mistake! The kitchen is no good; the stove is too far from the fridge, and there's no ventilation. It doesn't work. Plus this place costs an arm and a leg. I don't know how someone's supposed to afford the North End anymore. This used to be a place for immigrants—a place of opportunity."

I followed her downstairs and saw that she'd put everything back in the box and sealed it up with two strips of clear packing tape.

"You can sleep in your old bed," she added brightly.

"You still have my bed?" I asked, not sure whether to be pleased or horrified.

"Sure. I've been using the frame as a plant stand, but that won't take but a minute to fix." She paused, digging in her purse. She pulled out her wallet. "But first, let's go bra shopping. My treat."

I didn't really have a choice. Two hours later, I was outfitted with a dozen sensible bras. Though I was loath to admit it, they *were* more comfortable than the push-ups and nowhere near as frumpy as I'd expected.

⁓

Walking into our old apartment was like stepping into a whitewashed photograph from another era. The pale walls stretched up to the nine-foot ceiling quietly, without cracks. The very paint, the color of driftwood, looked taut, as though the room might have been holding its breath for the last decade. Though the morning light filtered into the tiny living room, soft and glowing, even the dust bunnies were suspended, seemingly on pause.

Everything but the windows was smaller than I remembered, but the space was also neater than I recalled. From the looks of it, our toys had long since been donated. Michael's bed was gone, too, a rubber plant in its place. But my bed was propped up just where I'd left it: my old, wooden castle just below the front window under the spider plant.

As Mom gathered her box of kitchen tools from the hall, I stood by my bed, watching her move through this space that was at once so familiar, and yet so foreign.

Those first few nights I tossed and turned, my body too long for the mattress. I awoke several times to find myself staring through the moonlight at the space Michael's bed had once occupied, watching the shadows dance on the wall and wondering through the clouded veil of fatigue if any of them were his. When the emotional noise became too great, I left Mom a note and escaped to John's parents' place on Cape Cod for the weekend, slipping into a blur of salt water and lattes.

When I crept back into the apartment a few days later, Mom was sitting at the kitchen table in a thick, chenille robe. The deep burgundy stood out in sharp relief against the white streaks in her hair.

"He's not your family, you know," she said, lifting her small chin slightly.

"He took me to find *you!* He was there for me when no one else—"

"Nonsense!" Her sharp tone stopped me in my tracks. "What about Connor, Tim, and Grace? What about me?"

"You think you can just claim to be my family, after all this time?" I hated the words as they came out, but I couldn't stop myself. "I've done pretty well without you all these years, you know."

"That's nice, Alex—really nice. Is that how you talked to Patricia and Pierre?"

We both knew the answer to that question. Suddenly, I could no longer take her calling me by that.

"Damn it! My name is *Sasha.*"

"The summer's going to be over before you know it," she said, pointing her finger at me. "You might never get this opportunity again, *Sasha.*"

The victory felt small. "What's that supposed to mean?" I gasped. "Is that a threat?"

"No one knows what the future holds. I could drop dead tomorrow."

Now I was at a boil.

"Speaking of *dead,* why did you send me a picture of Michael in his *coffin* back in Paris?" Old grief stirred my rage. *"That was disgusting."*

She sat back. "All the old Italian families honored their dead with beautiful photos of them laid out in their coffins. My grandmother slept with a photo of her dead mother across from her bed until the day *she* died!"

I grimaced at the thought. "This isn't the 1800s, Mom. What the hell were you thinking? In case you were wondering, I threw the card out."

Now it was her turn to grimace. "Wait a minute—that's my son you're talking about. I was honoring him. I thought they did a beautiful job. Since you weren't able to be at the funeral, I thought you'd appreciate the gesture." Her shoulders shook with anger. "You know what? Forget it. I don't need this abuse. Not from you."

She walked over to the cupboard and pulled out a large white teacup to which she added two mint tea bags, a spoonful of honey, and hot water. Then she slid it toward the empty seat across from her.

"Come on. Please. Let's talk about something else."

I stared at the greening water, conflicted. I wanted to yell. Or run to John. But if I wanted a mother, it seemed like the only thing to do was to respect her wishes. I sank into the chair and cradled the hot teacup in my hands.

In those few short weeks before my sophomore year, Mom moved smoothly from touring restaurants in the North End to a frenzy of home cooking, reaping the recipes of my Italian and Hungarian relatives. She served them up to me with methodical precision. The two of us holed up in the apartment around that old gas stove flanked by gallon jugs of apple cider vinegar and olive oil.

Mom was up no later than 5 a.m. making breakfast. Scrambled eggs were her favorite. She ushered me from the table to demonstrate how to whisk the eggs with heavy cream until they were pale but not frothy, just as she'd learned from *Mastering the Art of French Cooking*. Then she'd cook them over a double boiler into soft, wet curds. The whole spectacle took 15 minutes. I wasn't convinced the extra labor or dirty dishes were worth the trouble.

Mom encouraged me to start a recipe journal. I picked out a heavy-duty, spiral-bound sketch pad with a moss green cover and spent many hot afternoons at her worn kitchen table with glue and scissors. I filled the pages with recipes I loved and recipes I was curious about. When she clipped articles about the dangers of aspartame, the importance of salt, and how to make the best use of MSG, I added them.

Recipe by recipe, the food gradually became less Julia Child and more like that of my childhood. Like farmers in late August, we toiled with increasing intensity; from dawn until sunset, cooking was our only activity. In the morning Mom fried stacks of the homemade crepes I'd remembered so fondly, rolling them with plain yogurt, raspberry jam, and heaps of banana, strawberry, or pear.

For lunch, we enjoyed room-temperature slices of torta di riso, the savory rice casserole enriched with rendered bacon and a sprinkling of parsley. For dinner, we'd pluck the petals from Grammie's stuffed artichokes until we, too, were glutted.

When Mom prepped the artichokes, she didn't snip off the prickly tips of the petals, nor did she bother to trim the stem. She just hacked off the tops, stuffed the crevices with an eggy slump of Parmesan, bread crumbs, and garlic, and then steamed them until the fresh green turned muddy. As we dipped the petals in melted butter and lemon juice, the thorns jabbed my fingertips.

"Pricking our fingers," Mom said, "is a small price to pay if it means we get to the heart sooner."

🍴 Stuffed Artichokes

Mom got this recipe from her mother, who surely got it from her mother. Mom never actually wrote it down, so this version is the result of fastidious note taking while watching her work. The stuffing can be heaped rather decadently onto two globe artichokes, or spread more elegantly over four smaller artichokes. I prefer the former, as it makes a complete meal.

Artichokes cook best when there's room around them for the steam; a large oval pot (like an oblong Dutch oven) can hold two artichokes with room. In a pinch, multiple small pots can be used.

2 to 4 artichokes

For the stuffing:
3 large eggs
¾ cup Italian bread crumbs
A handful parsley, coarsely chopped (¼ cup)
½ cup freshly grated Parmesan (heaping is best)
1 large clove garlic, crushed
½ teaspoon baking powder
¾ cup milk
Salt and pepper

Finishing touches:
Paprika or parsley for color
Melted butter with a squeeze of fresh lemon juice for dipping

First, prepare the artichokes. Lay the artichokes on their side and use a sharp chef's knife to cut off the top 1½ inches. Trim the stems so they will stand up straight (and fit in the pot), and pluck off one layer of the outer petals (they're tough).

In a medium bowl, stir all the stuffing ingredients together. Pull the artichoke open slightly and spoon the filling on top and into the crevices behind the petals. Steam for 45 minutes to an hour, or until the petals are tender and pull easily from the artichoke (cooking time will increase dramatically if the artichokes are pressed up against each other when steaming). About halfway through cooking, check the level of water in the pot and replenish as necessary. Serve hot, garnished with a sprinkling of paprika or parsley.

To eat: Pluck off each petal, dip into melted butter and lemon juice. Use your bottom teeth to scrape the fleshy bit that connects to the artichoke base, and then discard the petal. When down to the petals as tiny as fairy wings, pull them away to reveal the hairy "choke." Use a spoon to scrape it away and reveal the heart—the most tender and flavorful bit.

Enough for 2 to 4

"Did you cook like this even when I was in Europe?" I asked Mom on my last night in Jamaica Plain before I returned to Wesleyan.

She shook her head and laughed.

"I weighed 89 pounds when you were in Europe. I lived off a Hostess CupCake a day."

Her voice softened. "I didn't have anyone to cook for. I wasn't very hungry."

"What *did* you do while I was gone?" The question felt brazen, but neither of us had made a move to talk about the past since our last blowup about the card. We were running out of time.

"Nothing." she shrugged. Her arms tossed indifferently, but her eyes begged to be left alone.

I waited.

She sat back and shook her right hand in the air, more Italian than ever. "I woke up, did data entry at the Trial Court for eight hours straight, came home, slept. After two years I worked my way up to the clerk magistrate's office. On the weekends I made pot holders from boiled sweaters—filled half a dozen crates with them. That was my life. You kids were gone. Michael was . . ."

Her face crumpled slightly before she recovered: "Sasha, I just want to forget that part of my life. I feel like *I* was dead all those years."

"You must have had a boyfriend . . . something?"

"There was nothing!" She paused and then shook her head. "I didn't talk to anyone after Michael died. Not Connor, Tim, or Grace—no one. I don't think I said his name for seven years. The whole thing just . . . blew me away."

"You didn't say his name for seven years?" I didn't even try to mask the sarcasm. "I find that hard to believe."

She stared at a stray crumb on the table. "Well, there was one person I talked to . . ."

"Who?"

She shook her head. "What is this, an interrogation? Come on, Sasha, this is our last night together for who knows how long. Can we just enjoy it without bringing up all that junk?"

I looked at her in disbelief. "I don't even know why you bother. You say you want me to consider you family, and then you shut down like this? How am I supposed to trust you?"

She looked at me unblinking.

"OK, then answer me this—why did you give up Michael and me? There had to be another way—something else you could have done?"

She slumped down into her chair again. "I had no choice, Sasha. The only way for you to have a normal life was to get you out of the Boston court system. Those social workers were like . . . vultures, circling our lives. They weren't going to stop."

As she spoke, darkness crept into her eyes. Her face changed until suddenly her expression looked so familiar that it took my breath away. She looked exactly as she had the day she announced we were moving in with the Dumonts.

If Mom really had no life except for work, it meant she'd spent the last decade living on nickels and dimes, scrimping and saving. A new realization hit me: Using some of her savings to get the loft in the North End was the same sort of lavish gift newly divorced parents get their kid. She couldn't sustain it on her salary, so she'd used the awkward kitchen as an excuse to cancel the lease.

I wanted to reach across the table and clasp her hand. To say I understood. But there were too many questions left unanswered.

"You know, Patricia and Pierre saved our lives, Sasha. They got you kids out of that mess." She looked down and shook her head. "They did . . . what I couldn't."

We were silent a moment.

"But you didn't even write, Mom. Not for years."

She sat a little straighter. "You were never going to connect with the Dumonts if I kept butting in. I had to create some . . . space. You have no idea what I went through, losing you kids."

⁓⤳

The morning of my departure, I found a few blanket-stitched pot holders and a greeting card propped up on the bedside table. The lithograph on the front depicted a formal dining table spread with a white-and-green cloth and set for a formal tea. Five tidy place settings were set under five vases filled with irises and wild ferns. Curiously, there were only two chairs, both empty.

Inside was the recipe for my grandmother's torta di riso, carefully penned in blue, green, and purple ink. Mom's handwriting was neat, legible, determined. It was a slip of paper, but to me it had all the trappings of a family heirloom. I pasted it in the book.

That was it. The summer was over.

Mom dropped me off at Wesleyan. Sophomore year was upon me. I felt a disappointment when the summer ended. I'd been able to spend time with Mom and had even answered a few questions, but they only seemed to complicate my understanding of my childhood. And I'd never mustered the courage to ask about my dad.

Still, I did know a heck of a lot more about my culinary heritage and food in general. Those recipes—and even the restaurant outings before them—made the reunion bearable. Mom and I had shared a project, something to take the focus off the intensity of coming back together after so many years. Perhaps that had been Mom's intent all along.

As she still likes to say, "You can't put the cart before the horse."

♟ Torta di Riso

This is a simple recipe that makes use of leftover rice—both practical and economical. Mom made torta di riso often, taking chilled squares along for our frequent walks in Boston's Blue Hills or drives up to Cape Cod, where we camped most summers. The traditional recipe uses salt pork, but I like the smoke and relative leanness of bacon. Sometimes I omit the meat altogether, opting instead for the clean taste of olive oil. As far as the parsley, anywhere from a sprinkling to a ¼ cup chopped is delicious. Tip: ¾ cup of uncooked white rice will make just over 3 cups cooked.

6 slices bacon, chopped
1 tablespoon olive oil, plus more for baking dish
1 onion, chopped
3 cups leftover, refrigerated white rice
½ cup freshly grated Parmesan cheese
6 eggs, lightly beaten
A little parsley, chopped
Salt and pepper

Preheat the oven to 400°F.

Sauté the bacon in olive oil over medium heat until the fat begins to render. Add the onion and lightly brown. Set aside to cool slightly. Meanwhile, add the cooked rice, Parmesan, eggs, chopped parsley, salt, and pepper to a large bowl. Stir together with the cooled onion mixture. Pour into a lightly oiled 2-quart baking dish (such as an 8 × 8-inch). Bake for about 35 minutes, or until golden brown on top. Cool 15 minutes before cutting into neat squares or diamonds.

Excellent served at room temperature or cold for a picnic lunch.

Enough for 6 to 8

CHAPTER 14

———

Sizing Things Up

L ESS THAN A MONTH into the school year, Mom took a job as a live-in baker for a small order of nuns in Newton, on the outskirts of Boston. They needed someone to make their daily batches of bread: sandwich loaves, baguettes, the occasional raisin loaf. When the abbess gave my mother the job, she also gave her the key to a small room on the fourth floor of the convent, barely bigger than the twin bed inside. The communal showers were down the hall.

Mom moved in without hesitation, finally severing ties with our old apartment in Jamaica Plain. Looking back, I think she had kept that apartment on the off chance I would come looking for her. Now she was as ready as I was to get away from it.

Knowing I would never again step foot inside those apartment walls, I put the past out of mind and turned my attention to school. That's not to say *Mom* didn't focus on *me*. The seven years of self-induced isolation since Michael's death seemed to make her ravenous for my time.

Every other week she'd send me a package, often including a few spices like dried Japanese chili peppers or half-sharp paprika, "just for fun." She called my dorm room several times a day, starting as early as 5 a.m., to discuss such issues as the merits of trenchers, the hardened planks of bread used for plates during the Middle Ages. When I hosted an Arthurian Cooking Tutorial, she mailed me pages of research photocopied from books in the culinary collections at the Schlesinger Library at the Radcliffe Institute for Advanced Study, then called at dawn to talk through the pages.

I always answered those calls with my arm draped across my still shut eyes. "WHY ARE YOU CALLING SO EARLY?"

"Aren't you awake?" she'd laugh, "I've been up for hours—I can't sleep past 2 a.m."

Her efforts did not go unnoticed, but since Mom had shut down any real conversation about the past, her intense focus on me felt a bit disingenuous. Next, she started just "showing up," regularly driving the three hours from Boston to my dorm unannounced. It felt like she was trying to get something from me, but I couldn't figure out what.

Once Mom drove all the way to Connecticut with a bouquet of sunflowers and pureed carrot ginger soup, surprising me mere hours after I'd had my wisdom teeth pulled. With this simple, selfless act, I recognized a show of pure maternal instinct, much more potent than any stalled conversation we'd had. It filled my heart. But I still needed her to *talk* to me, to explain her choices. Until she did, I was afraid to trust her affections.

I made a habit of spending my holidays with John's family or my three half siblings in New Jersey. I even spent a week or two with each of the Dumont girls, trying to maintain our bond. There just wasn't a lot of time for Mom. I built a wall around our relationship—less to control her than to protect myself—though from what, I wasn't sure.

The intensity of her attention was the opposite of the way Patricia and Pierre had encouraged my independence.

Even though I kept Mom at arm's length, my Russian roommate Katya and I had no trouble finding uses for the spices she sent. We made apple bread, apple fritters, and applesauce, all with the requisite shake of Mom's cinnamon, still labeled "sin." More than once, I found myself wishing I knew how to make Mom's famous apple pie that Michael and I loved so much. But each fall I forgot to ask her.

By the time I was a senior, I realized that Mom had been right when she said that I might never get the chance to spend so much time with her again. That summer after my freshman year was the first and last time in my adult life that we spent three straight months together.

I'd been dating John for almost four years when his mother leaned over to me at dinner one night at an Olive Garden and grabbed my hand. With John and his father, we'd just finished off a family-sized platter of spaghetti and meatballs, John's favorite, and were now enjoying tiramisu and wild berry Bellinis.

"I wonder what size ring you wear," she said, sliding off her gold wedding band, a smile trembling at the corners of her mouth. "Want to try mine on?"

I scanned the room, willing a waiter to send his tray crashing to the floor, or for the kitchen to set off the fire alarm. No dice.

John's mother slid the ring across the varnished wooden table. I smiled weakly and placed it on my finger. It felt cold against my skin.

"Interesting!" she said, and then took the ring back nonchalantly. "How are things with your mom?"

A week later, I broke up with John.

I was only 22, and though I loved John, I still had no idea how to *be* in love—to trust the feeling, own it as mine, and believe in it. Faced with the possibility of wearing that ring, I knew my only option was to run. This was more than fear of commitment: This was certitude that unconditional love could never exist—not for me. Good though John had been to me, his mother's hint of a proposal pushed me to end the relationship—in self-preservation.

That night I called Mom to tell her about the breakup, but she had something else on her mind. "Listen, I've been working through some of the loose ends—trying to piece together why Michael . . . had such a hard time." She lowered her voice. "Have you been following the sex abuse scandal in Boston?"

"Those kids suing the Catholic Church?" The story had been in all the papers, but I hadn't given it much thought.

"They're not kids," she replied, "These are grown men now. But the 'boy within' never recovers—these men can't hold down jobs, their emotions are all out of whack. Some never survived: When they hit puberty the trauma came flooding back. They get angry, depressed—many of them ended their lives. So it's the *parents* who are suing for their lost boys." She was quiet a moment. "The patterns are all there, Sasha."

I thought back to Michael's weekly counseling sessions with the priest he wouldn't let me near.

"Sash? Are you there?"

I shut my eyes and sighed. "Yeah . . ."

"I've been going through old papers, some of his medical reports. But I could use your help. Is there anything you can remember—anything that seemed off, that might help?"

I was already nodding.

CHAPTER 15

Moving On

S OMETIMES THE VERY ACT OF RUNNING entrenches the spirit more than it liberates. Two years later, not much had changed except my age. I was 24, haunting Wesleyan as a web designer long after most of my classmates had scattered. Mom continued to crash into my life with exhausting persistence while we worked on Michael's case against the Catholic Church, which by now had moved into arbitration. And—perhaps to insulate myself—three days after I broke up with John, I'd become involved with another man, a full-lipped Swedish weight lifter named Greg.

Mom hated his buzz cut, his motorcycle, our "shacking up" together, and how my years with him had turned me into a road-chasing GI Jane: "You're never going to figure out who you are if you don't get out from under these boys," she scolded.

Perhaps she was right that I'd leaned too much on my boyfriends. But on this sticky summer day, I was on my way to attend an older cousin's funeral in Boston. The highway propelled me into the city's inner circle just 30 minutes before the viewing was scheduled to begin. Disoriented by the knotted roads, I parked the car, unfolded a large city map, and squinted over the tiny print until a spark of something red caught my eye.

Patricia was walking down the street.

Though Pierre and two of the girls had come to my college graduation, Patricia had phoned in her congratulations. That was the last time we'd spoken.

The six years since we'd lived in Luxembourg had been kind; Patricia was slimmer than I'd ever seen her. A pair of black-and-white tapered slacks skimmed along her hips, stopping just shy of her gold flats; an orange silk blouse draped loosely along her torso. The shirt only served to ignite her scarlet hair to an even more furious shade than I'd remembered.

I flung open my car door right into the honks and whines of busy traffic and narrowly missed a passing bus.

"Patricia!" I waved as I caught up with her, stunned by the coincidence of seeing her in a city teeming with more than a half million people.

When she turned around, I rushed her with an enormous hug.

She stiffened, her hands fixed to her side, and pulled back. I let go, embarrassed.

"I'm sorry . . ." I began again. "Hi! How are you?"

"Sasha . . . w-what are you doing here?" She looked at me with widened eyes.

"I'm lost," I said, holding the map up high in my hand, "late for a funeral."

Her eyes softened slightly. "I'm so sorry, what happened? Are you OK?"

"It's one of my cousins—cancer. She fought for a long time but . . . yes, I'm fine."

"Do you have someone who can help you?"

I paused. "I can probably call my mom."

Patricia's gaze flickered. I winced, wishing I hadn't mentioned Mom. I flushed, too, as I remembered the gift Pierre had given me at graduation: a prepaid phone card. I'd looked at the plastic dumbly, wondering at what such a gift implied, but had been too uncomfortable to clarify its meaning.

I'd kept the card in my wallet for months, taking it out occasionally, trying to come up with a good excuse to contact the Dumonts. I must have done that a hundred times. When I got a new wallet, I moved the unused phone card to a drawer. One day I noticed it had expired.

Patricia looked at her watch, "Well, you're in good hands with your mom. Take care of yourself, Sasha."

"You, too . . ." I said, searching for the right words that would keep her there a moment longer. Suddenly, I realized we'd spent all the years since Michael's death in some variation of this game: she trying to keep my ticking time bomb emotions in check, me fixated on the mother and brother I'd lost. I never saw *Patricia*. She pressed her lips together in an ironed-on smile, and then stepped briskly past me.

She hadn't walked 20 feet before my shoulders shook and tears coursed down my cheeks. I knew better than to hope that our paths would cross again. Dozens of suits and skirts passed me by as I sobbed.

Though I felt the shame of their stares, I couldn't make myself stop crying. I was 9, I was 12, I was 19—a lifetime of endings, a lifetime unmoored.

~⁓

"What happened?" Mom asked when she came to retrieve me, taking in my blotchy eyes and frizzy hair. "You look like a ragamuffin."

"I bumped into Patricia." My voice was monotone.

"What?!" she scanned the sidewalk, turning this way and that, as though she might still be nearby.

"She was walking down the street when I pulled over to read the map."

"Wow! This is fantastic, Sash. What are the odds?" She beamed at me. "You'll finally be able to heal, the two of you."

"No, Mom, it was just a minute on a sidewalk. I don't know what's wrong with me. I didn't tell her I was sorry, I didn't make it ri—"

"Sorry for what? We should send her a note, maybe we can get some lunch—"

"Sorry for being a pain in the neck. Sorry for making her miserable. Sorry for being a brat. Sorry for being too scared to call."

I stood up, "Anyway, why do you keep stepping all over yourself, trying to make sure they're at the center of my life? They don't *want* to be. They want *you* to be my parent. It's over, Mom."

I gulped. "What happened in Luxembourg wasn't a mistake. I need to let them go. They *want* me to let them go."

On my way back to Connecticut I called Greg, unable to get the encounter with Patricia out of my head.

"You'll get through it, Sasha. You always have." He sounded weary, as if this latest drama was too much.

⌒

Perhaps it was. Running into Patricia made me stop and reconsider. At 24, I'd been in Connecticut for 6 years—2 years longer than I'd lived anywhere since I was 11. When I got the word that Michael's settlement from the church had finally come through, I was more than ready for change – both physical and emotional.

"It's not much," Mom said. "But he would want you to have the money. You two lived through so much together."

But instead of feeling vindicated on Michael's behalf, I felt tremendous responsibility. I'd seen enough of life to know that his bequest was a humbling gift, to be treated with care and respect. I wasn't going to piddle it away on lattes. I was going to honor his memory.

One day a light bulb went off as I watched the film *Babette's Feast*. The heroine wins the French lottery, 10,000 francs, and must decide how to spend the money. She could return to her hometown, Paris, and spend it on excess and entertainment, or she could spend it on a lavish French feast for her loved ones in rural Jutland, where she had arrived as a refugee years earlier.

She decides on the latter, celebrating her community but also honoring her past. She cooks her way through an opulent, sensual menu stocked with the most expensive ingredients in France. There's caviar and champagne, turtles and quail. Her simple guests swoon at every bite, dissolving into supreme pleasure.

By the time the film ended, I knew what to do with Michael's money. I'd immerse myself in the one thing that had kept me going through all the upheaval: cooking. And I'd do it at the Culinary Institute of America, one of the greatest cooking schools in the country, located in upstate New York. Though Mom had taught me a lot, there was so much more I wanted to know. I could use half the settlement toward the first year and half toward the second. When the money was gone, I'd carry what I'd learned wherever I went.

Greg didn't try to talk me out of it, but Mom did.

"What on earth do you want to go to the CIA for? You know how to cook," she said. I could feel her roll her eyes, even through the phone.

"Do I? I don't know, Mom . . . there's always more to learn."

I looked down at the shiny pamphlet, smiling at the photos of students in crisp white chef coats and checked pants serving up perfectly plated scallops, the crisp edges glistening with butter. "I want to figure out everything—the proper way."

"What's wrong with how you do it now? New York is too far away, Sash. That's a five-hour drive for me!" Her voice was getting louder. "You know that I can't help you from there."

"It's not like I'm going across the ocean, Mom!"

"Why don't you go to a school like Johnson & Wales, practically down the street from me? You could live with me." Mom was still living among the nuns in Newton, baking their daily bread.

"In a convent? Really, Mom? And then I become a nun?"

We both laughed.

"Come on, Sasha, what's this really about? Why are you running away again? Family is supposed to stick together."

She was trying so hard to rebuild our relationship, but with every push I just wanted to get farther away. "This is for *me*, Mom. It has nothing to do with . . . anything. I'm just doing something I've always wanted to do. Why can't you see that?"

"If you say so, Sash."

CHAPTER 16

The Other Side
of the Kitchen

HE CIA WAS ORCHESTRAL. Its gilded halls swelled with the
sounds of chopping, mixing, searing, a daily ensemble that
began at 2 a.m. with breakfast cookery and continued well
into the night. High-speed blenders trumpeted while the deep bass
of Hobart mixers spun hypnotically. Here was the whoosh of running
water, the staccato of lids on pots, the thump of wooden spoons on
metal pots. Even when a foot and a half of snow frosted the Hudson
Valley, the classrooms were steamy and warm. Their melodies played
out in rounds, corresponding to the array of service times.

The school was originally a Jesuit seminary; in the early 1900s,
young seminarians paraded these halls, heads bent in solemn prayer
on their passage toward priesthood. I could still feel the hushed
holiness of this place, though now the air had a succulence never
intended by the original occupants. On day one, the outgoing class

served us a four-course supper in Farquharson Hall. The arching, stain-glassed, frescoed walls revealed their former life as a chapel. We sat on the old chancel, 12 to a table, dotted around the draped tablecloths. Moving in somber procession, six crisp waiters delivered our food under silver domes, placing the plates before us in unison. Each dome reflected the vaulted, cloud-painted ceiling above us, more cathedral than mess hall. To this day, I cannot remember what we ate—only those shiny domes, the puff of steam when they were lifted, and the quiet adoration of the moment.

I worked my way through the prescribed course load, each class in three- to six-week blocks. Everyone, whether a seasoned chef or a rookie, started in the same place: "Introduction to Gastronomy." No longer could I cut into a plate of food, bring it to my lips, and smile with simple discovery. Chef Rosenblum taught us concentrated, studious awareness; she awakened *all* of our senses.

Blindfolds were de rigueur. One day we sampled ten kinds of lettuce until I found, with surprise, that I could distinguish romaine's crunchy sweetness from iceberg's watery bite, arugula's peppered tendrils from the slightly bitter petals of baby spinach.

It didn't stop there. As future chefs, we needed to glance down at a cup of white liquid and know whether it was skim milk, whole milk, or cream. Recognizing the slight curve of thick cream or the flat lines of skim milk soon became second nature. We learned to sniff out the difference between oregano and marjoram, a skill that could save us on a busy day in a disheveled kitchen. We stood in the humid, chilled stockroom, feeling for the long green point of an Anaheim pepper or the rounded nub of a jalapeño. Proper identification would keep us from inadvertently overspicing a dish.

Once our senses had been awakened, we were allowed into the kitchens. Each classroom released from under its door its own, signature scents: white wine and garlic, syrup and bacon, lemongrass and ginger. Behind those walls, I learned how to chiffonade basil, cut neat batons out of even the wonkiest potato, and make gallons of perfectly clear broth called "consommé" by removing impurities with a gelatinous web of egg whites.

In breakfast cookery, our drill-sergeant chef taught us how to make a perfect French omelet, tidy as a neatly folded blanket. There was one catch: I had only 90 seconds to create and deliver the dish to him on the other side of the busy kitchen. We lost marks if the buttercup-colored blanket was soiled with any flecks of brown or, like a Victorian showing her ankle, was crass enough to reveal any filling. I never thought I'd be able to do it, but, as Mom likes to say, practice really does make perfect.

I did it in 75.

🍴 The Perfect Omelet

A too-brown omelet, Chef always said, was never the fault of the hot pan but a lazy cook. This recipe is for those brave souls who may already have a delicious omelet recipe in hand, but enjoy the challenge of speed. Though we used clarified butter at the CIA (because it doesn't smoke at high temperatures), I've substituted more readily available ghee (look for it in the dairy case). A recipe like this, simple though it seems, takes several Saturday mornings to perfect. Once the basics are mastered, fillings such as fried mushrooms or peppers may be added.

A few tips from the trenches:

- *Have everything ready to go (eggs, ghee, filling, topping, plate, paper towel).*
- *Keep the eggs moving or they'll set too quickly.*
- *Julia Child was right: Flip the pan with conviction. Otherwise the omelet might slide to the side or, worse, to the floor.*

- **The times indicated are mere suggestions**—*variations in burner intensity and pan thickness will affect how quickly the eggs cook. The shape of the eggs, whether they're watery or fluffy, stiff or dry, is the best road map to a perfect omelet.*

3 large eggs
1 good pinch salt
1 teaspoon ghee
Small handful of shredded cheese, like cheddar or Gruyère

Finishing touches:
A sprinkling of fresh, chopped parsley or chives

In a medium bowl, vigorously whisk the eggs with a pinch of salt. Add ghee to a 10-inch nonstick skillet and preheat over high heat for about 2 minutes.

0:00 Pour in well-beaten eggs—they should cackle like a hungry chicken when they hit the pan. Immediately stir them, making quick, tight circles with a heatproof spatula—keep them moving—until creamy curds form.

0:36 Use the spatula to smooth across the top of the wet curds until they are flat and even. Sprinkle the cheese down the middle. At this point, any other precooked fillings may be added, such as sliced mushrooms or peppers. By now the eggs should be mostly set. Prepare to fold the omelet in thirds. Make the first fold by lifting one edge and bringing it to the center of the omelet. Flip onto a plate.

1:15 To complete the fold, use a paper towel to tuck the final third under the omelet, toward the center. Enjoy this neat, rectangular roll with a happy sprinkle of parsley or chives.

Enough for 1 omelet

When Greg broke up with me, I'd been at the CIA for two months. Even after three years of dating, I knew it was for the best. But for the first time since I was 14, no boy was waiting in the wings to catch me. Instead of reveling in my newfound freedom, I staggered. One Friday after class, unasked and unannounced, I drove the 200 miles to his front door.

When I arrived, I waited for him to invite me in, but instead he came outside. We sat a few feet apart on the top step of the stoop. I didn't say anything right away, though I'd rehearsed the entire drive.

"I don't know what you want from me," he finally said. His voice was flat.

One enormous teardrop, then another, trembled at the corner of my eyes. Barely audible, I offered, "A hug would be nice."

Greg didn't move. "I'm sorry—I really am, but I don't know why you're here."

The concrete step felt hard and cold. The tears came faster. When I dropped my face into my hands, he didn't seem to notice.

Then he gave me a gift, the single best thing to come out of our relationship: "Sasha, I understand that your life has been a struggle, believe me. But you have to work through that on your own."

He paused. "I never had time for my own problems when we were together. There was always something going on with you. You need to figure it out, Sasha—*yourself*."

I caught my breath.

"Horrible things happened to you," he went on carefully, looking over at me for the first time. His green eyes softened. "But you have to learn to fix your own problems, and not put them so much on other people. Like that afternoon when you bumped into Patricia . . . there's nothing I could have done to help. *You* have to decide to be strong without her. *No one can create peace for you*."

He sat there for a few minutes in silence as the winter sky turned orange. I stared unblinking at a small, gray pebble between my feet. Finally, he stood.

"OK," I murmured.

He turned and walked back into the house, pulling the heavy door quietly behind him.

I drove back to culinary school in a daze. Greg had tapped into the heart of the matter. I'd hungered for peace for as long as I could remember, but it had been a mistake to think that someone else could fill the emptiness. I had to get over it. And I had to do it alone.

When choosing our summer internships, most of my classmates went with area restaurants. They slapped spatulas as line cooks or cleaved their way through ten-hour shifts of solid prep work. They were fast, skilled, and heat tolerant.

I didn't want that sort of pressure. For my internship, I looked into food writing, food science, food styling—anything other than the front line. And with these jobs I'd have weekends off. At our school recruitment fair, I found my match with an international product development company called Bama Pie, headquartered in Tulsa, Oklahoma.

Bama works for the biggest names in the fast-food world, and also has its own line of frozen pies and biscuits. I'd be working with their chefs and scientists on new product ideation, which was a fancy way of saying we'd be dreaming up new foods all day. As a bonus, I'd be halfway across the country, about as far from Greg as I could get.

Mom met the idea with her usual resistance.

"There are plenty of internships right here in Boston. Maybe you could bake bread with me at the convent."

"Greg and I broke up, Mom. I just need some time to get away for a bit."

Mom was silent. Then she said, "In that case I'll go with you. You can't do a big cross-country drive alone."

"There's not going to be much room. I'll have my whole life in the car."

"I don't take up much room."

"Can you limit yourself to one suitcase?"

"No problem."

We crammed every inch of my life into my green Civic on the last day of school. My chef knives slid into long folds of cardboard. My clogs and flip-flops piled into baskets. My yard sale cookware filled three milk crates. My giant blue duffel bag and a few scattered trash bags held the rest. True to her word, Mom squeezed one tiny suitcase on the floorboards by her feet.

We began the drive early the next morning.

"Why did you decide to come with me, Mom? This is a big trip; don't you have something better to do? I'm sure the nuns are going to miss their bread."

"A mother knows when she's needed," she said, smoothing her pants. "Plus I need to get away from those nuns. They have more drama than we did with the courts in the eighties! Did you know that one of the nuns has been punching holes in my daily loaves of bread? They finally caught her in the act. They made her say 12 Hail Marys . . . hasn't happened since."

We both laughed. I should have left it at that, but I couldn't.

"Why is someone always mad at you, Mom?"

She leaned back in her seat and closed her eyes. "Bad luck, I guess."

"No one can have *that* much bad luck."

"People get jealous. A nun saw I could make really great bread . . ." She shrugged her shoulders. "Nuns get mad and petty and jealous, just like everyone else."

"I'm not buying it, Mom."

She opened her eyes.

I went on, "You never tell me anything. Like that summer we lived together before my sophomore year, when I asked you about what you did while I was in Paris, after Michael died. You said 'nothing,' but then, in the next breath, you started to say there *was* someone you talked to. How can I trust you, if you can't trust me?"

"We're back to that?" she huffed.

"So who is the one person who had the privilege of talking to you?"

She sighed. "Gloria had a little gift shop on Beacon Hill with the cutest greeting cards, all kinds, for birthdays, anniversaries—funerals, too. She helped me with the card I sent you in Paris—the one you *threw out*."

She met my eyes briefly; then we both looked back at the road. "She was the only one I could talk to about Michael. I visited that woman's gift shop during my lunch breaks and after work every single week for two years after the funeral. In rain, snow—it didn't matter. I went. Each visit I made some small adjustment. The photo never changed, but the card stock, the envelope, the font—it all went through so many changes. One day, probably after the 50th font change, I apologized to Gloria."

Mom laughed softly. "I'll never forget what she said: She told me designing that card was my way of working through Michael's death. She'd lost a daughter many years back, so I guess she'd figured me out."

I imagined Mom packing up at the end of a long day at the trial court—that same court, I realized with astonishment, in which she'd fought for us. I pictured her trudging through a downpour, along the cobblestone alleys to a little card shop on Beacon Hill just to look at Michael's face in that coffin. I thought about how sick it made me to look at that photo for a few short minutes, and realized she'd done that to herself every week for two years—104 times.

The thought took my breath away. "You know, I don't even remember our goodbye back when you gave us up," I told her. "I don't even know where we said goodbye."

"I'm not surprised," she said, staring at her hands, "the whole thing was so traumatic." She looked me over and clasped her hands. "I'll always regret not hugging you."

"What do you mean?"

"I gave you a kiss, but I didn't hug you kids. I don't know why. We were in the vestibule of the apartment by the staircase when the caseworker pulled up. He beeped—I gave you each a quick kiss. You had your hands full with your little suitcases. You were so loaded down . . . it all went by so fast. A moment later, you were gone."

I sat with the image for a moment; but even with her prompting, the shadows of this memory wouldn't come to life.

The sun marked our progress toward Tulsa, rising and setting over a tapestry of towns. Some patches were green, others rusted and crumbling. Eventually waitresses began to assume we meant cold tea when we ordered it instead of the steaming hot cups we took for granted in New England. They spoke in lyrics, indiscriminately calling us honey, sweetheart, child. Every sentence became slow. Deliberate.

With each passing mile, Greg faded a little. But the release wasn't satisfying the way I'd hoped. Instead I felt tearing, a shearing, an unraveling. As we snaked along the spine of the Blue Ridge Mountains, I gasped at every hairpin turn. We were one breath away from plummeting over the rippled mountains on either side.

"You need a break. Sasha, let me take over awhile."

"I've got it under control," I told her. *No one is going to drive me,* I thought to myself. *Not any more.*

"You can't do this totally alone, Sasha."

"Of course I can. This is *my* car."

Eventually the black soil turned red. We passed through Memphis and into the dusty center of the country. Quilted fields stretched into the horizon, fences so spread apart that cows and horses appeared to roam freely. Little else stirred. Finally we crossed a long, metal bridge. Three skyscrapers popped into sight—Tulsa.

As I took in the city's scrawny profile, Mom leaned back in her seat, shut her eyes, and laughed, "You're probably going to live in Tulsa forever."

Something about her announcement felt a little too much like a premonition. "Yeah, right," I scoffed as I looked over the ragged horizon, wondering what on earth Tulsa had to offer that I hadn't already experienced in Paris, Luxembourg, or just about *anywhere.* "Spiderman would go out of business here, don't ya think?" I said.

Mom laughed. But I couldn't shake the eerie feeling her words had cast over me.

PART FOUR

Stirrings

*"When one is in love,
a cliff becomes a meadow."*

—Ethiopian proverb

CHAPTER 17

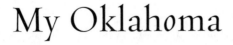

My Oklahoma

I RENTED A STUDIO APARTMENT on the west side of Tulsa—little more than two rooms right off the Arkansas River, tucked between the billowing smokestacks of the city's industrial zone. Mom helped me set up my scattered belongings. We unloaded the car in less than 30 minutes: a milk crate of kitchenware on the counter, my old blue duffel bag heaved into the closet, my favorite pillows in a pile where the bed was supposed to be.

A veil of humidity hung in the air, sticking to my skin. Even the walls seemed to sweat. Setting up with Mom felt like a true mother–daughter moment and I realized, warmly, that many parents wouldn't drive halfway across the country to help their kids settle in like this, certainly not at my age. In less than a month, I'd be 26 years old.

A few hours later, the furniture arrived on the backs of two horse-faced men. For $150 a month, I'd rented the bare minimum from a local furniture store: a bed, a twill love seat, and a round white lamp.

The hungry apartment swallowed up these tokens, the empty rooms echoing and emaciated. It would have cost another $50 a month to get a dining table and chairs, coffee table, and nightstands. We made do by standing at the thin island counter for meals.

Mom had only two days before her flight back to Boston. The morning before she left, we drove down to the nearest big-box store and picked up a few necessities, like shampoo and a blanket. Mom also grabbed a ten-pound bag of Granny Smith apples and hoisted it into the cart.

"It's almost your birthday. Let's make an apple pie."

"Like the kind we had when we were little?"

"It's the only kind I know how to make," she shrugged with a smile. She sent me down the aisles to grab a couple of lemons, brown sugar, a few sticks of butter, flour, and a glass baking dish.

"Don't we need cinnamon and nutmeg?" I asked.

She patted her purse. "Never leave home without it."

At the apartment I leaned over the laminate island and helped Mom peel the apples, then watched as she sliced them up. The knife landed with a dull thud against the cutting board, laborious and arrhythmic. Her cuts were nowhere as thin or as even as the chefs at the CIA would have required, but rather a mishmash of wedges, rounds, and blocks.

She squeezed an entire lemon over the pieces so they wouldn't brown, and then tossed on a palmful of sugar and the spices. Almost immediately the sugar pooled onto the apples—a syrupy condensation. She used a fork to press butter, flour, and water together into a quick piecrust. First there was too much water, then too much flour. She worked more of each into the dough until it began to shape up, and then rolled it out with a bottle. It stuck in places, but she still managed to drape the now warm parcel across the glass baking dish. In went the apples, along with their juices. She used her knuckles to crimp the pastry crust together and popped the whole shebang in the oven.

I dug out my recipe journal to jot down some notes.

"I didn't catch how much flour you used—what was the ratio?"

"Recipes are no good when it's this humid," she said, her voice pinging off the hard, tile floors. "You just have to wing it and hope for the best."

I put down my pen and stared into the oven. "I can't wait," I said. "Michael always asked for this pie for his birthday, remember?"

She smiled at me. "I remember."

Thirty-five minutes later, Mom pulled the pie out of the oven and heaved it onto a thin metal trivet with a clang. Cinnamon, nutmeg, and lemon floated through the air, the scent warm and sparkling.

"It's too hot to cut into right now," she said. "Let's go for a walk."

Mom unfolded four dramatic, wide-brimmed sun hats from her carryall, each more colorful than the last. I laughed, amazed that she owned headgear worthy of the Kentucky Derby, but even more impressed that she'd thought to bring them—and found a spot to squeeze them into her small suitcase. She chose a cherry-red silk hat to pair with her jean shorts and wide-neck sweatshirt. I chose a cream hat with long orange feathers. The feathers rose and fell with every movement, waltzing as I walked.

As we strolled along the river, all eyes were on those hats. At first the attention felt awkward, but soon I settled into the panoply. I could be whoever I wanted to be in Tulsa. Joggers dripped by us with the glow of a hundred-degree morning on their faces, yet I stayed cool.

Back at the apartment, Mom sliced into the still warm pie before either of us had taken off our hats. I stood at the counter and took a forkful. My eyes closed as I brought steaming apples to my lips. But instead of the glorious flavors I'd remembered from my childhood, I tasted a limp, chewy crust and slightly underdone fruit. The acid from the lemon juice made the inside of my mouth sour and my teeth hurt.

Mom looked at me, waiting. I took off my hat, smiling weakly while chewing, wondering what on earth to say.

Finally, I managed, "Wow, Mom—it's good." She beamed. I looked away, unable to keep the lie out of my eyes. I continued to eat. Slow. Deliberate. Dutiful. Eventually I scraped the juices off the plate. And truth be told, the pie wasn't bad; it just wasn't what I remembered.

Had the CIA ruined me, with its professionally perfect desserts? Was I expecting too much of my mother? Or had my memory been nothing more than wishful thinking?

Mom took a bite and chewed thoughtfully. "It's pretty good, considering . . ."

I emptied my plate. Mom beamed and cut into the pie again, sliding a new, larger piece in front of me.

I ate the second slice, too.

Mom's Apple Pie With a Twist

I've updated Mom's recipe, so I can remember the past with feet planted firmly toward the future. Though Mom likes to add several Granny Smiths, I prefer my pie granny-free, on the sweeter side. I use Pink Lady apples, though many varieties will do, as long as they are firm. To catch the spiced apple drippings, I sprinkle steel-cut oatmeal on the bottom crust. Mom doesn't thicken her juices, but I like some cornstarch for body. Either way is delicious. But there's plenty to keep from Mom's recipe, too—the bewitching "sin" of cinnamon perfuming the fruit, the touch of brown sugar, and the spirit of the thing—a dessert that gets made, in the face of—and perhaps because of—all odds.

For the pie dough:
3 cups all-purpose flour
1 teaspoon salt
2 teaspoons sugar
½ pound (2 sticks) cold butter, cubed
A little ice water

For the apple filling:
4 pounds firm baking apples, such as Pink Lady
The zest and juice of 1 lemon
⅓ cup brown sugar, packed
⅓ cup white sugar
1 teaspoon cinnamon
½ teaspoon nutmeg
3 tablespoons cornstarch (optional, for thickening)
¼ cup steel-cut oatmeal (any kind that's "ready in 5 minutes")

Finishing touches:
1 egg white, beaten with 1 teaspoon water
1 teaspoon sugar

Make the pie dough by whisking together the flour, salt, and sugar, and then cutting in the butter with a pastry cutter (Mom used two knives held like an "X" and drawn across each other). When the butter is mostly pea-sized, switch to a large fork and drizzle on the ice water, tossing until a shaggy dough forms (6 to 10 tablespoons usually does the trick). Press the dough together and form two disks, one a little larger than the other. Wrap in plastic wrap, and refrigerate for about an hour.

Meanwhile, peel and cut the apples into ¼-inch-thick slices. Add to a large bowl and drizzle with the lemon juice and zest, then toss with the sugars, cinnamon, nutmeg, and cornstarch.

Preheat the oven to 400°F. Roll out the larger disk until several inches wider than the pie dish—15 or 16 inches. I like to work between two floured sheets of parchment paper so I don't have to worry about sticking. Alternatively, dust a clean work surface with a bit of flour. Place this first round of dough on the bottom of the pie dish, sprinkle with oatmeal, and fill with apple mixture, being sure to scrape in all the accumulated juices. Press with the palm to flatten the apples (this reduces the air pocket created by an all-butter crust).

Roll out the second disk. Drape it across the apples and cut three vents in the center. Roll the top edge under the bottom edge to seal and crimp with the knuckles. Brush all over with just enough egg white to lightly glaze the pie. Sprinkle with sugar.

Bake for 30 minutes, then reduce the temperature to 325°F and bake another 30 to 35 minutes, or until the crust browns agreeably. Let cool on a rack for 3 hours before slicing. This gives the pie time to set up, though only refrigeration will make the slices perfectly firm. Serve warm, with a scoop of vanilla ice cream or, as Mom likes, a dollop of yogurt.

Makes one 9- or 10-inch deep-dish pie; enough for 8 to 10

The next day Mom flew back to Boston, 1,587 impossible miles away. Back at the apartment, I settled into my rented love seat. I didn't move all morning. I watched the gray laminate kitchen flicker in the fluorescents. I looked at the cabinets. A few of the doors gaped, revealing a tin of mint tea, a quart of coffee grounds, three cans of tuna, and five cases of Diet Pepsi.

Finally, as the sun towered overhead, I cut into the last slice of pie and ate it slowly while thinking about the journey ahead. Four months in Tulsa. That's when the real tears came. I thought they'd be about missing Greg, or being alone. But more than anything else, they were about that stupid pie.

I'd been waiting to taste it for more than a decade. It wasn't just a botched dessert. For the first time, that pie showed me who Mom *really* was, not who I wanted her to be. That pie was *her*. No matter how much I needed her to be the perfect mother, she could only be human. And though her choices had always been made with the best of intentions, the results spoke for themselves.

As I washed the pie plate and put it back on the empty shelf, I told myself that I had to love her despite it all.

As often as I'd changed homes in a life buttressed by closed doors, Tulsa was my first foray into total solitude. For four months, I'd have no boyfriend to lean on, no family nearby to check in on me: I'd washed up manless, motherless, and friendless. I felt cornered by the loneliness, the disconnect, and the dissolution into anonymity. Yet I knew this self-induced isolation was exactly what I needed.

Those first days, I operated on strict autopilot. Once the apple pie and tuna fish were gone, I survived on gas station beef jerky and hourly jolts of coffee. I shuffled to and from my internship at Bama Pie Factory, filling the required eight hours each day, trying to come up with new product ideas for our fast-food clientele. White potions and powders lined our 30-by-30-foot kitchen lab, stretching from floor to ceiling.

There was no natural light, though the shelves glowed brilliantly, windows on a chemical sunrise. Some of the potions were designed to make food last longer; others added flavor or enhanced dough elasticity. No concept was considered a success unless the scientists could find a way to integrate them into fast-food products (in the name of food safety and longevity, of course).

I soon learned to pass on the fancy ingredients I'd so loved at the CIA. Instead of Gruyère, I experimented with processed cheese in pizza crust. Instead of exotic star-fruit salads, we explored the possibilities of deep-fried cheesecake squares. Since I hated to see anything go to waste, I ate the results. After the first month, I could no longer zip my pants.

From 5:01 p.m. until 8:59 a.m., I stood in the shadows of the real work to be done: scaling the loneliness. Sleeping in my rented queen bed was a perpetual reminder that there was no man to hold me, make me laugh, make me forget.

This was my rainy season. I fell asleep crying. I woke up crying. One morning I cried so hard while jogging that I had to stop and use a leaf as a tissue.

It was ridiculous.

These were the tears of coming face-to-face with the past; of coming face-to-face with my mother and accepting who she was, instead of who I wanted her to be; of relinquishing the Dumonts; of letting Michael go. They were cleansing. Purifying. Cathartic.

I never told anyone what was happening. My co-workers were nice, but it was easier to keep my distance. Somehow Connor, Tim, Grace, and Mom knew. I wasn't in Tulsa long before little notes began to arrive in the mail. One clipping from Mom read:

"All you can be is you. Your true self shines with more beauty than your mind can ever know."

I framed the quotation, not because I believed the words, but because I knew that one day I must believe them. And the thought of *that* terrified me more than anything.

❧

It was late August when the deluge finally stopped enough for me to look around. I had about two months left in Tulsa. The first morning I woke up with dry eyes, I realized Greg had been right.

I was never going to get better if *I* didn't do something to make my life better. Plus I was sick of crying. Now, I was ready for a full-to-the-brim, straight-up glass of joy—the kind I'd experienced when Mom gave us the cranberry juice in our cereal instead of milk, before I realized that the treat was born of want. I wanted to return to that feast of innocence. And yet for the first time in my life, the thought of cooking wore me out.

One afternoon a cherry-red motorcycle slid past my car. I remembered the freedom I'd felt on the back of Greg's motorcycle: *Why should I have to be on the back of someone else's bike to capture that lovely abandon?*

So one day at work, instead of researching new pizza crust flavors, I holed up in my cubicle and Googled Tulsa-area motorcycle clubs. The first result was Tulsa Sportbike Riders. The tagline read: "Riding's more fun when there's more than one."

Perfect.

I showed up at the very next event, a meet and greet at a local motorcycle shop. I half-expected to find a group of punks doing wheelies in the parking lot, but all I saw were silver-haired fathers and grandfathers, apple-bottomed mothers and grandmothers. Despite the weather (98°F, 50 percent humidity), everyone sported tall boots and thick leather jackets. They eyed me with mild curiosity as I exited my car.

Inside a brassy voice asked, "Where's your bike?" I whipped around to find a fleshy woman with long, silver hair looking me squarely in the eyes.

"I'm still figuring out what I want to get," I replied, "I'm new in town. My name's Sasha." I held out my hand.

The woman tilted her head to the side and scanned me from top to bottom, considering my pigtails and torn jeans. "I'm Leona. Have you ridden before?"

I shook my head slowly. "I've taken lessons. I was thinking of getting an SV 750. My ex-boyfriend had one."

"Honey, that's much too big of a bike for the likes of you. You only need a 250cc engine if you've never been on the road. Unless, of course, you have a death wish . . ."

She didn't say the words unkindly, but they popped out with just enough snarl that I took a half step back. A few other riders perked up, and soon I was surrounded by a living, breathing public service announcement for wearing my helmet, gloves, and boots.

"You all are so responsible," I joked, overwhelmed by the depth of instruction they were giving me. Maybe this wasn't the best place to find my freedom after all.

"He wouldn't have it any other way," the woman chortled, her enormous bosom shaking like a semi on a gravel road. She jerked her thumb toward the corner by the door at a quiet man with salt-and-pepper hair, nineties "dad" jeans, and a black leather jacket. He was of average height, husky in the middle, with broad shoulders that looked like they could row a boat to Timbuktu and back.

I leaned to the side, trying to make out his face. But just then he walked out the door, popped on his helmet, and revved up his bike. I expected him to crack open the throttle, but he zipped smoothly down the road, several of the lounging riders waving to him as he passed.

"Who's that?" I asked.

"Keith Martin, the founder of our club."

The idea that this dowdy man had started a motorcycle group tickled me. "Doesn't this go for another two hours? He's leaving kind of early if he's the founder."

Leona leaned closer but didn't lower her voice. "One of the riders went down on a group ride earlier today. It's no big deal, a little road rash . . . but he always makes it a point to go by the hospital whenever something like that happens."

Two months earlier, the words "nice guy" might have piqued my interest. I might have asked more about him. I might have made sure I sat near him at the next gathering. But I was done letting guys fix me.

With Leona's advice and encouragement, I purchased a perfectly safe 250cc yellow-and-black Kawasaki for $900. I had no idea how I'd get it back to the CIA in a few months, but I wasn't looking that far ahead.

I rode every day; under the hot sun, in the thundering rain, through the fog. The hush and gush of wind in my helmet lulled me. The rain purified me. The scent of warm engine and gasoline clung to my skin even at night. I loved how Oklahoma roads kept going, a straight-forward grid stretching farther and farther into the grassy horizon.

There was no reason to stop—ever. I drank in the rushing humidity the same way I drank in the breeze on the swing in Jamaica Plain, insatiably. Some days I rode on my own, but mostly I rode with whomever wanted to get away for a while.

There was no shortage of takers. Weeknights, we prowled highway on-ramps and giant country sweepers at 90 miles an hour. Weekends, we nosed around the foothills of western Arkansas about an hour away. For big trips, Keith and his buddies led the pack, a few miles ahead of the rest of us. By the time I'd roll into the scheduled pit stops, they'd be pulling out.

I asked Leona about it.

"Those guys aren't here to socialize at pit stops. They're here to *ride*. They go to the racetrack. They *practice*, work the corners, rub the pavement like erasers." She looked at me with a knowing grin. "Don't even think about trying to keep up with those guys."

I laughed. "To be honest, I'm too chicken to ride on the track."

"Hate to break your heart, honey, but you couldn't even if you wanted to. You don't have full leathers and a back protector."

The thought made me chuckle. "I'd look like Iron Man."

"You'd be safe."

Halfway through my internship, Mom phoned to find out how things were going.

"You got a motorcycle?" I could hear her exasperation through the phone line.

"Don't worry, I wear my helmet."

"What on earth for?" she gasped. "You'll never feel the wind in your hair with a helmet in the way."

"Oh . . . I thought you'd be happy . . ." I began, confused. "You know—that I'm keeping my brain safe."

"You don't need a helmet to keep safe, Sasha. That's a false sense of security—it takes the reality of the situation away. Without a helmet you have no choice but to respect the road. Pace yourself a little more. Trust me, I know," Mom said. Then she paused: "How are you going to get your bike back to New York?"

I looked around my yawning apartment, no more furnished than the day I'd arrived. I spotted the bumblebee yellow of my bike outside the front window and smiled.

"I don't think I want to come back."

"Do you mean to cooking school?"

"I—I don't know. The CIA's great and all, but I feel happy here, Mom. Like . . . I've found my footing. If I can find a job before Christmas, I think I'm just going to stay."

I hadn't planned to say the words, but there they were. Going back to school felt wrong, especially considering that it would use up the last of Michael's precious money. And I didn't want to leave Tulsa. The checkerboard roads and flat terrain were plainer and less exciting than anywhere else I'd ever lived. And yet this honest, sunburned land fed me exactly what I needed: my own space, a place to run, ride, to move through the pain to the other side. Tulsa held me when I needed holding.

"Does that make me a failure, not to finish school?" I asked Mom.

"Maybe to some people—but you know what, Sash? The better part of wisdom is turning a failure into victory. You have to complete the transition."

I chuckled at her dramatic choice of words. "What do you mean?"

"You're almost out of the fire, Sasha. Now you have to learn what it is to be a ph—" she cut herself short.

"A phoenix?"

"You just have to unfold your wings and fly."

*

I met Leona at Eddy's Wings to tell her the news: I was staying. As we munched on a platter of spicy chicken, Keith walked in.

"Hey, I want to introduce you," Leona called across the small restaurant. She jerked her chin in my direction.

Keith walked over to our table and smiled. "I've seen you on some of the group rides." He reached over to shake my hand. As his fingers touched my wrist, I looked into his eyes for the first time. A flash of something—a snippet of a scene as real as any memory—bowled me over. I was several years older, sitting in a darkened office, working side by side on a website with this man. The computer screen glowed blue on our faces. Somehow I knew it was our office. I knew we had a life together—a home.

Now you've really lost it, I thought. You've been single way too long.

I blushed. Keith smiled deeper, his eyes softening. They were dove gray, his gaze cashmere.

"Nice to meet you."

His words stretched out in a smooth southern drawl. I felt a settling, a natural comfort take root deep within me. I snapped my hand back quickly.

"I thought you two kids would make nice friends," Leona said.

"It only takes a smile to make a friend," he beamed.

When I glanced down at Keith's mouth, I noticed fine white scars along the upper part of his lip, just under his goatee, like the stitching on a rag doll. I looked back up quickly, embarrassed to have stared.

"Mine's a little broken," he acknowledged, tracing his finger across the scars.

"What happened?"

"I was 14, tooling around on my minibike out in the country about a quarter mile from my parents' house. A huge dog came after me. I lost control and turned the bike too hard. The gravel road ate my face."

He chuckled and shook his head. "They found me walking in a daze, covered in blood, headed the wrong way from the house. I ended up in the hospital for two weeks because I let fear get the best of me. They had to completely reconstruct my upper lip. My whole face looked like a smashed tomato. Not exactly the best way to start high school."

"They did a great job," I said. "I'm amazed you still ride."

"I have dogs, too." He laughed. "Small ones."

He was a head taller than me, with a round face, arched eyebrows, and those gorgeous, half-moon eyes. He looked shockingly like Billy Ray Cyrus. I told him as much.

"You should see my high school picture. Our mullets were twins, separated at birth." We laughed.

"Thank God the eighties are over," I said.

Twenty years had removed all traces of Keith's mullet; silver threatened to edge out his clipped brown hair. His goatee was completely white. From the side, his nose was straight. From the front, it looked more Roman. I found myself resting my eyes again and again on his. It felt curiously like coming home. But I dismissed the sensation.

A few minutes later, a young guy walked up to Keith's side. He had shaggy brown hair, a round, baby face, and the most enormous feet I'd ever seen. "This is my son, Ryan," Keith said, putting his hand on the boy's back. They were the same height.

I nodded to Ryan, smiling vaguely. I looked down at Keith's hand; a gold band traced along his ring finger. After more pleasantries, I pulled Leona aside.

"He's married . . . with a teenage son?"

"Son, yes, but married? No. He wears that ring just because. He's dating Ryan's mother. They *were* married—for eight years, I think— but divorced. He married someone else for a couple of years, and now he's dating Ryan's mom again."

She looked me over, smiled knowingly, and then added: "His love life would give *The Young and the Restless* a run for their money."

Keith and Ryan went outside to look over the line of motorcycles. Keith ruffled Ryan's mop. I smiled. He looked like a good father.

"How old is he?" I asked Leona.

"He had Ryan three days before he turned 20; he's 35."

And I'm 26, I thought. All logic told me I should be alarmed, but every time I looked in his direction, a curious sense of peace washed over me.

———

When my internship ended a couple months later, Leona invited me to crash with her while I looked for a job. I checked with the head of my internship at Bama to see if any relevant departments were hiring—nothing. I scanned the newspaper for some kind of food styling or food writing position—again, nothing. The lack of food positions shook my resolve, but I'd already missed the deadline to return to the CIA.

The next week I sent out two dozen more applications, this time to any job I was remotely qualified for, from web design to graphics to waitressing. I checked my email every 15 minutes—nothing.

When word got back to Keith, he suggested I help him with a few freelance web design jobs. I'd barely logged five hours when the phone rang. An interview later, and I'd landed a gig as marketing coordinator for a chain of regional auto body shops. It wasn't remotely food oriented, but the pay was decent, I knew how to do the job, and my boss was nice, even if the hours were relentless. And *anything* was better than going back north, which increasingly felt like the epicenter of all my failed relationships.

I called Keith and told him I wouldn't have time to help him with his projects after all. He sounded disappointed, but I figured it was for the best. Though he never flirted with me or made an inappropriate remark, I kept thinking of those dove gray eyes. After I hung up, I stared at his name in my phone contacts, my finger hovering over the delete button. Finally I pressed it. My other contacts slid into place as though he'd never been there.

With the new job, everything seemed to be falling in place, except for one thing—Michael's money. I had no regrets about spending the first half on cooking school. No matter how far or hard I rolled, I knew the CIA's lessons would creep back into my kitchen and life. But the question remained: What to do with the second half? The answer came to me almost before I'd asked the question.

I must make a home, to honor Michael's memory—a home no one could take away from me. All the comfort food in the world wouldn't matter if I didn't have a home. I could use the last of the money for the down payment.

Just three weeks into my second-ever job, I found a real estate agent and got to work. Off my motorcycle, Tulsa's streets didn't gush by with quite the same urgency. Details came into relief, like the art deco buildings sprinkled downtown and throughout the old neighborhoods.

These stunning properties were remnants of the early 1900s, when Tulsa was known as the Oil Capital of the World. Many were now abandoned, ghosts of another time. Though these pouting beauties might one day be converted to trendy lofts, they were most certainly *not* for sale to the general public. To the north and south of downtown were solid craftsman houses, many built before statehood. These architectural gems were too expensive or too run-down for me to renovate on my own.

Then there was the trendy Brookside neighborhood near my new office, filled with a mishmash of homes from different eras. Some sold for more than a half million, whereas others cost $140,000. There was a shabby chic vibe to many of these more affordable homes, their puckered yards filled with lawn art, sprawling vines, and puffing, potbellied chiminea (those stubby, onion–shaped, front-loading fireplaces).

One day on a whim, I rode through the southernmost edge of Brookside behind my office. Just a mile south of the restaurants, the houses were even more affordable: Most were less than $100,000, and many only went for $75,000. Just across from a sun-beaten triangle knotted with weeds, a flimsy red-and-white sign caught my eye: "For sale by owner."

The mid-century ranch wasn't beautiful from the outside: a squat two-window facade with a cinder-block stoop. Except for the cherry-red shutters, it looked exactly like all the other houses around the triangle, some shade of drab beige. But it was surrounded by an eight-foot privacy fence, and the sign promised a hot tub and walk-in closet. I called my real estate agent from the street.

Inside, the living room walls were also cherry red. The two front bedrooms were bubblegum pink and sky blue. As if in rebellion, the windowless galley kitchen slumbered in a perpetual state of darkness; walnut cabinets and black appliances blotted out any glimmer of light, even during the daytime. The kitchen's only saving grace was the faux Tuscan wall. The brickwork and plastering was a clear DIY job, but if I squinted just right, I could imagine myself in Italy. I loved it.

And then I walked into the master bedroom addition. The ceiling there was higher, at least nine feet, and built out with three long, lean windows that funneled the sunlight onto the shag carpet. I stood in the rays, eyes shut, and felt the warmth soak into my skin. I must have stood there a long while.

When the owner finally plodded into the bedroom, he pointed to the dark wood trim. The crown molding rippled along the ceiling, ornate and complex, different from the rest of the house—clearly the work of a craftsman.

"Looks British, doesn't it? My wife wanted to paint that there trim white. I told her it'd be a crime." He squared his jaw and arched his back as though contemplating fine art at the Louvre. Tilting his head sideways, he crinkled his eyes as if to say, "You better not paint it, either."

~⌒

Right after the New Year, I closed on the house. At the time, buying it felt exciting and important and adult, the way I felt sliding into my mother's heels as a kid. I suppose I needed something to be all mine, as most unattached people do.

I was blind to the house's faults, the way new lovers are: the roof that needed a thousand dollars worth of repairs to pass structural inspections, the mold-infested leak in the bay window, and the sloping dining room (a sure sign that it had been the back porch in a former life). I signed the contract without setting foot in the backyard. It just didn't seem important. A quick scan through the window was enough.

Oh, but I was young.

My first night in the house, I finally stood in the backyard, keys in hand. An unseasonably warm wind blew through, carrying the scent of mud and melting snow. I craned my neck to stare at the stars, pinholes in the darkness. I'm not sure what happens after we die, but if ever there was a time to believe my brother's spirit was with me, this was it.

I thought about what had led me to this spot; all of it had started with Michael's money. "Thank you," I whispered. "I love you. I wish you were here."

As I looked up at the vinyl siding, the simple stone foundation, I recognized that this house was just the shell of a home. I couldn't help but wonder if, as in *Babette's Feast,* there was more to come, if Michael's money would build something much greater than the sum of these parts.

～⁀)

My new job bled into my evenings and weekends until most days, I only had time for the house. The first order of business was covering up the red paint in the living room. I slapped on avocado green, then a yeasty sort of yellow before settling on beige. I added a couple of thrift store couches, also beige. I picked up a scallop-edged dining table from the dent-and-scratch room at the furniture store. And I slept on the beige shag carpet until I could afford a bed. When I stitched sheer curtains from fabric scraps, Mom reminded me she'd hung sheets and towels over the windows during our first weeks in Jamaica Plain.

When the first bills showed up, I realized I was going to need a roommate.

Vanessa, a friend from the motorcycle club, moved into the front bedroom the next month. Ten years my senior, she was more like a big sister than a friend. With cheekbones like Marilyn Monroe's, acrylic nails, and straight-ironed hair halfway down her back, she made my perpetual pigtails and dirty fingernails look as ramshackle as they were.

After she moved in, finances eased up. I got a cat. I did laundry. I mowed my lawn. Once in a while Vanessa would ask me to teach her a recipe from the CIA, but I could never find the time. The days droned by, one more ordinary than the last, until winter backflipped into summer. I'd been in Tulsa for one year. Work was only getting harder, as we were trying to roll out a new series of ads for the fall, a big season in the auto body industry.

"You need a break," Vanessa said one day after a motorcycle turned both our heads. "Let's enjoy the summer before it's over." Over the last several months, Vanessa and I had done very little riding. We crammed it in the space between work and sleep. So we decided to go check out a track day.

We hung our arms over the fences all morning. Even though we could only see a sliver of the knotted course, the bikes floated, sighed, dove, groaned, and screamed, each one marking its unseen place on the track.

"I want to do this," I said to her, eyes wide.

"Me, too!" she said.

"Hey there, stranger," a voice said behind me, "I still need to pay you."

Keith was standing a few feet away. I hadn't seen him much since I'd bought the house months earlier. Every time we did meet, he offered to pay me. And every time, I skirted the subject because whenever our eyes locked, I had the sensation of seeing an old friend. And we couldn't *be* friends. Not with those eyes. Today though, he looked different. He was leaner, his race leathers hanging off his hips, his goatee gone.

"Don't worry about it."

"What do you mean? Five hours—that's a hundred bucks!"

"I suppose . . ." I looked at Vanessa, then back to Keith, "I *could* get a back protector with the money."

I fished a scrap of paper from my pocket and scratched down my address. "Send me a check and you just might see me out there next time." I pointed to the faded asphalt.

"Well, you're going to need to learn a few things, then," he laughed.

Early the next evening, the doorbell rang. Vanessa was still at work. I peeked out the front window. Keith was at the door looking trim in black work boots, a pair of jeans, and a Superman T-shirt. I leaned forward to get a better look, but bumped the window with my forehead. His head turned in my direction. I jumped behind the sheer curtain: Had he seen me peek out at him? *Good job, Sasha.*

I took a deep breath, then gripped the door handle and pulled it open. "Hey, what are you doing here?" I tried not to look overly pleased.

He smiled. "I hope you don't mind me stopping by like this."

"Of course not. It's great to see you again!"

"Can you come outside for a minute?"

"Sure. What's up?"

He motioned me toward his white pickup, swung open the door, pulled a large shopping bag from the cab and held it out to me. As I peered inside, recognition hit me.

"You got me a back protector?" I gasped. "Wow. Thank you!"

I rushed him with a hug, my arms clasped around his neck. His body was warm and smelled like summer. My tank top moved up just enough for his arm to graze the skin of my lower back above my shorts. Something about that moment, our two bodies pressed together, made me want to lean on him a little more. I fought the urge, pulling back, but the hug had lasted too long. I looked up at him, swallowing hard.

"What's that look?" he asked.

"N-nothing. Listen, I'll see you later." I forced a quick smile. "Probably at the track!"

I turned and headed toward the house. *Shoot. Shoot. Shoot.*

He strolled along behind me, hands in his pockets.

"Your grass is looking a bit long. You gonna mow it?" he teased. I looked back at him. His smile was half hung, like a little boy's.

I paused a moment, surveying the crabgrass shooting up past the still trim Bermuda. "If I had to choose between mowing the lawn and making memories, I'd choose memories, every time."

By now I'd reached my front door. He caught up with me. "Hey, back there, I saw—" he stammered, "something in your eyes. What was that all about?"

I opened the door and stepped into the cool shadows. I paused a moment, hand on the doorknob, trying to think of something to say. He had one foot on the middle step and one foot on the landing.

"Nothing. It was nothing."

His eyes searched mine. "Are you sure?"

Despite myself, the words came rushing out: "It's just that I . . . I like you."

What am I, in middle school? I could have died right then and there.

He stepped into the house, pulled the door shut behind him, and stood in the cool shadows with me. A minute ticked by, then two. I tried to think of an excuse to leave, but this was my house.

"I like you too," he finally said. The corners of his mouth flitted up, and then pressed in a straight line. "I've always felt a connection to you."

He opened his arms. When I didn't move, he stepped forward and pulled me toward him. I thought of his son, his girlfriend/ex-wife: Self-loathing washed over me.

"This is not who I am. I won't destroy a family." I pulled away from him, leaning against the back of the couch.

"I understand. It's just that—"

"I've spent my whole life being second choice. I need to be some-one's first choice. I can't . . ."

He took my face in his hands.

"Will you just *listen?* You Yankees talk so fast!" He cleared his throat. "Sasha . . ."

He took his hands off my face and held up his left hand. The ring was gone. "I moved out. It's been a long time coming. I left last month."

"Oh my goodness! How's Ryan taking it?"

"We sat down with him and explained that it isn't his fault. We've barely been more than roommates for a long time. He's decided to live at his mother's."

"Well," I shook my head, "I had no idea—"

Before I could finish, he pulled me toward him into another full-body hug. This time our bodies pressed closer. He slid his cheek across mine and then, there it was—his lips on mine.

CHAPTER 18

Mr. Picky

THREE WEEKS LATER, Keith and I lay in my bed watching the afternoon sun flicker through the trees and ricochet off the ceiling. He kept an apartment across town, halfway between my Brookside home and his son, but he often ended up at my place on Saturday afternoons. Since Vanessa had moved in with her boyfriend, we had the place to ourselves. This was our space. Our time.

Things were good—really good. When we weren't together, we text-messaged several hundred times a day. When we were together, we were worse than a couple of teenagers. I spent my days giddy, smiling. On this particular golden day, I felt the stirrings of love flit around my heart, as delicate as they were unnerving.

"I know it hasn't been very long—you and I, I mean—but I . . . I don't want to waste my time," I began.

I took his hands in mine, rubbing my thumb along his tough palm. His life line was deep and creased, like an old letter. This was the only part of him that really felt nine years older than me.

"It's just that . . . this is going to sound really silly . . . but I'm almost 27 . . . I'm going to want a family—a baby—the whole thing. I really like you and . . . well . . . I don't want to go down this road if you're—"

"Done?" he finished for me.

I pulled my breath in quickly and nodded. I stared at my hands cradling his. My fingers draped soft and olive against his fair skin. I would have never dreamed of talking babies with Greg or John, certainly not after three weeks.

"I just don't think my heart could take it if . . ."

He propped himself up on a couple of pillows. "Not that long ago, I thought I was done. My heart's tired, too. High blood pressure and atrial fibrillation—it runs in the family. But it's more than that. I'm about to turn 36, I have a mostly grown son. I even got . . . a vasectomy."

He looked at me earnestly. "But that can be reversed. This is going to sound weird, but I can see it. I can see it *all* with you."

Something somersaulted inside me. The stirrings of love became stirrings of more. I tracked the ceiling fan as it beat slow circles through the light.

"Then you're going to have to meet my mother next month when she comes to visit." I closed my eyes. "Just so you know, she's kind of tough on the guys I date."

Almost exactly a year after I'd last seen her, Mom arrived. She was positively beaming, all aglow, gushing about the house. She tore through the rooms like an opera singer, tossing her arms about, admiring their size, the colors, the flow. She adored the kitchen and inspected every leaf, blade, and bud in the backyard. She peeped at the neighbors through the knotholes and turned on every faucet. When she was done, she collapsed on the couch.

"I still have the voice mail you left me when you bought this house," she said, pulling her cell phone from out of her purse.

Over the scratchy speakerphone came a squeaky voice that sounded something like mine. "I did it, Mom! I just signed the papers. I have a home!"

Mom laughed. "You were so happy—I *had to* save it."

"I didn't even know you could save voice mails for eight months."

She looked out the window and gasped. "There's a house for sale? Next door? I wonder what it costs!"

I didn't want my mother nearby, and couldn't quite figure out why. "Trust me, you don't want to buy a house next door to me. There's a lot more to it than I expected."

Mom waved her hand. "Reality? That part always works itself out."

"The thing is, Mom, I need a little . . . personal space."

She frowned and tossed her cell phone in her bag.

***

Keith and Ryan came over two nights later. I'd told Mom that Keith was a guy I liked and left it at that. Since I hadn't cooked much lately, I decided to keep things simple: a roast chicken, green bean salad, and homemade rolls.

My chicken recipe was a blend of Mom's and Patricia's: a sprig of rosemary and two of thyme crushed into the skin with butter, a nose flare of orange zest and enough paprika to tingle. I pressed half an orange into my hand—just enough to crack open the pulp and spill some juices out—and then slipped it inside the cavity.

Along the bottom of the roaster, I scattered quartered potatoes, petals of onion, and an overabundance of garlic nubs. Halfway through cooking, the bird crackled and hissed, potent rosemary greening the air like an exclamation mark even as the oven's heat tightened the skin into a deep crust. No need to fuss with the bird— my house smelled like a home.

The guys were right on time. I threw open the door and waved them through with a grin. Ryan hadn't been over yet. He stepped forward a few feet, tracked around the living room with his eyes, and then turned to me.

"Are you going to . . . decorate?" The words were blunt, but not accusatory.

Still, I flushed.

Keith fired him a look.

"It's OK," I said, nodding as I scanned the mishmash of thrift store finds, the stacks of papers and books where shelving should have been, the dust. Nothing matched, or even seemed to go together. There were no end tables. No coffee table. No TV. The two front bedrooms were as empty as the day I'd moved in.

I didn't even have a guest bed for Mom; she was sharing my king bed in the master bedroom. This was not a home to a 17-year-old— more like a glorified bachelor pad.

"I guess I'm going to need to work on that . . ." I smiled sheepishly.

Mom didn't look up when I led them into the kitchen. She was perched on a bar stool at the counter, trimming green beans and tossing the ends into the trash can at her side. *Plink. Plink. Plink.*

Keith stepped right up to her, bent a little at the waist, dipped his chin to his chest, and offered her his hand. I smiled involuntarily.

When Mom looked up, the green bean she'd been handling fell into the bowl, forgotten. She reached toward Keith's hand, and narrowed her eyes slowly. *Was she frowning? Or just processing?*

"Nice to meet you, Ma'am," he said as he clasped her small hand in his. His smooth southern drawl draped the words through the air. "How was your flight?" He locked his eyes on hers, taking her in as though she were the only person in the room.

She let out a small, girlish laugh, furrowed her brow, and shook her head. "Oh, good, yes." She almost sounded embarrassed. She glanced from him to me, and then started trimming the beans again.

After Keith sat beside her and reached into the bag of green beans to pluck browning stems with her, I made myself busy setting the table. I had exactly four plates to my name. When I placed a pair of stamped silverware by each setting, the cheap metal plinked against the oak veneer. Indigo picnic cups finished off the look.

The table looked naked. For the first time in my life I thought, rather dejectedly, *I could really use some place mats.* I rummaged around my pantry and closets for some semblance of mature adulthood. I scavenged some yellow napkins from the back of a kitchen drawer and pressed them against the counter to try and smooth out their wrinkles. They'd have to do.

I found a few lavender candles and a cotton cloth Mom had given me. She said it was like the lavalavas the ladies wear in Samoa. But it looked like a tablecloth, swirling with bold bands of emerald green, white, and navy. I cleared off the plates, draped it across the table, and reset it.

When the green beans were done, I tossed them with chopped tomatoes, a pucker of cider vinegar, olive oil, salt, and several grinds of pepper, and then popped them on the table with the chicken and rolls.

"Looks great, Sasha," Keith said.

"Did you make this?" Ryan asked, wonder in his voice. He studied the still crackling chicken skin. Juices hiccuped from within the bird and dripped onto the roasting pan. Rosemary bloomed on the air, thyme trailing behind.

"Yup."

"How?"

"I put it in the oven and baked it for a while—maybe an hour or so. Have you ever had roast chicken before?"

"Just rotisserie from the grocery store."

Mom raised her eyebrows. Ryan leaned closer, "What's on it?"

"Just a few herbs . . . like rosemary. Thyme. Oregano?"

Keith and Ryan both had blank expressions on their faces. I opened my mouth to explain, then thought better of it.

"Well, whatever it is, it looks good," Keith smiled. "I had no idea you could cook like this."

"Oh, this is nothing," I began, "you should see the stuff we made at cooking school."

"If you can cook like that, how come you and Dad eat out all the time?" Ryan asked.

I looked down at the roast, then around the table. "I don't know . . . I haven't wanted to cook much since I got to Tulsa. I'm not sure why."

When Mom cleared her throat and lifted her fork, we all followed suit. Bite by bite, the chicken, potatoes, and rolls disappeared. Keith ate three rolls. Between mouthfuls, he praised the soft, doughy interior, marveling that I'd made them myself.

Then I noticed that Keith and Ryan weren't exactly eating everything. The skin, onions, and garlic languished on their plates. Neither touched the green bean salad. Keith did a better job of pushing his food around, while Ryan's scraps were left exactly where they'd landed. From what I could tell, the only thing Ryan did eat was a bite of chicken and half a roll.

After Keith and Ryan left, Mom busied herself with the dishes. I stood at her side, patting them dry and then placing them in the cupboards. I waited for her to mention Keith. Five minutes went by, then ten.

Finally, I put down my towel, leaned on the counter, and asked, "So . . . what do you think?"

She passed me another wet plate without looking up.

"About what?"

Irritation tightened in my chest. When I rubbed the plate a little too hard against the terry cloth, it slipped out of my wet hand. There was a sharp clatter as the ceramic hit the corner of the counter and ricocheted into the thickest part of my thigh.

"Shoot," I took a deep breath. "*Keith*—what do you think of Keith?"

"Oh. I don't know . . ." She hoisted the roasting pan into the sink, scraped the congealed chicken fat into the disposal, and began scrubbing. She peered under the sink. "Don't you have any steel wool around here?"

"It just takes a little elbow grease. A regular sponge will get the job done." I took the pan from her, shooed her away, and started scrubbing. "What do you mean, you don't know?"

"I only just met him."

"But you knew right away with all those other guys! You've never *not* had an opinion."

She scowled. "That's neither here nor there."

"Well, you have to admit, Keith's a real gentleman. He holds the door open for me and everything—so different from the guys up north."

I looked at her out of the corner of my eyes, trying to decipher her expression.

She shrugged her shoulders. "Sure."

"I'll be honest, Mom. A twice-divorced man with a 16-year-old son wasn't what I expected, especially at the age of 27. But I'm in love with him."

"He's been married twice?" she asked, furrowing her brow. "You never told me that." She paused, considering. "Well," she tossed her hand dismissively, "those women obviously weren't right for him. An ordinary girl can't hold on to a guy like that."

"What do you mean?"

"Exactly what I said—he's different. Put it this way: He's not going to put up with a bunch of nonsense. He's *serious* about you," she said, drawing out the words slowly. "But you're in for a ride if you think he's going to embrace all that cooking you did at the CIA. That's much too fussy for him."

"I had no idea he was picky—"

"His son's right. That's what happens when you eat out all the time. It's all so . . . sterile. No one has to order anything they don't like." She nodded toward the door, "You've got a real Mr. Picky on your hands. The question is: What are you going to do about it?"

In that moment she gave herself away. I grinned, despite myself. She really, really liked him.

▮ Orange & Herb Roasted Chicken

. . . .

I've seen many fussy ways of making roast chicken. For me, the only requirement is the crackle and hiss—a refrain heard as much in my mother's kitchen as Patricia's. If the orange is particularly juicy, it'll gurgle through much of the cooking process—a comforting sound any time of year.

A couple generous sprigs fresh thyme
A generous sprig fresh rosemary
2 tablespoons butter, melted
½ teaspoon paprika, heaping, plus more for sprinkling

1 teaspoon salt

1 orange

One pasture-roaming chicken, 4 to 4½ pounds, giblets
removed

A couple garlic cloves, bruised but not peeled

A few drops vegetable oil

Preheat the oven to 400°F.

Tear off most of the green matter from the thyme and
rosemary, mince, and add to a small bowl (reserve the woody
stems). Stir in the melted butter, a teaspoon of salt, a half
teaspoon paprika, and the grated zest of the orange. Slice the
orange in half, and set aside.

Rinse and dry the chicken. Sprinkle the cavity with salt
and paprika, toss in the woody stems, the garlic cloves, and
one of the orange halves (pressing it in the hand to crack it
open). Truss the bird, and rub the butter and herb mixture
all over the outside. Roast on a lightly oiled V-rack until the
breast meat registers 175°F (1 hour for a 4-pound bird; add
another 5 minutes for a 4½-pound bird). For well-done dark
meat, cook an extra 10 minutes or so—until the thigh registers
180°F. Let rest 15 minutes before carving.

Enough for 4 to 6

CHAPTER 19

—●—

All That I Could Want

FTER MOM LEFT, I tried to learn how to ride the track, but found my craving for adrenaline had a threshold: I wasn't built for such speeds. Instead, I spent more time on the sidelines talking with Keith, filling him in on my past. When he asked about my father, I explained that there was a man who fathered me, but whose face and name I never knew. And there was a man whose face I'd seen, but who no longer acted as my father.

Keith never balked, never judged, and never changed his attitude toward me. He just accepted it all, perpetually focused. I wonder if it came from his job as a 911 telecommunications technician. Sometimes he got calls in the middle of the night to troubleshoot a failed emergency call. While he worked on the lines and computers, he occasionally had to replay the recordings of panicked spouses and petrified children in order to help identify what had gone wrong. He really knew how to listen.

It's a rare thing to feel truly heard. Keith teared up when I cried, laughed when I laughed, and challenged me on occasion. It was as if he were channeling my every story—as though he were there with me and had been from the beginning.

Instead of telling me about his life, Keith brought me to see it with my own eyes. He was raised three hours away in Geronimo, Oklahoma, population 1,282. In all my travels, I'd never seen anything like it. Downtown Geronimo is a glorified crossroads. This is the heart of the Bible Belt; an abundance of steeples inch ever skyward. The people are settled in their homes, in their bones, in their souls. They trust their land and their God. On Sundays, they raise their hands and shut their eyes, giving in with an abandon I can only marvel at. It is the middle of nowhere, but for these people it is everywhere.

Keith's parents, Clint and Wanda, hugged me the moment they met me. Acceptance is the Geronimo way. For the last 35 years, the two have lived several miles out of town on a forgotten piece of farmland tucked between the Lawton prison and the old creek. Keith's younger brother Daniel lives just on the other side of town.

Wheat fields, emerald green in the winter and barren in the summer, line the quarter-mile drive that curves up to Clint and Wanda's one-story brick house. They lease the land beyond their windows to farmers, never once sinking their teeth into bread made from that red soil.

Eight plum trees grow crooked in the south winds that push across the land, stubborn survivors of heat, hail, and whirling-dervish wall clouds (those testy harbingers of tornadoes). But the trees haven't fruited yet. There's no fresh produce in sight, save for the remains of the tomato bed Wanda once shackled over the cracking clay.

There's a waiting in Geronimo, a settled acceptance that all things bear fruit with time. Baseball-size hail, howling tornadoes strong enough to flatten a town, and minor bouts of indigestion are waited out with equal patience. There's no pining for anything more than the sun to rise, catfish to bite, dinner to be hot, and smiles to be quick and frequent.

Keith is the salt of *this* land.

￼ Okie Catfish

....

I don't like catfish, but I love the Martin family recipe. In Clint's hands, the muddy fillets become mild, the crisp coating sweet. It's not just that he catches the whiskered fish fresh from nearby lakes. It's that, even before mooring his boat, Clint and Wanda rinse and pack the fresh-gutted flappers with salt and ice. Although I could add bells and whistles, there is something beautifully Oklahoman about the simplicity Clint's recipe offers. The creole seasoning is a nod to Keith's Louisiana-dwelling aunt—if this or the Jiffy Mix is unavailable, try the substitutes provided for an equally delicious meal.

1½ pounds catfish fillets
Salt

For the crust:
¾ cup flour
¾ cup Jiffy Mix (or substitute ½ cup yellow cornmeal, 3 tablespoons sugar, and 1 tablespoon baking powder)
Enough Tony's Creole spice blend to make the flour blush (about 2 teaspoons) (or substitute ½ teaspoon cayenne pepper, ½ teaspoon black pepper, ½ teaspoon garlic salt, and ½ teaspoon chili powder)
Vegetable oil, for frying

Cut the fish into 2-inch-wide sections. Sprinkle both sides with salt. Refrigerate overnight (no more than 24 hours). The

next day, whisk together the flour, Jiffy Mix, and creole spice.
Rinse the salt from the fillets, and dredge their wet flesh with
the flour mixture. Deep-fry at 350°F until golden brown, turning once after 3 to 4 minutes and cooking for 6 to 8 minutes
total. Drain on paper towels and eat immediately.

Enough for 4

There's something mandatory about experiencing a buffet in
Oklahoma. Aside from the depressing chain restaurants, of which
there is no shortage, every small town seems to have at least one
quiet gem. Although I wasn't specifically seeking one, I did find it in
Talihina, a town of a thousand in the hills of southeast Oklahoma,
150 miles from Tulsa.

Keith and I planned the motorcycle ride with a dozen other
members of Tulsa Sportbike Riders. We'd been dating almost a year;
it was our first getaway since I began my new, laid-back job as a
marketing coordinator for the Girl Scouts. The group would stay
two nights at Queen Wilhelmina, a lodge founded in 1898 and once
dubbed "Castle in the Sky." Keith reserved the King's Suite, assuring
me with a wink that we'd have plenty of alone time. During the day,
we'd rev along ribbons of cloud-capped roads, flanked by lush forest.
At night, we'd sink into the lodge's extensive buffet. As we packed,
Keith described green bean casserole (topped with crunchy onion
strings), biscuits cloaked in woolen sausage gravy, and a tender
slump of roast beef or ham. I could almost hear the steam table
hissing, beckoning.

But the morning of the trip, I woke up with a pounding, clogged
sweatiness between my temples. When I told Keith I didn't think I'd
be able to make the ride, his eyes darkened.

"Do you think some medicine would help?"

Between his allergies, high blood pressure, and atrial fibrillation, he had a full medicine cabinet.

"I'm sorry." I shook my head. "Are you upset about the room fees?"

"No, no." He patted my leg. "You need to rest. I'm sure we can get our money back."

While he retreated to the kitchen to make me a cup of tea, I dragged myself to the bathroom and splashed cool water on my face. I got dressed slowly, through bone-deep shivers, hoping to hide my misery.

"I think I can make it, Keith. I just—"

"Great! I'll get the bikes ready." He grinned and squeezed me tight.

I winced, but when Keith looked at me again, I made it into a smile.

We zigzagged through the countryside for two and a half solid hours. The long line of motorcycles ahead shimmered and blurred. I lifted my visor, but still had trouble seeing. Even over the engine, I could hear my breathing, short and shallow.

When we arrived at the lodge mid-afternoon, I slumped over the bike, my head on the gas tank, helmet and all. My limbs continued to vibrate, as though the road was still moving beneath me. Finally I hauled myself off the bike, leaning on the metal frame for support. The next thing I knew, I was on the ground with the bike on top of my legs. Keith rushed forward.

"Are you OK? You forgot to put the kickstand up."

He half-carried me to our room; I had a 102.6-degree fever. He filled a champagne bucket with ice and sat by my side, holding my hand.

As my eyes fluttered shut, I heard him whisper, "I'm so sorry, Sasha. This is not what I planned."

I woke up a few hours later. My temperature had dropped to 101.4°. After the afternoon's inferno, the fever now felt like a cool breeze. I could hear the group outside, laughing. I felt badly that Keith was missing the fun. "Let's go outside to get some air," I offered.

Once outside, Keith waved but led me past the group, toward a weathered bench at the top of a remote, grassy slope. We sat side by side looking out across miles upon miles of forested hills.

"Sasha?" he asked, a slight strain to his voice.

His eyes were cast downward, toward a black velvet box cupped in his palm. He held it toward me, his temples tinged with red. "Would you do me the honor of spending the rest of your life with me?"

Suddenly, I knew that his hasty behavior that morning had nothing to do with lost deposits, and everything to do with this moment. I didn't need to ponder my decision. "Yes!" I cried, hugging him. "As long as you do one thing . . ."

"What's that?"

"Get down on your knees," I laughed, pulling him down off the bench and letting myself tumble down into the grass with him. I lay my head on his chest, listening to his heart beat.

"Your heart is racing, Keith," I murmured.

He smiled and brushed the hair out of my eyes. "I guess I can get nervous after all."

We lay there a long while, watching the sun dip quietly into the darkness, serenaded by the rising chatter of crickets and winking fireflies.

"Did you talk to my mom, your parents . . . Ryan?"

"Yup." He smiled. "I called your mom first. She wanted to know what *my parents* thought. I told her that I had to get by her first." He chuckled. "She liked that. Everyone else was good."

"Even Ryan?"

"Really." He squeezed my shoulder. "They want us to be happy."

I took a deep breath and smiled.

"I love you." I pressed my lips against his, as I had so many times before. This time, though, my kiss became a laugh.

That night, when we approached the much anticipated buffet, the ring gleaming on my finger, I found something much sweeter than the green beans, gravy, and roasts I'd expected: hot peach cobbler. Hundreds of wedges, deep orange like the sinking sun, nestled in the hotel pan beneath buttery rubbings of crust.

Softened from cooking in their own molten juices, the wedges sang of brown sugar and cinnamon. They whispered of the tender pink blossom and rich earth from which they sprang. The hot peaches sank into our shared scoop of vanilla ice cream, their warm nectar flowing like honey.

¶ A Quick Peach Cobbler

I'm of the mind that a cobbler should be "cobbled." There's no peeling of peaches or fancy equipment here; just fruit passed quickly from bushel to table with a touch of cinnamon and a generous crust. Look for peaches with good blush that give slightly—but if they are hard or tart, there's no shame in using frozen. I don't care for candy-sweet cobbler, but I've known many who would add more than a half cup of sugar to this recipe— especially if the peaches need a little coaxing to draw out their natural sugars. Although I like my cobbler wet (the better to sauce my ice cream), very juicy peaches will want a tablespoon of flour to thicken the mix.

For the crust:
1½ cups all-purpose flour
½ teaspoon salt
1 teaspoon sugar
8 tablespoons (1 stick) unsalted butter, cubed
A little ice water

For the filling:
2 quarts fresh or frozen peach slices, from 8 peaches
A couple heaping tablespoons brown sugar, more if peaches
   are tart
A couple good pinches cinnamon
1 tablespoon flour for thickening (optional)

Finishing touches:
1 egg white whisked with 1 teaspoon of water
1 teaspoon sugar

Make the cobbler dough by whisking together the flour, salt, and sugar, and then cutting in the butter with a pastry cutter (or two knives held like an *X* and drawn across each other). When the butter is mostly pea-size, switch to a large fork and drizzle on the ice water, tossing until a shaggy dough forms (6 to 8 tablespoons usually does the trick). Press the dough together and form a disk. Wrap in plastic wrap, and refrigerate while prepping the peach filling.

Preheat the oven to 350°F.

Slice the peaches in eighths and add them to a 2-quart baking dish (such as an 8 × 8 inch). Sprinkle with brown sugar and cinnamon. Toss with flour, if using. Roll out the dough on a clean work surface with a bit of flour to prevent sticking. When it is an inch larger than the baking dish, drape it across the peaches and roll the edges under, tucking them against the inner edge of the dish. Cut three vents in the center, and brush with just enough egg white to lightly glaze the crust. Sprinkle with sugar. Bake 45 minutes to an hour, or until the fruit is tender and bubbling, and the crust is browned. Serve under a softened ball of vanilla ice cream.

Enough for 6 to 8

Six months before the wedding, I asked Mom and Wanda to send me their guest lists. Wanda's had come back with about 30 people on it. Mom mailed me a list of 300, seven pages long.

"I have three hundred family members?"

"And friends."

"Mom, I only have a hundred stamps!" I drew a red line through the name of my childhood therapist. The next five names on the list were the Dumonts. My hand began to shake.

"Mom, the Dumonts aren't going to come."

"You *have* to invite them Sasha. They took care of you. They paid for your college! Let *them* make that decision. You might be pleasantly surprised. If not, you made the gesture. Are you really trying to cut family because you don't have enough *stamps?* I can *buy* you more stamps."

"It's not that." I swallowed hard. "Mom, who's going to walk me down the aisle?"

"Things like this have a way of working themselves out."

"Mom, a father isn't going to show up out of thin air."

I knew my brothers Connor and Tim would do it in a heartbeat. But that felt contrived. And every time I saw a photo of a bride in a magazine, her escort was gray haired. Leaning on the older generation seemed proper. "Do you think your dad will come?"

"At 95, I think a cross-country wedding is a bit much for him."

"What about you, then?"

"Me?" She laughed. "I don't think that's my pl—"

"Well, whose place is it?" I stamped my foot impatiently. "Can't you just do this *one* thing for me, Mom?"

She paused. "Let's just wait and see what the Dumonts say, OK?"

Toni responded first, sending warm wishes but sincere regrets. She'd just switched jobs and moved into a new apartment. She signed the card for her two sisters; they wouldn't be able to come, either.

A few weeks later, Patricia and Pierre's regrets came in the form of 13 boxes. Each battered, musty container held long-forgotten memories from my time in France and Luxembourg, stored for a decade. I'd now lived as long without the Dumonts as I had with them. And yet, I still missed them.

As I peeled back the flaps, yearbooks, photos, and the trinkets of a teenager piled up in my living room. Then my hand touched something soft and fuzzy. I reached in farther and squeezed. I knew what it was even before I unearthed him: my old white teddy bear, that cotton friend from all those foster homes, all those transitions, all those goodbyes.

I sat down on the floor and held the bear for a good while, forgetting for a moment that I was nearly 29 years old. I closed my eyes and imagined walking down the aisle. The grass was emerald, the sky aquamarine. Each of my two fathers held one of my arms, but when I turned to look into their eyes, they'd vanished.

Once I released the idea of Pierre attending my wedding, I considered my birth father. For the first time in my life, I hungered for his presence. But I knew that even if I could find him, there'd be no connection, no reason for him to walk me down the aisle.

The next time I spoke with Mom, I told her that it was time to face reality: She was the only parent I had. I asked her one more time to escort me. In the lengthy pause that ensued, I lost my cool.

"You know what, forget it! I'll just walk myself down the aisle."

"No, I'll walk with you," she said quietly. "I want to do it."

Finally, I thought, relief washing over me.

But all I said was, "Thank you."

⁓

Thunder cracked and rolled the morning of our wedding. Over my first cup of chai, I sat at the bay window and watched black clouds dump torrents onto Tulsa. At 10 a.m., my brother Connor, our volunteer photographer, reported that the earth around the old barn we'd rented for the occasion was thick with mud. But by early afternoon, a scalding sun had beat the water back. By 5 p.m., the ground was dry again.

Mom guided me from the old barn, down the hill, between the trees. We were a vision of moss and cream. My lace, corseted gown ballooned out from my hips, while her crocheted shift hung straight to her knees. I wore my hair long and straight, held back with a ribbon and punctuated with a veil. She wore an airy woven hat the color of sand.

Mom squeezed my arm gently as we stepped between 45 family and friends onto the runner I'd made from a bolt of burlap. They weren't the 300 she'd wished for me, but love is love, and they were enough. Grace, my maid of honor, and my dear friends, Katya and Rebekah, stood to the left in coral sundresses. Keith's brother, Daniel, my brother, Tim, and Ryan stood to the right in pistachio shirts and sand-colored linen slacks. Connor flitted about, taking photos—his wedding gift to us.

In the middle was Keith, stunning in his linen ensemble, his snow-white shirt set in relief against the shimmering pond behind him.

As I approached, I saw that Keith's eyes were wet with tears. With each step closer to him, my smile grew.

Mom kissed my cheek and handed me over to Keith. Fifteen minutes later, he kissed me. I felt the most curious feeling burst through my core: an expanding, a bubbling, an overwhelming shortness of breath. And then it hit me.

This must be what it feels like to be full. Content—a hundred percent happy.

CHAPTER 20

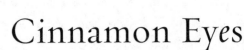

Cinnamon Eyes

THE ACHE BEGAN AT 4 A.M., three months after our wedding and an unlikely eight weeks after Keith's reversal procedure. My hand flitted to my abdomen: It felt different, somehow. I was pregnant. There was no test, no doctor to confirm it, just the brazen confidence of intuition. In this foggy awakening, I even imagined that this baby would be a girl.

My sister, Grace, phoned me early that same morning.

"Are you asleep? Sorry. But the most amazing thing just happened," she gushed. "I was sitting in my office, doing some paperwork. You suddenly . . . popped into my mind. I looked up at the bookshelf across the room, at your picture. At that exact same moment, it tilted, and get this, a baby grasshopper jumped in front of it. What do you think it means?"

I sat up against the headboard. "What time did it happen?"

"Maybe 5 a.m.?"

It was an hour later on the East Coast. "I woke up at that exact same time," I chuckled. "Grace, I'm pregnant!"

"Are you serious!? Congratulations! How far along are you?"

"I have no idea. No more than two weeks; that's the soonest Keith could—you know—after his procedure. It sounds crazy, but I just know it. I think it's a girl."

Keith did his best to accept my premonition with cautious hopefulness. When the doctor who performed the reversal heard our happy news, he gave Keith a high five. It takes six weeks to heal post-op. The doctor had never had someone show up for a three-month follow-up appointment with a wife nearly two months into her pregnancy.

This would be our miracle baby.

By my five-month checkup, I'd sold my bike, my boots, and my leather jacket. I even gave away my back protector. There was no way I was going to risk a miscarriage by taking my little miracle on a bumpy ride.

Baby things soon took the place of my motorcycle paraphernalia: a borrowed crib, a flea market rocker spray-painted white, and a Craigslist changing table. Even my nightstand became a pregnancy shrine, spilling over with *What to Expect When You're Expecting* and *Your Self-Confident Baby.*

One day I grabbed my diary and settled into the couch for a moment of reflection. From the kitchen, doughy ravioli bloomed on the air, mingling with the tomato sauce Keith had promised to make earlier that day. The pasta was frozen and the sauce jarred, but the rising scent of that simple dinner made my mouth water. I'd taught Keith how to cook the pasta on a gentle bubble. It all felt so ordinary, so comfortable—so right.

I cracked open my diary and wrote: "I have my happy ending. Thank you, thank you, thank you."

Just then my laptop chirped on the coffee table, announcing new email. "My name is Phoenix," the message read. "I'm your sister. We have the same father. I've been looking for you for a long time. I'm writing to let you know that our father died last year."

I gasped as I read and reread the words.

Keith ran into the living room, sauce-covered spoon still in hand.

"What is it? Are you OK?" He looked down and, seeing my hand on my belly, knelt by my side. "Is the baby OK?"

I pointed to the screen, hand trembling.

He leaned over and read the message. He looked up at me, tears in his eyes.

"Oh, Sasha, I'm so sorry."

"I thought I didn't care. Now I'll never meet him." I shook my head in tight bursts, willing the email away.

"What are you going to do?" he asked.

I thought of Greg's words: *No one can create peace for you.*

"The only thing I can do. Go to her." Even while sniffling, I laughed. "And get a therapist." Aside from a few halfhearted attempts, I hadn't seen one since Michael died.

⁓⁓⁓

By my second therapy session in as many weeks, I was ready to call Mom.

"I got an email from Phoenix the other day."

I could almost hear her hackles go up over the phone.

"Oh?" she said noncommittally.

"When were you going to tell me about her?"

"I *told* you he probably had kids all over the country! You need to stay away from those people. Please, you have no idea what I went through to get away from that man . . ." The fear in her voice was palpable.

"You mean Oliver? My *father?*" I paused. "That's his name, isn't it? Mom, you've never told me anything about him except that he was a charismatic con artist."

"There's nothing else to—"

"Let me finish. I'm going to do for you what you couldn't do for me. I'm going to share some information you might want to know."

"I want nothing to do with him, Sasha. And if you know what's good for you, you'll stay as far away from him as possible."

"He's dead." I winced as I said the words.

"What do you mean?"

"Phoenix gave me his full name. I went to the Social Security office two weeks ago to confirm it." I gulped. "I can send you the paperwork. He died two years ago."

Mom didn't say anything right away, so I continued. "I'm going to California to visit Phoenix."

"How did he die?" she asked.

"Some sort of cancer. Lung, I think."

She sighed through the phone.

"Did you hear what I said, Mom? I'm going to California."

"Why?"

"Because she's my sister! I want to get to know her."

"She's a space cadet."

"Wait a minute, Mom," I yelled. "I thought you didn't know her? For once in my life, this is *my* decision. I only told you as a courtesy."

I hung up on her and was slamming open the refrigerator just as the phone rang.

"I'm sorry, Sasha," Mom began, her voice softer than before. "He wasn't all bad, you know. He was beautiful and smart, and always inventing something. If you ever want to know something about him, you don't need to go to California—you can just talk to me."

She spoke the way a prisoner speaks about a guard, even years after being released: with breathlessness, fear, and admiration.

I couldn't bite back my sarcasm. "You're ready to talk about him *now?*"

She chuckled, indifferent to my rising indignation. "Not really. It's different with him . . . gone. You don't understand what a relief it is."

I gripped the handle on the refrigerator tighter, the cool air pressing onto my reddening cheeks.

"No, I don't."

Our flight landed in San Jose, California, a few weeks later on a dewy morning in February. The air was almost warm, the sun sharp. Our rental slugged through one sticky traffic jam after another, a grid of offices and retaining walls framing the mountains beyond. While Keith drove, I phoned Phoenix.

"We're here! If you want, we can come straight to you—grab some lunch, maybe?"

"Oh, that's great, honey! But the thing is, I'm in the middle of a few things. And at 3 p.m., I have a manicure. Why don't I meet you later—say, 6?"

"Six *tonight?*" I stammered. "OK, where?"

Phoenix offered to take us to see her mother, Lotty, who'd been married to my father for two years back in the sixties. She clicked off with a cheery goodbye.

I put the phone in my lap and turned to Keith.

"She's . . . busy."

Keith tilted his head to the side and opened his mouth, then shut it again.

In the background, the GPS crowed: "Recalculating route . . ."

～✺

That night Phoenix met us at her mother's impeccable brownstone, a retirement complex with tall ceilings and grand hallways. Phoenix was 16 years older than me, now cresting her 40s. I could see the years marked along her face. She was soft in the middle, but carried her weight like a woman who was once thin.

We had the same flat cheekbones and eyebrows, and the same brown hair, though hers skimmed the waistband of her peasant skirt. Her big brown eyes were my eyes. When she smiled, her upper lip almost disappeared, just like mine.

Astonished, I realized we must have *his* cheekbones, *his* eyebrows, *his* eyes, *his* lips. She gushed over my belly and hugged me warmly, her bracelets making soft music as they collided with my shoulder blades and each other.

Upstairs, Lotty invited us into her apartment with a gentle smile. She was a slight woman with turnip-colored hair, but she hugged me with the force of a linebacker.

Keith and I sat on a couch in the living room, a wide-open space lined with windows from floor to ceiling. They were cracked open, a natural breeze ruffling the silence. I reached for Keith's hand and squeezed.

Lotty brought in a pitcher of Mexican horchata and invited us to sweeten our glasses with sliced strawberries. A moment later, she emerged from the back bedroom with a worn shoe box and a manila envelope. She slid the contents of the box onto the coffee table: two dozen photos. "Here are the ones you'll be interested in," she said.

In the first photo, I am sitting on Phoenix's lap in the water. I must have been a year and a half old. Together, we're splashing the waves and clapping.

"This is astonishing!" I said. "We used to play with each other? We've actually *met?*"

Lotty explained that Phoenix had come out to the Cape to visit her father every summer. I locked eyes with her. This was, in fact, a reunion.

Phoenix smiled weakly and turned back to the flowers. Her mother picked up the next photo, folded in half.

"You might recognize this lady," she winked.

On one side of the crease was my mother, on the other: a man. The two stand shoulder to shoulder, their faces frozen in a moment of stillness. Though the photo is tight around their arms, I can still make out a grove of pine trees in the distance. Mom almost disappears: Her eyes are at once expressionless and intense, like an old black-and-white portrait from the late 1800s. The man is half a head taller than she is, bearded, wearing a rumpled, plaid flannel shirt.

I took the photo from Lotty, trying not to snatch it. Even under the beard, this man's face is thin, his eyes shining. No, not just shining—they are beautiful, the color of cinnamon. The left side of his mouth lifts almost imperceptibly. He looks like a stranger, but even more like someone I knew. He looks like Michael.

This was my father's face. I looked at every detail over again, trying to read him like a bedtime story.

Keith put his hand on my leg and squeezed. "Hey, Sash . . . ?"

I looked up. Lotty was holding out a third photo.

The faces were hard to make out: a mess of shadows and poor exposure in a grassy knoll. There's a small child in a blue gingham sundress, maybe two years old. There's a man with a floppy-brimmed hat, like the kind Jed Clampett used to wear. He's resting on his haunches, arm wrapped around the child. His face is mostly dark, but I can still make out the smile; it's him again—my father. To the left, another child leans in, with a dimpled smile and baby-blond hair—Michael.

"Is that Sasha?" Keith asked Lotty, his voice drawn out with wonder. I don't need to look up to know the answer.

This little version of me leans toward her father, squirming with uproarious laughter at some silliness long since sublimated. One of his arms drapes around me; the other lies behind Michael's shoulder.

A lump formed in my throat.

"You can keep that one," Phoenix said from behind the flowers.

"T–thank you." I pressed the photo to my heart. In this moment, I wanted nothing more than for my father to walk out of the photo and say hello—just once.

"What happened?" I asked Lotty. "My mom never told me why—"

"That's your mom's story to tell, and what's more, I don't know it," she responded. "But I can tell you, your father was a complicated man. I met him out at Lake Tahoe when I was 20. I was at a resort with my parents, and he was the cook. He always smelled delicious and, oh, God, he was a looker. He proposed to me two weeks after we met on a bench at the end of a dock." She laughed. "When you have eyes like that staring into your soul, there's nothing to say but yes."

Lotty pulled out a photo of my father holding baby Phoenix. He was beardless, clean-cut, and at 22, looked even more like Michael.

"He wasn't just a cook. He was an artist. A poet. A brilliant inventor.

"But there was darkness, too. His mom was only 14 when he was born. He started off in a boys' home. He spent Sundays on the front steps, waiting for her to visit. She never came.

"We did alright for a while. The darkness, his fits of anger, happened after Phoenix was born. We divorced, but saw each other every week for her sake."

Phoenix was looking over at her mom for the first time since we'd arrived.

Lotty sighed. "I showed up one day with her when she was maybe a year old. He was painting furiously in his studio. He was convinced that he was the Count of Monte Cristo. I couldn't talk him out of it. He spent a year of his life in an asylum. I checked him in myself."

She leaned forward.

"He climbed over the fence and escaped to New England. He still deserved to see his daughter, so I sent her out there every summer until she was out of the house and old enough to make her own arrangements."

Lotty pulled out a stack of letters from the manila envelope. "He wrote her about boys, about love, about everything a father should. But his return address always changed. And sometimes there was no way to reach him."

She dropped the letters on the table, and I picked one up, addressed to Phoenix. I soaked in his words, pretending they were for me: "If this guy you say you like doesn't treat you with respect and give you the attention he should, then he's not worth your time. You deserve better, honey."

Lotty continued. "He became a mountain man—that's what Phoenix called him. He lived out his life deep in the woods of New England, camping, wandering. He was his happiest far away from it all. Being in society was like a cage to him. But when he died, I do think he'd managed to find some kind of peace."

I looked up at Phoenix. "What was his funeral like?"

She shook her head.

"She didn't go," Lotty said.

"You didn't *go?*" I spat back, incredulous. Phoenix looked away. I immediately regretted my tone. "I'm sorry." I turned to Lotty. "Did you?"

She hesitated, and then shook her head: "Phoenix hasn't seen him since that photo." She paused. "He put her through . . . a lot. We spoke on the phone every few years, when we could find him. He got lung cancer, his smoking caught up with him. The state called to let us know he passed; there was no money for a funeral, and she was his oldest kin."

Phoenix cleared her throat and spoke for the second time since we'd entered her mother's apartment. Her voice trembled. "When I was looking for you, I found a picture of you and Michael with your firefighter cousin. Antonio—was that his name? I got the idea to call the firehouse where he worked. When I called, I guess you were already overseas. He had no idea where you were. He said Michael had . . ."

She sighed. "When I called Dad to tell him about Michael, we cried together over the phone."

"It's hard to believe that was 16 years ago." Lotty added.

Mom had been right on every count. My father had been a man without roots, without stability. But what Mom hadn't said was that he *cared*. The photos and the stories painted a man conflicted, a man who battled to love his world and be loved, sometimes with less success than others. I left California with one shadowy photo and more questions than when I'd arrived—questions that could only be answered by a man six feet under.

CHAPTER 21

A Baby and *a* Blog

I CONSIDERED SEEKING OUT my father's grave, but decided against it. It was time to focus on our baby—transitioning from my job at the Girl Scouts to raising our child full time. I moved my old white teddy bear into the waiting crib.

Mom came to visit in late June, about a week before the baby was due. She brought along a few balls of tan-and-white cotton-cashmere yarn and taught me to knit while we waited for my body to kick into gear. Day after interminable day, we sat side by side, our needles clicking out two pairs of booties and two tiny caps.

We cooked together, too: three of Mom's zucchini pies, made with a couple of white-flecked zucchini, three eggs whipped until frothy, and—as always—more Parmesan than seemed proper. For a finishing touch, Mom chopped a handful of parsley from my flower bed and stirred it into the egg.

I relaxed into her company, content *not* to talk about my father, *not* to fight about the past. I was simply grateful she could be beside me in this time of endless expectation. Finally, when it seemed every ounce of water I'd drunk over the last ten months had pooled under my skin, I went into labor.

It was 2 a.m. on the Fourth of July. According to the doctors, the baby was ten days late. Of course, Mom had told me that was hogwash. "Babies know when they want to be born," she said, "They're stronger if you listen to your body, not some *chart*."

Now Mom's door was open. I could see her small, sleeping form in the moonlight. It surprised me how a twin bed swallowed her up. When I knocked lightly, she sat up like a rocket, her frizzy curls bouncing forward.

I nodded through the darkness: It was time. She grabbed a skinny, green mug off the desk, handed it to me, and told me to drink the contents. Then she turned to shut the door.

"Aren't you coming with me?"

She looked me up and down.

"It's going to be a while. You're just getting started." She pointed to the mug: "Drink that. I'll come by in the morning."

On the way to the hospital, I sipped Mom's lurid brew, a bitter and potent blend of chamomile tea, turmeric, and honey. The combination made my stomach churn. Almost immediately, my contractions quickened and I abandoned the mug in the cup holder of the truck.

At the hospital, when the nurses checked me, I was a half-centimeter dilated. Under normal conditions, they'd send me home, but since the baby's sluggish heartbeat indicated it wasn't responding well to stress, they wanted to monitor us. More to the point, I was getting sick with every contraction. Once they added antinausea medication to my drip, there was no sending me home.

Finally, after four hours in triage, a penguin-shaped nurse wheeled me over to labor and delivery. "You're going to have a baby today," she twittered as we rolled down the long, shiny hallway. I looked up at Keith and smiled.

Around 8 a.m., Mom breezed into the hospital room. I was between contractions. She inspected all the beeping, blinking computers, and groaned. "This is exactly why I had you at home. It's a *baby*, not a disease."

The nurse stared at Mom with pinched face and large, unblinking eyes. Mom screwed up her brow, primed for a debate.

"Hey, Mom..." I called, loud enough to distract her, "you made it!"

Mom softened her expression and pulled a chair up to the side of the bed. "We can't have a *birth* day without a few gifts," she said, smiling. She dug three wrapped packages out of her leather tote: a sketchbook made with recycled paper (to draw the baby), a jade necklace (for me), and an old three-dimensional valentine from 1914. Mom got the card from her father, who happened upon the unused card in his piles of paperwork.

The brittle card was a good ten inches tall, scalloped along the edges. On it, a Victorian mother held her child to the sky, smiling up at the baby's face. I was moved that Mom had saved it all this time.

Mom pulled a small bottle of champagne from her purse. She'd sneaked it past the colony of nurses who bumped and jostled in and out of my room. Mom said the bubbles would help me relax. Hastily, I pushed the bottle back into her purse, worried that we'd get kicked out if we were caught.

Our eyes were still locked while I wheezed through the searing pain of another contraction, my hand gripping the pillow. The nurses glanced at me, and then frowned at the monitors. Quickly, one strapped an oxygen mask to my face. Mom stood by, helpless, while Keith grabbed my hand.

Mom's eyes brimmed over. She busied herself smoothing the sheets at the foot of the bed. A few stray tears rolled down her cheeks, which she quickly wiped away. As the contraction passed and my breathing slowed, she mumbled something about getting some cups for the champagne and rushed off to the cafeteria.

I don't ever remember seeing my mother cry. Not when she thrust us into the arms of the Dumonts, not when Michael was in the hospital—*never*. She'd always been able to keep it together in front of me. Even in the courts, she'd worked to exude the sort of strength one would expect of a mother. But in the process, I realized, she'd made herself appear cold and uncaring.

Her tears now revealed the truth I needed to see: My pain was her pain. Everything that hurt me, hurt her.

It really was that simple.

While Mom was gone, the doctor administered my epidural. I insisted on not being completely numb for the birth, so they gave me a walking dose. The relief was instant and complete. Keith and I were playing Boggle when Mom returned with two Styrofoam cups.

"How are you holding up?" she asked, sizing up my relaxed countenance with surprise.

"I got an epidural. I'm going through a huge contraction now," I said, "Do you see it?"

She pointed to the top of the digital mountain on the screen, "This? I suppose these gadgets are kind of neat after all, aren't they?"

We clunked our foam champagne glasses with a dull thud.

By midday, real labor began. Keith was at my side, Mom a few feet away by the window. I hadn't planned to invite her to stay, but after I saw her struggle through my contraction, I knew she belonged at my side.

I was ten days overdue, but the labor went quickly. Four strong pushes later, my child greeted the world with a mighty wail.

"It's a girl," Keith grinned.

We named her Ava Marie. She floated in my arms, her soft skin warm and redolent. In the first instant I held her, my heart cracked open. I would do whatever I could for my child, this soft, sweet stranger of my heart's creation. I knew I would never abandon her; like Mom, I'd give her the life I knew she deserved. I would protect her with my *everything*.

Mom stayed another week to help me and fawn over Ava, but then had to get back to work. She'd recently taken a job as the business manager at a local seminary in Boston. After I dropped her off at the airport, I found a chubby-cheeked baby doll in the crib next to my old teddy bear. I recognized the blue eyes and yellow knit cap instantly: It had been Michael's. Unbeknownst to me, Mom had kept it all these years, and now she'd left it for Ava.

For the next several months I cradled, nursed, rocked, and read to my daughter. She learned to hold her head up, roll over, sit up, cuddle Michael's baby doll. I cheered her on like a crazed soccer mom. For the first time since I'd become an adult, I saw the world through a child's eyes: I understood that it was an incredible place, but also a place of surrender. She could do nothing but trust me and her surroundings.

Nursing her was the ultimate reminder of this: I was literally Ava's food. The responsibility was humbling. I called Mom eight times a day with questions. When the all-night sessions wore me down, Grace, who'd successfully nursed two babies, talked me off the ledge, reminding me to drink plenty of water and to eat right. Our calls always ended with, "I wish you weren't half a country away."

While Keith was at work, Ava and I were left to figure each other out as best we could.

There is terror in every happy ending: terror that it's not real, terror that it cannot be sustained. Though I'd settled into mine when I was pregnant, it was a naive sort of complacency. Phoenix's sudden email had dredged up the tough reality that no joy is impervious to misfortune. This was on my mind as I floundered through my first months as a mother.

Sure, I now had the American dream: a husband, a baby, a house, two cats, two cars. Friends and family regularly affirmed I was doing everything right. "Motherhood suits you," Keith whispered one night, while I cradled her. "It's like—you're all lit up."

And yet the intensity of my love for this child overwhelmed me. When I considered the future, I saw a deeply rooted probability that I would somehow fail as a mother and wife.

By Thanksgiving, I was crumbling at the corners. Now that I had forged a family of my own, the cracked foundation of my own childhood had finally caught up with me, incapable of withstanding the pressure I put on it: my fantasy of what a home should be. I found myself waiting for the other shoe to drop.

I put my nervous energy into watching reruns on the Food Network, scanning through cookbooks, and surfing the Internet for kitchenware. I fixated on a set of "French square" spice jars listed on a wholesale website; I must have looked at them 50 times. I imagined that my dusty spices would glow anew within the glass, their rightful color restored: the warm goldenrod of turmeric, the deep plum of sumac, the royal green of dill, the moss of oregano.

I shouldn't have been surprised when Keith got me the jars for Christmas. He said he couldn't watch me ogle them one more time. He could tell I was at loose ends and gently suggested that some old-fashioned "home cookin'" might be a good distraction from my anxiety as a new mother.

The box of spice jars sat on the Formica counter for a month before I got a chance to move them into the drawers beside the stove. There they stayed until one sleepless, snowy night in February.

It must have been midnight when I padded from my warm bedroom to that dark kitchen. I could almost hear the walls around me creak, brittle against the press of cold air. By now the snow was done falling. I couldn't see five feet into the yard, and yet a universe away the stars shone clearly. The shrouded planet felt at once enormous and much, much too small.

I stood barefoot on the kitchen tiles, thinking about why my kitchen had fallen into disuse. Sure, Keith was picky, and at seven months old, Ava was barely eating solid food. But there was something more. I pulled open the spice drawer and held one of the empty jars to the dim light. In it, I saw my childhood—Mom's improvisation, Patricia's determination, and the 12 countries that fed me: France, world famous for pastries, tarragon sauce, and lacy lavender; Greece, known for thick yogurt topped with golden pools of honey; Tunisia, where the markets burst with baskets of spices so heady the scent lingered on my clothes for days.

Marcel Proust, the 20th-century novelist, knew how easy it is to bring the past to life: When he bit into a tea-soaked madeleine, the shadows of his childhood took on color, snapping into full dimension. If I put the right ingredients in my spice jars, I realized, they'd be portals to that bygone era.

My thoughts turned to all the countries I hadn't been to yet, to all the exotic foods I had yet to experience. What would it be like if I could fit this uncharted world in those jars, if I could use them to season my future? Perhaps I could bypass Proust and enjoy a madeleine of my own making.

Suddenly, I knew what I had to do. I ran to the bedroom and shook Keith's shoulder.

"I'm going to cook the world!" I exclaimed.

"What time is it?" he said, lifting his head from the pillow and squinting.

"Recipes from every single country!" I gushed, "One per week—I'll start a blog!"

While he rubbed the sleep from his eyes, I explained that I wanted to help him learn to love new foods, become less picky—that, together, we could raise our daughter with an appreciation of other cultures. I could wake this kitchen up and hopefully quell some of my wanderlust. And then there was the reason I could not yet give voice to: I could begin the next chapter of my life afresh.

Little did I know that it would be nearly impossible to separate my history from the future I wanted to create.

PART FIVE

True Spice

"Follow your bliss and don't be afraid.
Doors will open where you didn't know
they were going to be."
—Joseph Campbell

CHAPTER 22

Afghanistan or Bust

I CAN COUNT ON ONE HAND the number of times I've used a shopping
list since Keith and I got married. I always get the same things: frozen fish, macaroni and cheese, canned beans, Pink Lady apples, and
if I'm feeling particularly naughty, a half-gallon of mint chocolate chip
ice cream. But not today: Today I am on an entirely different mission.

Today, I will cook Afghanistan. Thanks to the alphabet, this
mountainous country in south-central Asia is the first of the 195
countries awaiting me on our family's journey to eat our way around
the world. When I'm done, I'll share my recipe adaptations on my new
blog, Global Table Adventure. There's something comforting about
knowing that for the next four years, this will be my quest: one meal
per country, one country per week. Straightforward. Structured. A
check-it-off-the-list-for-immediate-satisfaction kind of adventure:
the yin to the yang that is motherhood.

But none of my cookbooks have Afghan recipes. I expand my
search and find a blog by an Afghan man living stateside, who says

that community is the heart of Afghanistan's nomadic culture. Nowhere is this more apparent than at mealtime. Families gather together on dusty floors and eat with their hands out of communal platters, and anyone who comes into the home is treated with the respect afforded a close relative.

There's an old saying: "The first day we meet, we are friends. The next day we meet, we are brothers." I choose recipes to reflect this Afghan hospitality: *burani bonjon,* a braised eggplant dip; *sabse borani,* a spinach yogurt dip; *firnee,* a sweet saffron and rosewater custard; and *kabeli palau,* a seasoned rice dish with raisins, carrots, and chicken. Because the food is traditionally scooped up with bread, I'll also make a batch of *noni Afghani,* this country's version of naan. I find a recipe to adapt for the cumin seed–topped flat bread from *The Best International Recipe* by Christopher Kimball, a book I buy that very afternoon. For after dinner, I decide on a few dried apricots.

I call Mom to tell her my plan.

"Are you going to make German Tree Cake?"

"Well, I'm starting with Afghanistan," I say, repeating myself. "I'm trying to expand my horizons." I add, silently, *this is about the future,* not the past.

"What's wrong with your heritage?" Mom reminds me that leathery coins of dried apricot are loved beyond Afghanistan. "Grandpa ate one a day for years," she says, "And apricot jam is the best part of the German Tree Cake."

For supplies, Ava and I head out for Laxmi Spices, a market tucked away at the forgotten end of a strip mall. Inside a haze of cumin, coriander, and cinnamon drifts like incense, clinging to my skin as I meander through the dim aisles. A mosaic of curling Bollywood movie posters blocks the only window. I've lived in Tulsa for three years, but never set foot in this shop.

From behind a newspaper, the owner eyes me curiously. He's brown and wrinkled, like an autumn leaf. "Can I help you find something?" His accent is thick and lush.

I glance at the scrap of paper in my hand where I'd scrawled "rose water" in red ink. I'm not entirely sure it exists outside of the perfume aisle. I'd certainly never seen it at my regular grocery store, and none of my classes at the CIA used it. Rose water sounds so exotic, like something the women in the *Arabian Nights* would dab on their racing pulses before slipping into bed on their wedding nights.

"No, thank you," I say, shaking my head slowly. It's been so long since I cooked—*really* cooked. I want to smell every package, peer into the frosted cases, and dream of the faraway places these foods come from. I want to linger a while.

Next to me a wide, long shelf bursts at the seams with heavy sacks of rice and lentils. Basmati. Cracked red rice. I trace my fingers along the woven bags. Most of them weigh 25 to 50 pounds. It would take me ten years to eat all that rice, I think, not to mention the quarter-pound bags of cracked mustard seed and cumin seed one shelf over.

In the next aisle, I find dozens of carbon steel woks—some as small as a teakettle, others nearly three feet across. All have two small handles for maneuvering. When I kneel on the dusty floor to examine them more closely, I see a faded price sticker: $20 for the medium one, about 18 inches across.

It would cost $60 at Williams-Sonoma.

"You want one?" the man asks. Without waiting for me to answer, he carries it to the front of the store.

"Is it a wok?" I ask, trailing behind him.

He makes a slow, circular motion with his arm: "Stirring pot."

"What do you cook in it?"

"Everything," he says. "You imagine. Stirring pot does."

Perfect, I think, smiling at his broken English. His white mustache dances as he explains that I must give the stirring pot attention; I must oil it to keep it from rusting. I must bake it in the oven between uses. I must keep it dry. I nod impatiently, thinking only of how enticingly different the rugged black metal looks from my shiny, stainless-steel, 11-piece pot set gathering dust at home.

Twenty minutes later, I turn down the last aisle, arms bulging with a pile of eggplant and a half dozen spices like whole cardamom pods that smell like the first sweet flower of spring, as well as whole coriander, cumin, and saffron. Even though saffron is one of the most sought after spices in the world, it still feels scandalous to spend seven dollars for a tiny box of squiggly red crocus stamens.

"And where do you keep the rose water?" I finally ask. I think of how my great aunt used rose water in her linen drawers and quickly add, "To eat."

The old man cracks his first smile and nods. "Yes, to eat. We have all sizes," he adds and reaches toward a one-liter bottle below the counter. I quickly shake my head and take the smaller four-ounce bottle. I give it a little shake, and Ava watches as the water laps lyrically inside. She giggles, and then reaches toward our new stirring pot.

"Isn't it beautiful?" I whisper. "I have a feeling this pot is going to change everything."

❧

When I burst through the door with an armful of eggplant, it is Keith's turn to groan.

"What is that?" he says, staring at the shiny black orbs.

"Keith, meet eggplant; eggplant, meet Keith," I say lightly. "It's dinner in Afghanistan. And it's going to be your dinner tonight."

He takes a deep breath, frowning.

"For Ava's sake," I whisper to him. He shifts on his feet.

When I'd initially suggested the project, Keith had been on board—he even helped me look into its feasibility. Despite his picky tendencies, he'd agreed to taste every recipe, no matter what was on the menu. He said the adventure sounded *fun*—that it'd probably be good for him. Considering his medical history we agreed to emphasize heart-healthy foods along with a dose of celebration foods. But today, face-to-face with the eggplant, he doesn't look convinced.

I sneak into the bathroom and call Vanessa.

"Would you like to come over to eat an authentic Afghan feast?" I ask, trying not to sound desperate. I explain the project and add, "I need a little . . . peer pressure to get Keith on board."

She agrees.

For the next five hours, I stumble through the recipes while Keith entertains Ava. Every time they poke their heads into the kitchen, I'm deeper in the trenches.

First they find me kneading the bread. There's yogurt in the dough, making it yielding and soft. After much clatter and fuss, I wrestle the mixture into a smooth ball and tuck the bowl in a sunny spot on the couch to rise.

The next time they peek in, I'm blistering eggplant slices in hot oil, dancing around the splatters. I reduce the heat and braise the strips in their own juices along with turmeric, garlic, cayenne, and chopped tomatoes. By now, the kitchen counter is riddled with spills, open containers, and discarded vegetation.

For the yogurt sauce, I mix in caramelized onions, chopped spinach, garlic, and mint. The flavors are sharp, even for a garlic lover. I slip the bowl into the refrigerator, hoping it will mingle and mellow by dinnertime. Meanwhile, the sweet custard bubbles on the stove, nearly forgotten, the rose water and spice making the house smell like a field of saffron roses.

Finally, I pull out my new pot and prepare the kabeli palau. Keith and Ava watch while I toast the chicken, saffron, and garam masala in ghee. The spice blend gives off a surprising sweet note from the cinnamon and cardamom – a stark contrast to their stout companions, cumin, coriander, clove, and black pepper. Then I layer on the pureed onion, garlic, tomato paste, and rice. Only once the pot is full do I realize it didn't come with a lid. A lid serves to trap the steam, create pressure, and evenly plump up the thirsty rice. I bang through my cupboards. None of my lids fit. Keith, who watches my feverish cooking display with stupor, suggests a round pizza pan.

It doesn't create a seal, so I opt to go without. I add some extra stock to make up for the dry oven and then pop the whole thing in.

When the doorbell rings, I'm cooking the bread while nursing Ava in a sling. Stray saffron threads and cumin seeds fleck her fine hair. I have 25 seconds to tidy the kitchen, just enough time to slide an entire pile of dishes into the sink. When Keith brings Vanessa and her boyfriend Gus back to the kitchen, they peer at me through the haze. Vanessa asks if she can help.

"That's OK!" I say with a strained smile, slapping another piece of homemade naan onto the skillet. The cumin seeds crackle and fill the air with a white cloud of earthy fragrance.

When we finally sit down, I feel as though I've run a marathon. Gus looks over the spread. The stirring pot sits in the middle of the table, brimming with rice and chicken laced with saffron and garam masala, topped with fried carrots and golden raisins: a new feast, a new memory in the making.

"Where is the silverware?"

"There is none," Keith explains. "Sasha says they don't use any in Afghanistan."

Vanessa leans forward, points to Gus, and whispers, "He hates touching food with his hands."

Keith squints at the eggplant dish, now unrecognizable in its red and ocher cloak. "I don't really like to, either," he muses.

"That's the eggplant," I offer, hoping the homey scent of garlic will entice them.

No one moves an inch.

Afghan music tiptoes softly about the room. Steam rises from our plates. Like the first one to drop their towel before skinny-dipping, I slide my hand into the pot, take a few fingers of warm food, and hope everyone else will follow suit.

The flavor explodes in my mouth, unlike anything I've ever eaten. It's smoky from frying, rich from the oil, and heady from the spice. The cayenne pepper makes my eyes water. "Wow. This is *good*," I say.

Then I try the yogurt dip. The flavors have mellowed, and now they sing. Finally I reach into the giant pot of rice, still steaming. The cinnamon note from the garam masala works beautifully in the savory dish.

The tension gives way to giggles. Everyone—even Keith—gingerly digs their fingers into the communal pot—the stirring pot. I wait, searching their faces.

One by one, they smile. *Yes, this is good,* they say.

Soon our hands find their rhythm. With no silverware to clink, the room fills with the silent concentration of busy eating. Eating with our fingers does not come naturally, so we eat slower and talk more. Thirty minutes goes by, then an hour and two.

"When you blog about this, are you going to write about the war?" Vanessa asks.

I look long and hard at the beautiful display in front of us. For the most part, this is food I'd never heard of a week before. This is a real feast.

"No, I'm not," I respond. "There are enough people talking about the bad things in that part of the world. It's time for some good. The food is enough." I surprise myself with the forcefulness of my answer.

That night, as I stand in front of the sink washing a stack of dirty dishes notably lacking any knives, I make a vow to be a voice for the good, the happy, and the downright silly. Food, I realize, is family, not just survival. It's peace.

This, I decide, will be my goal for the next four years—to create a place of calm inside and outside of my heart. Before I go to bed, I move the remaining spices from the market into the spice jars. They don't fill them all, but it's a start.

Kabeli Palau

The national dish of Afghanistan is a highly spiced basmati rice dish made with lamb, chicken, or beef, piled onto a large platter that everyone dips into with bits of noni Afghani *(naan). The festive atmosphere this creates makes kabeli palau an important celebration dish, ubiquitous at weddings and festivals. The rice is colored—commonly with a touch of caramelized sugar, though many use browned onion and saffron with similar effect, as presented in Terri Willis's* Afghanistan, Enchantment of the World. *The Afghan season theirs with char masala—here I've substituted more readily available garam masala. And although some like a few chopped tomatoes, I opted for the concentrated smack of tomato paste. A skyward platter brimming with spiced rice, tender chicken, and cardamom-laced carrots and golden raisins will feed a crowd in more ways than one.*

1 pound basmati rice, rinsed
1 large onion, peeled and chopped
⅓ cup ghee
2 heaping tablespoons tomato paste
A couple large cloves of garlic
2½ pounds bone-in chicken (legs, thighs), extra fat trimmed
1 tablespoon salt
1 tablespoon garam masala
1 good pinch saffron
¾ cup water

Finishing touches:
½ pound carrots (about 4 large), peeled and cut into match-
   sticks (2 cups chopped)
1 teaspoon oil
1 teaspoon sugar
½ cup golden raisins
A good pinch cardamom
¼ cup slivered almonds

Rinse the rice in cold water until clear. Soak for an hour, more if you have it. Meanwhile, in a large, heavy-bottom pot with tightly fitting lid (something like an oval Le Creuset), brown the onion in ghee. Use a slotted spoon to remove the onion. Puree it with tomato paste and garlic. A food processor will do nicely, but a blender will work, too (just add the water to make the job easier). Set aside.

Brown the chicken pieces in the same pot over medium-high heat. Patience is a virtue here: The browner the chicken, the better the flavor. This can take 5 to 8 minutes per side. Move the chicken to one side of the pot and add in the onion mixture, salt, garam masala, saffron. Let it toast a moment in the hot ghee, and, if it hasn't already gone in, add the water.

Stir the chicken back into the mixture, lower heat, cover, and let bubble very gently.

Preheat the oven to 350°F. Meanwhile, prepare the garnish. In a large skillet over medium heat, cook the carrots in oil with the sugar until glossy (but not cooked through). Add cardamom and raisins. Cook another minute until plumped. Set aside.

Bring a pot of salted water (at least 6 cups) to boil. Drain the rice and dump it into the boiling water. Boil 4 to 5 minutes—no more—until half cooked. Drain.

Remove the chicken from the pot. Add the rice to the pot, stirring to coat with spiced broth. Put the chicken on top of the rice along with the carrot mixture. Cover and bake 30 to 35 minutes.

Finishing touches: Setting the chicken and carrot mixture aside, mound half the rice onto a large platter. Add the chicken, then bury with remaining rice. If a crust has formed on the bottom of the pot, be sure to scrape it up as well—some consider this the best part. Scatter the carrot mixture over the top, along with the almonds.

Serve immediately with a thick, doughy flatbread such as naan, preferably without silverware.

Enough for 6 to 8

CHAPTER 23

World on a Plate

THE FIRST FEW COUNTRIES GO BY like a *Where's Waldo* of world cuisine. I spend hours looking for authentic, viable recipes, subsumed by the curiosities I uncover—the more unfamiliar, the better. At home I lie on the carpet next to Ava, flipping through cookbooks. At the library I scan the reference section with her on my hip, only leaving after we find a cookbook for me and a picture book for her. I research the foods of dozens of countries in one sitting—sometimes resorting to the help of a Peace Corps site, an expat blog, or a YouTube video for help. But there's a silence around many, as if they don't exist.

The hunt is maddening and satisfying. It fills the cracks and crevices of motherhood, at once smoothing my nerves and stretching them to their limit.

Even at eight months, Ava is my little helper. When I show her my selections, she pats the cookbooks with her hand. She watches the cooking videos, hiccuping and cooing. I cannot bring myself to select just one or two recipes, so I choose a half dozen for each country. Each Saturday I race to prepare the food before she wakes up, using the blender in the laundry room to protect her from the commotion. I cobble together the posts after she goes to bed for the night. With each country, I select increasingly exotic dishes, relishing excitement but especially the shock on Keith's face when I present him with each meal.

He heaves a great sigh, his lower lip blowing out into a pout when I offer up Albanian lamb roasted in a quagmire of yogurt and rice, called *tava elbasani*. He's never had lamb before, and he hates plain yogurt. The meat emerges from the oven with a brown crust, each bite tenderized by the lengthy yogurt bath turned golden custard. Albanians are known for simple spicing, and one bite—filled with the citric warmth of paprika—says it all. But the revelation is lost on Keith. He cannot get past the homely presentation.

Dessert fares no better. Rose water–flavored Turkish delight—a sugar- and starch-based confection now enjoyed worldwide, but especially in the former Ottoman Empire—should be blushing, translucent, like the glow of a window covered in frost. A dusting of powdered sugar only enhances the illusion. But mine clumps together, a miserable failure none of us can bring ourselves to enjoy. Keith pokes his with a knife, brow crinkled.

For Algeria, I go beyond adaptation to create my own recipe inspired by Clifford A. Wright's *A Mediterranean Feast*. I take traditional ingredients Wright recommends—chickpeas, potatoes, onion, and wide sheets of pasta in a spiced tomato sauce—but assemble them in an Italian-style lasagna to catch Keith off guard. For kick I add the requisite cocktail of spices: cayenne, cumin, coriander, and *harissa*, a scorching North African spice blend made with chili peppers, garlic, and oil. I spoon the warm mixture between lasagna sheets with ricotta, Gruyère, and mozzarella. Even before it goes in the oven, the cheese begins to melt.

When I pop the browned "lasagna" on the table, Keith smiles. But when a chickpea rolls from his slice, he raises his eyebrow. Still, I urge him on. We sink our teeth into the spice, our tongues catching fire even as the ricotta cools us. Only then does it occur to me that the combination of layered pasta with potato is an echo of my family's own Genovese spaghetti with hunks of boiled potatoes.

Four bites in, Keith asks for seconds, and then begs me to make the lasagna again. But that would be too easy. Instead, I remake the less familiar Turkish delight to redeem myself, relieved that Algeria enjoys the tricky confection as much as Albania. I stir vigorously and get the lumps smooth. When Keith eats two pieces, his brow smooth, I consider it a triumph.

Hot Algerian Lasagna

This dish blends traditional Italian lasagna with chickpeas, potatoes, ground lamb, and a healthy dose of cayenne pepper. Although the recipe is an invention of my own, inspired by the work of Clifford A. Wright, Algeria does have strong connections to Italy—not the least of which is the Trans-Mediterranean pipeline, which runs from Algeria, through Tunisia, into Italy.

Harissa and cayenne pepper provide the punch for this dish. Dried harissa mix can be found in the spice section of some supermarkets, whereas wet pastes are more often sold in Middle Eastern markets. A teaspoon of cayenne makes the lasagna mild—double this for good burn. Cayenne pepper's heat is rated in "heat units." This recipe was made with a 35,000 cayenne, which is on the low end of the scale. With a 90,000 cayenne, only ⅓ of the cayenne pepper will be needed for the same kick. Most spice companies include this information on their spices.

For a more budget-friendly version, ground chicken or beef may be substituted though the result will be leaner, too.

For the filling:
A few glugs olive oil
1 medium onion, chopped
1 pound ground lamb
A couple cloves garlic, crushed
½ teaspoon ground cumin
¼ teaspoon ground caraway
1 tablespoon harissa, prepared
1 teaspoon cayenne pepper, or more to taste
Salt
1 heaping tablespoon tomato paste
One 15-ounce can tomato puree or sauce, plus an 8-ounce
   can (2½ cups total)
One 15-ounce can chickpeas, rinsed and drained
2 medium Yukon gold potatoes, peeled and ½-inch diced
   (about 2 cups or 10 ounces diced)
½ cup water, or as needed

For assembly:
15 ounces ricotta
2 eggs
2 cups (½ pound) shredded Gruyère
2 cups shredded mozzarella
1 pound no-boil lasagna sheets

In a large skillet over medium-high heat, sauté the onion in a couple glugs of olive oil until golden. Add the lamb, and brown for a good 5 to 10 minutes, breaking it into small chunks with a wooden spoon along the way. Reduce heat and stir in the garlic, cumin, caraway, harissa, cayenne, and salt. Cook for a few minutes, until fragrant. Add tomato paste, 15 ounces of puree, chickpeas, cubed potatoes, and ½ cup water. Increase heat to bring to a bubble. Cover and simmer until potatoes are just tender—about 15 to 20 minutes, adding extra water if needed. Check seasonings, adding more salt and cayenne if desired.

Preheat the oven to 350°F. In a small bowl, mix ricotta with eggs and 1 cup Gruyère cheese. Add salt to taste.

To assemble lasagna:
Spread a glug of olive oil and half the remaining tomato puree on the bottom of a 9 × 13-inch (3-quart) casserole. Next, add a layer of lasagna noodles, a quarter of the ricotta mixture, a quarter of the lamb mixture, and ⅓ cup mozzarella cheese. Repeat three times. Finally, end with a layer of noodles and remaining puree sprinkled with remaining Gruyère and mozzarella. Cover with aluminum foil, and bake 55 minutes. Remove foil, and bake 5 minutes further to brown. Let rest a good 30 minutes before slicing.

Enough for 8

The blogging and cooking adventure consumes me so deeply that I wonder if I'm taking too much time away from my family. If, by flailing headlong into some imagined, perfect future, I'm stretching Keith too far, perhaps testing his steadfastness—and by extension, his love for me. Is this culinary adventure adding to the joy of the moment—or circumventing it?

When I get to Angola, I happen across a five-volume collection called *The World Cookbook for Students,* an encyclopedia of world recipes. It's like the global cookbook jackpot, with recipes for every country in the world plus many territories and principalities. Even though the collection costs more than $200, I order it immediately. I tell Keith it will free me up since I won't have to spend so much time researching. He nods in agreement a little too readily, relief written on his face.

When the book arrives, I flip to Angola and pick out a recipe for *bâton de manioc,* a grated cassava root packet steamed inside a skinny banana leaf envelope. Cassava root looks like a fat, brown carrot, with the texture of a hard potato. A South African friend explains that I'll be able to find the cassava and the banana leaves at the African market down the road. She says it nonchalantly, as though it is totally normal to have an African market a mile and a half down the road, in the middle of Middle America. I must have driven past it a thousand times, yet never noticed it.

As I work on my adaptation, I compare the recipe with a few others. Several suggest I soak the cassava for two days, then grate it, mound it into packets, and steam them for six hours. All this work seems a bit over the top, but I have no one to ask. So I follow the instructions and soak the cassava.

On cooking day, I peel through the tough brown exterior, more like bark than skin. The inside is pristine—white and smooth. I tell Keith I cannot wait to taste it. He doesn't look so sure.

The initial excitement fades when I spend the next hour and a half grating the cassava. Tough fibers thread through the woody core, making the job even more difficult. My biceps and shoulders burn as I hurry to grind them down and make the packets before Ava wakes up.

My cheeks flush. My forehead glistens. Bits of cassava flick onto the counter, the floor. In the midst of this mess, I imagine myself living in Angola. I read that in the small villages equipped only with outdoor kitchens, neighbors come together to help each other make food. The social contact makes quick work of the arduous task.

But my kitchen, ample though it is, is silent. There is no grandmother, no mother at my side. I spoon the paste into the banana leaves
and roll them up into long, green cigars. By the time Ava wakes up,
my knuckles are raw, and the sun is low in the cotton sky.

That night, we eat the bâtons de manioc with some friends and
their small child. Keith takes one tight-lipped bite before putting the
packet down. Ava does the same. Our guests nibble politely around
theirs. Everyone reaches for the traditional Angolan stew I prepared,
made with chicken, okra, pumpkin, and red palm oil.

I should be happy they're enjoying *something,* but I cannot help
staring at the neglected green bâtons. There are 20 in the stack. I think
about the hours I spent grating. Unwilling to let the work go to waste,
I wolf down one, then two, then three. The gummy mixture tastes like
a combination of steamed artichokes and a mild starch, like potato.
I'm not sure if I'm eating them because I'm hungry or because I want
to show Keith what a *real* appetite is. By the time I get up from the
table, I've eaten six.

After our guests go home and Ava goes to bed, Keith and I argue
about the leftovers. I want to save the cassava and the chicken, but
he says there's only room for one. His vote is for the chicken, which
I take as blatant disregard for my bloody knuckles. It's a stupid fight,
but for some reason it feels like it matters.

The longer we argue, the weirder I feel. There's no pain, just a
stretching, an expanding, as if there's an enormous balloon in my
stomach. The distention becomes so uncomfortable that I switch into
sweats and go to bed early, leaving Keith to deal with the leftovers.
I drift into a fitful sleep, waking up around midnight when Ava
cries out for her first feeding of the night. I'm still nursing, so I am
surprised to hear Keith get out of bed. His footsteps are muffled, as
though I'm listening from inside a fishbowl. I wonder if she's been
crying a long time.

I slide out of bed to go to her, but no sooner do I stand up than I crash to the floor. I land on all fours, but the carpet fibers feel like knives. My bones, my joints feel like the edges of a shattered chandelier. Still, I know Ava needs me. I stumble to my feet and track through the bedroom, dragging my hand along the wall to steady myself. By the time I reach the dining room, my ears buzz, my temples throb, and stars flood my vision. The room shrinks like a candle without oxygen. I wonder, vaguely, if I'm dying.

The room goes completely black just as Keith thrusts Ava into my arms. I open my mouth to say something, but the words don't come.

Suddenly I'm sideways, crashing into something hard. The last thing I hear is a grating metal sound.

~

"Sasha, Sasha, wake up." Keith shakes my shoulder.

My face is pressed against the living room carpet, my left arm lies across one of our bar stools. Keith kneels beside me with Ava in his arms, whimpering.

"What happened? You almost dropped her, Sash. She was dangling upside down when I took her from you. Her head was two feet from cracking onto the kitchen tiles," he whispers.

When I shake my head, the small movement brings on a wave of nausea I cannot control. Afterward, Keith helps me back to bed.

The next day, the doctor listens to my story with squinted eyes and pronounces the culprit: dehydration. I've been dehydrated before, I tell him. This has nothing to do with dehydration.

I ask him if the two falls could be the result of something I ate. I mention the bâtons de manioc, the strange ingredient, and the complex preparation, but he just smiles over his spectacles. He hooks me up to an IV of fluids and sends me on my way.

The dismissal irritates me. That night I look up cassava poison-
ing, finding my way to several sites including Ohio State University's
Research News. One word jumps off the screen: cyanide. Apparently, the woody fibers inside cassava contain a form of the poison:
"An unprocessed cassava plant contains potentially toxic levels of a
cyanogen called linamarin. The proper processing of cassava—drying,
soaking in water, rinsing, or baking—effectively reduces cassava's
linamarin content. But shortcut processing techniques can yield toxic
food products."

Even though I soaked the cassava and cooked it for hours,
nothing would change the fact that I grated the tough fibers right
into the packets. With such small traces of the toxin, no one else was
affected. But eating so many of them was another story. I'd emptied
my stomach and then some; only spending an hour hooked up to the
IV had brought color back to my cheeks.

Continuing my search, I land on a page from Hong Kong's Centre
for Food Safety site, which warns: "The clinical signs of acute cyanide
intoxication include rapid respiration, drop in blood pressure, rapid
pulse, dizziness, headache, stomach pain, vomiting, diarrhea, mental
confusion, twitching, and convulsions. Death due to cyanide poison-
ing can occur when the cyanide level exceeds the limit an individual
is able to detoxify."

The people of Angola grow up knowing these dangers inherently.
Their elders teach the others to soak and grate the cassava. In Angola,
the risks of cooking are balanced out by cooking in community.

In the afternoon, I look over the kitchen, peppered with creature
comforts: a microwave, a bread machine, an indoor kitchen, for
goodness' sakes. For the first time, I feel the emptiness of cooking
without the wisdom of the ages at my side: How little these conve-
niences matter when there's no guiding hand to help keep us safe.
I pull the cassava sticks from the refrigerator and toss them in the

trash. The next day I donate my microwave and give a friend my bread machine.

When I tell Mom what happened, she groans. "Doctors are such idiots. I hope you fired him. Of *course*, it's the cassava."

"But the website says the cassava in the United States is supposed to be cyanide free. They treat it with some kind of . . . wash?"

"Nonsense! Are you going to trust your body or what's *supposed* to be?"

"Well, it sure would be easier if I knew what the hell I was doing," I say. "What kind of mother am I, to risk my child's life like that?"

"Yes, that's scary," she agrees. Then she brightens. "Maybe you should focus on recipes that are going to *work* for your family, Sash. That's all. Don't try so hard to be shocking. I'm sure Keith's not a fan of all this fuss, anyway."

⚏ Muamba de Galinha

This spicy Angolan chicken stew presents none of the difficulties of bâtons de manioc. *It's a homey chop-and-simmer, one-pot dinner. The unique red tint and bold flavor come from red palm oil, the oil of choice in West Africa. Expats say it tastes like home, but the carrot-colored paste (that sets up at room temperature, like butter) is certainly an acquired taste. Angolans use the oil with abandon—doubling the amount I used here would not be unheard of—but I find a restrained hand goes a long way. It is available in ethnic grocers, certain natural grocers, and online.*

Although this rendition makes my nose sniffle, feel free to add more chilies to taste. Angolans don't hold back. The stew certainly can be served on its own, but it tastes great with boiled yucca, or served over rice.

Juice and zest of 1 lemon

4 large garlic cloves, crushed

A generous pinch of salt

1½ teaspoons chili powder

4 to 5 whole chicken legs

¼ to ⅓ cup red palm oil

2 large onions, chopped

3 tomatoes, quartered

1 habanero pepper, as desired

1 cup water

Salt and pepper

1 small pumpkin (about 1½ pounds), to make 1 pound cubed

½ pound okra (fresh or frozen), sliced in rounds

Mix lemon juice, zest, crushed garlic, salt, and chili powder, and rub into the chicken. Cover and refrigerate for an hour or overnight.

Heat a large pot or Dutch oven over medium-high heat. Add the oil, and brown the chicken, 5 to 10 minutes a side. Avoid crowding. Do this in several batches if needed. Next, cook the onions until soft and beginning to brown. Tip in the remaining marinade and tomatoes. Slit the habanero in half (or, for more fire, chop it), and toss into the mix. Splash in the water, and season with salt and pepper. Cover and cook at a gentle bubble for 30 to 45 minutes, or until the chicken is tender.

Meanwhile, peel, seed, and cut the pumpkin into 1.5-inch cubes. Stir the pumpkin and sliced okra into the broth, cover, and continue bubbling until all ingredients are cooked through, a good 30 minutes. Adjust seasoning. Serve hot.

Enough for 4 to 6

CHAPTER 24

—🥄—

Stove Top Travel

B Y NOW MY BLOG, Global Table Adventure, has a sprinkling of devoted readers, and I cannot imagine telling them I almost killed myself with the very recipe I suggested they try. I don't want my ignorance to reflect on the Angolan people; it's not their fault I screwed up. Ultimately, I decide to modify the recipe with clearer instructions and to keep my mouth shut about my reaction.

Still, the incident has repercussions. Keith is increasingly cool on the project, and I find myself wondering if the adventure is a risk to my daughter's safety. After all, I could have unwittingly passed the cyanide—or whatever it was—through my milk to her.

But somehow I cannot stop cooking. Though I've yet to make a meal from a country I've lived in or experienced firsthand, this adventure reawakens deep-seated yearnings. The photos and stories of the world's people lure me, inviting me to taste, explore, and imagine myself elsewhere. I feel young once again, as I was in Europe, with infinity at my fingertips. But where those voyages were bandages for a broken heart, these new journeys will launch me toward the uncharted life I crave. They *must*.

That March, we sip bittersweet grapefruit sparklers from Antigua and Barbuda. Even the summery glow of our curried chicken salad sandwiches and the heat from our jalapeño-studded mango and avocado salad do nothing to take the chill from the air.

"Did you know 'Antigua and Barbuda' is actually made of more than two islands? Behold Redonda." I pull up a photo on my laptop.

"It looks like *The Little Prince*'s planet," Keith laughs. At less than a square mile, the barren spine of rock looks oddly out of scale.

"There are 82,000 people in the country, with Redonda contributing exactly zero. There's no fresh water. Heck, it's more cliff than anything," I add "But get this—there are *four* kings who claim Redonda as their own."

A daydream is born: We sit in oversize thrones on that bald rock while sipping tumblers of the pink grapefruit drink. We finish our meal warm.

With Tulsa under an icing of snow, we imagine heating our hands over the crackling campfire kitchen of the famous Argentine chef Francis Mallmann. As we bite into our smaller rendition of the enormous pumpkins he roasts beneath embers, we can almost smell the same charred crust of the oven-roasted acorn squash, and see Patagonia's yellowed grasslands through the eyes of a gaucho, a South American cowboy.

For Australia, we're stockmen journeying into the heart of the great down under. We tear into kangaroo kebabs (purchased frozen four miles away, at Harvard Meats), palmfuls of damper bread (pretending we've cooked the baking soda mixture in ash), along with beet- and fried egg-topped Aussie burgers. When our motorcycle buddies contribute to the potluck, the backyard becomes the outback.

On my face, I feel the orange glow of Uluru—that enormous sandstone rock that burns at sunset above the brush.

These daydreams give the weekly feasts dimension. We are no longer just eating like tourists; our imaginations now reside in a different country every week. "It's better than TV," I tell Keith. I ask if he thinks I should include our daydreams in my weekly posts.

"Absolutely!" he says, "You can be your readers' tour guide."

But our fantasies feel private, like the fairy tales Toni, Michael, and I reworked once upon a time in Atlanta—too silly to share beyond our small circle.

I hold back.

Roasted Acorn Squash With Arugula & Chèvre

This unusual salad is adapted from Francis Mallmann. To streamline the recipe for home cooks, I swap his campfire-roasted pumpkin for a more manageable oven-roasted acorn squash (a grill works well here, too). One half makes the perfect portion size, enough for a light meal, or as an impressive starter in a larger feast.

I suggest letting guests assemble their own hot salad at the table. Provide a shallow bowl to hold the squash and 2 small spoons per person so that they can smash the ingredients together themselves. Oregano-mint dressing pulls together the peppery arugula and tang of goat cheese, making this hot salad an unforgettable experience worthy of regular rotation.

2 acorn squash
1 glug of olive oil
Salt and pepper

For the vinaigrette:
1 handful fresh mint leaves, finely chopped (about 2 tablespoons)
1 handful fresh oregano leaves, finely chopped (about 2
   tablespoons)
¼ cup red wine vinegar
½ cup olive oil
1 teaspoon salt
½ teaspoon pepper

Finishing touches:
1 small bunch (2½ ounces) baby arugula
8 ounces aged goat cheese, like bûcheron

Preheat the oven to 400°F. Cut the squash in half and remove
any seeds and strings. Brush the cut ends liberally with olive
oil and sprinkle with salt and pepper. Roast for 45 minutes
to an hour, or until browned and a fork pierces the flesh with
no resistance. Meanwhile, whisk together ingredients for the
vinaigrette in a small bowl.

Finishing touches:
Transfer the roasted pumpkin to serving plates. While still
steaming, fill the cavities with baby arugula and crum-
bles of goat cheese. Spoon on vinaigrette to taste, and toss,
being sure to scrape the warm squash flesh into the greens.
Eat immediately.

Enough for 4

Each country becomes a palpable moment in time, guiding
our days just like Ava's development. Just as we learned to eat with
our hands as Ava learned to crawl, we also learn the Austrian art of
romance when she drops down to one nap.

Everyone likes to tell new parents to make sure they carve out time for their relationship between diaper changes and all-night croup fests. But no one explains how to do it without child care. Whenever Keith and I discuss hiring a babysitter, I always say the same thing: "No way am I leaving my baby alone with some stranger. She's not even a year old. She can't tell us if something goes wrong."

When I ask Mom what she did as a single mother when she needed a little downtime, she tells me there was no time to date, and she didn't have friends. But Tim remembers that when Michael was nine and I was seven, she'd put us to bed and then take Tim, Grace, and Connor across the street to the park to blow off some steam, saying of Michael and me, "Don't worry, they're good sleepers. They'll be fine."

We must have been, because I have no memory of waking to an empty apartment. Perhaps I'd be more willing to leave Ava with a babysitter if she had a sibling closer to her age, a guardian of sorts, to watch over her the way Michael had watched over me. For the time being, Keith and I remain homebound; our romance will have to be kindled within these walls.

Austria turns out to be the perfect catalyst. Austrian romance is epitomized by the Sacher torte, a bittersweet chocolate cake layered with apricot jam, enrobed in a shiny chocolate glaze. One of the world's first chocolate desserts, it was invented in 1832 for Prince Metternich by a 16-year-old chef's assistant. The Hotel Sacher claims to be the point of origin, but could only claim this credential after a seven-year lawsuit in a tooth-and-nail litigation that captivated the entire country.

While researching, I learn from Chef Schorner, an instructor at the Culinary Institute of America, that "chocolate is everywhere now, a common thing. But if you go back 200 years, people who made something with chocolate created romance. Today, we have nostalgia for that simple time. Sacher torte represents a way of life without Google or Twitter, when people sat next to each other and simply had a beautiful conversation over cake." Today, Austrians eat slices of the shiny cake at cafés in a quiet, face-to-face, device-free time.

I spend one day whipping and swirling chocolate into a light, airy cake. The method feels like I'm stoking a fire, willing the batter to inflate, rise. And it does. When I put the cake in the oven, the batter looks so full that I half-expect it to burst into flame. When I place the completed cake under a dome on the kitchen counter, I can almost hear the light glinting off the glaze, crackling.

That night, as a family we eat a simple preparation of schnitzel and green beans cooked with speck, a cured meat product similar to bacon that I found at the local German market. As with the African market down the road and the kangaroo at Harvard Meats, I had no idea Siegi's Sausage Factory & Deli existed. Tulsa has proved its international mettle yet again. If I can make this adventure work in a small city like this, I realize, people could do it from most any city. I make it official and decide not to order any ingredients online. A motto is born: *Cook global, shop local.*

Over dinner, Keith and I talk. "I don't know why I never saw all the culture here in Tulsa," I say. "I'm sure Mom would have discovered these markets years ago." I remember how she dug up the German Tree Cake recipe all those years ago at one of the many folk dancing festivals she took us to. I watch Ava gum her green beans for a moment and sigh. "I wish our families could share some of this with us."

Keith jumps up and grabs my Canon Rebel. He points it at Ava, peering over the lens at me. "They might not be able to fly here every week, but we can make all this real by filming. For my parents, too."

In his footage, nine-month-old Ava looks like a cherub while she eats, all rosy-cheeked. "I can do this every week and post it with your meal reviews," Keith says.

I love the idea. After dinner I tuck Ava into her crib with a kiss, then lift the chocolate cake from the darkened kitchen. Since Keith and I cannot gallivant around to cafés, I invite him into the backyard for our first date since Ava was born. Under the balm of night, we enjoy one enormous slice, nearly a quarter of the cake, with two forks. I serve it with Austrian hot cocoa thickened with whipped egg yolk.

The cake is soft, chocolaty, but not cloying or particularly moist. What makes it memorable is the layer of tart apricot jam—a flirty little tease peeking out from between the two cake rounds. The bittersweet glaze drapes each bite like a satin sheet.

When we get down to the last few morsels, I slide the cake over to Keith and let him finish it. I pull out two poetry books Mom once picked up for a quarter at a yard sale, and we take turns reading from them.

A line from the Austrian poet Georg Trakl speaks to me most forcefully: "A smile trembles in the sunshine / Meanwhile I slowly stride on / Unending love gives escort / Quietly the hard rock greens."

"You know I couldn't do this without you, Keith," I say, turning to face him. His skin looks silver in the moonlight.

He nods and holds my hand.

"Thank you for not giving up on me," he says. "I know I'm a picky eater, but . . ." He smiles a sheepish sort of grin and points at the crumb-laden plate, "This cake was delicious. Who knew a tiny country in the Alps was holding out on us all this time?"

I laugh. "Well, it's not like I've always made the adventure easy for you."

"Seriously, Sasha, I guess I didn't realize . . ." he bites his lip, "how much of the world I was missing out on, you know, by only eating hamburgers."

I nod, leaning into his embrace. "Austria came along just in time. When was the last time we did this together? No laptop, cell phones, dirty diapers?"

We're both quiet. Somewhere in the shadows, the cicadas and crickets are in a humming, clicking frenzy. Fireflies puncture the darkness. I stare into the light, but soon I'm distracted, thinking about how to describe all this for the blog. I release my breath slowly and linger in that space so rarely visited, between yesterday and tomorrow, for once truly present.

We sit together for hours. At the end of the night we slip to the bedroom and once again consume each other like new lovers. When the passion we tended so carefully before parenthood rises up in me, I find it older, wiser, as resonant as a well-aged violin.

Over the next days, the warmth of Keith's touch stays with me, as a hot cup of cocoa leaves the table beneath it warm.

🍴 Sacher Torte

For romance to reach its full potential, the very notion of perfection must be tossed aside. Like the bitter note in chocolate, struggles draw out love's sweetness in a more sophisticated, less cloying way. When we come back together after challenges, we reveal what we—and our relationships—are made of. In the Sacher torte, one of the world's first chocolate cakes, dark chocolate is combined with a moderate amount of sugar to make the perfect bittersweet blend.

For the cake:
12 tablespoons (1½ sticks) unsalted butter, softened, plus
    more for cake pan
1 cup confectioner's sugar, sifted
A good pinch salt
8 large eggs, separated (reserve the whites in a large bowl)

A good 1½ teaspoons vanilla extract

7 ounces dark chocolate, melted

½ cup sugar

1⅛ cups cake flour, lightly whisked to remove lumps

Finishing touches:

Apricot jam (one 9- or 10-ounce jar)

¾ cup heavy cream

3 tablespoons light corn syrup

1 teaspoon vanilla extract

1 cup (6 ounces) semisweet chocolate chips

For the cake:

Preheat oven to 350°F. Grease and line a 10-inch springform pan with a round of parchment paper.

In the bowl of a standing mixer fitted with a whisk attachment, cream softened butter at medium speed until light and fluffy, gradually incorporating confectioner's sugar and salt, scraping as needed. Incorporate egg yolks, one at a time, and then splash in the vanilla extract, scraping again. Whisk melted chocolate into butter mixture, taking care that it is warm, not hot. Scrape.

In a large bowl, beat egg whites on high speed with a hand beater. Gradually add the sugar and beat until medium peaks form. Fold both the cake flour and the egg white mixture into the butter mixture, alternating in thirds—starting with the cake flour and ending with the egg white mixture.

Pour into a prepared springform pan, and bake 30 to 35 minutes or until the cake springs back when pressed with a finger and an inserted toothpick comes out clean.

Let cool completely. Slice in half, making two evenly sized discs. Warm the jam in a small saucepan, to spread easier and soak into the cake better. Working on top of a cooling rack set over a sheet pan, spread the bottom disk with half the jam. Top with the second disk, and cover the top and sides of the cake with the rest of the jam to seal in the crumbs.

Finishing touches: In a small pot, heat the heavy cream, corn syrup, and vanilla until the first few bubbles break the surface. Remove from the heat, add the chocolate, and whisk until smooth and glossy. Cool about 10 minutes to thicken the glaze and ease its application. Pour over top of the cake and spread over the sides. Refrigerate to set glaze. Serve cool, but not cold.

Enough for 12 to 14

CHAPTER 25

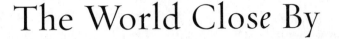

The World Close By

YOU LOOK STRESSED," Mom declares, glancing at my sweats and low ponytail.

We're on our way home from the airport. She's here for Ava's first birthday party—her first visit since the blog began six months earlier.

"Things are different now. With the blog there's a lot to do, and not a lot of time to do it in," I muse. "Keith's videos add a whole other element. He's up every Sunday night until 2, 3, 4 a.m."

"But that's worth it," Mom interrupts.

"It's *all* worth it," I snap, but I wonder if I'm saying it for her benefit or mine. Ever since Austria, 15 countries and four months earlier, Keith and I have redoubled our efforts. There's been some media attention—mostly local TV—and I feel increasingly in the spotlight, with a heightened need to "perform."

As soon as we get home, Mom shoos me away. "If there's that much to do, make good use of my time here—get caught up!"

She plunks Ava and the books down on the living room carpet and settles in for an afternoon of play.

When I hesitate, she says, "We're fine," her chest puffed up with grandmotherly importance. She'd never admit it, but I can tell she's glad to be needed. And I'm relieved to have her help. I thought her mission was to spend time with Ava, but I notice her eyeing me from the sidelines, as though she's keeping her finger on my pulse, too.

I pile my cookbooks on the dining table and flip through them in search of Bulgarian recipes. Then I watch as Mom teaches Ava to feel the warm sunshine on the carpet, to tear sheets of paper, to throw balled-up socks into a laundry basket. Mom's ability to transform everyday objects into toys reminds me that it was her creativity that kept me from realizing we were poor all those years ago.

Mom pulls several books out of her suitcase and starts reading them to Ava. Suddenly, some of the words sound familiar.

"I don't mind a dragon THIS size," said mother. "Why did it have to grow so BIG?"

"I'm not sure," said Billy, "but I think it just wanted to be noticed."

Intrigued, I come over and see that Mom is reading my old copy of *There's No Such Thing as a Dragon*. I pick up a few of the other books: These are mine and Michael's.

"Mom, I can't believe you saved our books all this time—what, 20, maybe 30 years?" I hug her to my side. "Wow."

"I hope you want them, because if you're just going to donate them, I'll ship them back to Boston myself."

"Don't you think," I begin carefully, putting my hands on her shoulders, "that Ava can have *more* than one set of books—that she can have the old and the new?"

When the doorbell rings, Mom answers. A few moments later, she leads a tall, lamppost of a man into the house. He looks young, perhaps 20, but has the long face and sunken eyes of someone much older. I cannot imagine why Mom would have invited him in.

"Sasha, this is Nick—from *Bulgaria.*"

I furrow my brow, wondering what kind of joke she's pulling.

"Where did you find him?"

"I didn't—he just rang the doorbell!"

He says "Hello," but the word comes out all chewed up. He's clearly not from Tulsa.

Mom laughs with delight. Nick's in town to sell educational books—his summer job. "Come in," she says, pulling him right up to the dining room table to my teetering cookbooks. "Your timing is impeccable; my daughter is cooking Bulgarian food this week."

Now it's his turn to look surprised.

For the next 30 minutes, I quiz him about the traditional food from his homeland. He laughs at some of the recipes I've dug up, claiming they're out of date or, worse, that he's never heard of them. He says I absolutely *must* try a dried fruit drink called *kompot,* a chilled cucumber soup called *tarator,* and a snail-shelled cheese pastry called *banitsa.* In appreciation, I buy a set of science books for Ava and invite him to dine with us. He declines with a bashful shrug.

After he leaves, I show Mom the glittering world map above the dining table, now studded with gemstone stickers on the 26 countries we've cooked so far: Afghanistan to Azerbaijan; the Bahamas to Brunei. All in all, six months have passed. It feels like a lifetime.

"Ava might not remember any of these meals, but some things you just *have* to do, even if the purpose isn't initially clear. I have to believe it will be worth it." I glance back at her stack of books on the living room floor. "Like how you saved those books all those years. Who knew that you'd be reading them today, with my daughter—your granddaughter?"

Mom softens. "You're right. And how amazing that Nick showed up today—what are the odds of that? Something's going on here."

She laughs like a giddy schoolgirl: "This project, it's not just helping your family." She glances over to the front door and shakes her head. "It's like you're pulling in the whole world, Sash! No wonder you're stressed. That's a lot of responsibility."

I wonder if she's right. I wonder if, after Nick, the doorbell will continue to ring as we let in someone from Burkina Faso, then Burma, and so on, until the entire world is sitting around my dinner table. An enormous global table. No arguments. No food fights. Just people there to share a meal. What could I learn from them? What could we learn from each other?

I think back to my rough-and-tumble childhood and try to imagine all the players of my own life coming together around such a table: It's a motley crew, to be sure.

Mom's flight is scheduled before I serve the Bulgarian feast, but I make her a glass of kompot anyway. The Eastern European Christmas drink is inky with currants, prunes, and scattered sparks of dried apricot. The fruit plumps agreeably when simmered in sugar water, clouding the pot with a brown plume of sticky syrup.

I dig my spoon into my glass and lift one quivering prune to my lips.

🍴 Kompot

Kompot (also known as Oshav) is a glass of summertime for all seasons. In the winter, Bulgarian children enjoy kompot as part of the Christmas celebration. Most any dried fruit will make a lovely addition—especially apples, pears, and cherries. When serving, be sure to give everyone a few bits of fruit at the bottom of their glass!

10 cups water
1 cup sugar, or to taste

1 cup prunes
1 cup dried currants
1 cup dried apricots

Add all ingredients to a large pot. Cover and bring to a bubble. Cook until the fruit is well plumped, about 15 minutes. Serve chilled with several lumps of fruit in each glass. Although a straw isn't necessary, a long-handled spoon will be much appreciated.

Makes 3½ quarts

I never considered the question of taking a vacation when I decided to cook my way around the world. Then in August, my brother Connor invites us to spend a week with his family in Virginia. I cannot pack my suitcase with all the cooking paraphernalia I might need. Keith isn't set up to edit a video on the road.

"Why don't we just take a week off," Keith suggests. "Isn't the blog about the journey, not the destination?"

But hundreds now click through my blog daily; I don't want to disappoint our readers. Before we leave, I cram in cooking Cambodia with Burundi.

I need a few dried, brined limes for a sour chicken soup. I lay the heavy citrus on a scorching patch of driveway. On one 104-degree day, the side exposed to the sun fades from green to yellow, the once glossy skin withering into leathery hide. I flip the limes, and the next day they're done. They should have taken one, maybe two weeks.

While Keith packs our bags, I look into Cambodian grilled eggs, street food mentioned in Steven Raichlen's *Planet Barbecue*. There's just one problem: no recipe. I reach out to Karen Coates, the former Asia correspondent for *Gourmet* magazine and whose blog I follow. She contacts a Khmer friend who helps explain the dish.

Turns out, it's no small trick. A dozen raw eggs must first be blown out of their shells into a large bowl. Whip in a few fingers of sugar (palm or brown for depth) and a pucker of fish sauce. Some suggest minced kefir lime leaves, but I don't have time to scurry over to the Asian market; the empty shells must still be painstakingly refilled with the glop and then steamed. Once firm, the eggs (shell and all) are skewered with bamboo rods and grilled.

The concept reminds me of Mom's Jell-O eggs. But unlike hers, which we propped up in an egg carton to fill and set, these eggs need to be *steamed* upright before grilling. Some Cambodians steam them for eight hours. Finding the right vessel proves to be difficult, and I spill several batches until I discover the sides of a collapsible steamer basket can be lifted and closed around the eggs, then tied.

But the eggs boil over, coating the steamer in what looks like foam insulation. In our haste to head east, I leave the mess in the sink. It is only when I'm lounging on the beach with my family that I realize I could have probably just steamed them in the cardboard carton they came in. Back home, I tackle the dishes and consider trying again. But the breakneck pace of the blog demands I move onto another country, another meal.

⫯⫯ Cambodian Grilled Eggs

Despite the challenges I had with this recipe early on, I couldn't get the brown sugar and fish sauce delight out of my mind. I've since made dozens of batches to streamline the process. I'm glad I took the time; with a little planning this popular Cambodian street food will be a showstopper at any barbecue. While I kept the core of the process—steamed, seasoned eggs, served skewered, from a warm grill—I learned three key things: Although some cracking is normal, thin eggshells crack excessively while

steaming—opt instead for sturdier organic eggs; instead of blow-
ing out the eggs, create a larger hole so the liquid simply shakes
out (this will also reduce cracking); and to avoid stress the first
time making them (and allow for backup), steam the eggs one
day ahead. Before serving, just reheat them on the grill.

After mastering the basics, play with the flavors: A few
splashes of soy sauce or sprinkles of minced kefir lime leaves,
chives, or hot chilies make lovely additions. For a hassle-free
option, this egg mixture would make wonderful scrambled eggs
for a Cambodian-inspired brunch.

6 whole, large organic eggs
1 tablespoon brown sugar
2 teaspoons fish sauce
A couple good pinches pepper

Cut a cardboard egg carton to fit inside a large pot. Set aside.
Add ½ inch water to the pot, cover, and bring to a gentle bubble.

Meanwhile, using a large clean needle or safety pin, carefully make a 1-inch hole in the top of an egg. Flick shell frag-
ments out, away from the egg so that they do not fall inside.
Shake the egg over a large bowl to release the insides. Repeat
with remaining eggs.

Rinse the empty shells in hot water, then stand them in
the cardboard egg carton.

Prepare the filling:
Whisk the eggs with all ingredients, and funnel into the
eggshells. There will be some egg leftover. They expand while
steaming so leave ¼ inch of space at the top of each egg. (If any
eggs do bubble over, the foamy egg easily scrapes off the shell.)

Right before placing the carton of filled eggs directly into
the pot of water, turn the heat to a notch or so above the lowest

setting. Cover and steam gently for about 35 minutes without lifting the lid, or until the eggs are cooked through. The water shouldn't bubble or they'll boil over, but there should be enough heat and steam in the pot to gently cook them.

At this point the eggs can be refrigerated overnight if desired.

Although they can be served straight from the pot, it's more fun to finish them the Cambodian way: Thread onto pre-soaked bamboo skewers and grill until hot. Serve as is, letting guests delight in peeling their own eggs.

Makes 6

Ava is busy learning to walk and talk. Shortly after she takes her first steps that autumn, I take her to the park to stretch her legs.

But we don't stay long. "Papa will be home soon," I remind her, "and we're going to eat a special meal tonight, from Chile."

She giggles and chants, "Chile, Chile, Chile."

At that very moment, 33 Chilean miners are trapped 2,300 feet under the earth. They'd been there for nearly two months.

Half a world away, at the edge of the playground, I have no idea if they will survive. What I do know is that, as I hold my daughter close, the miners' families and friends are certainly hugging each other as well, clinging to fraying hope with circles under their eyes. Two months is such a long time to be in darkness.

I don't tell Ava about the miners. Instead, I try to make Chile real for her. I tell her about how the Chilean people like to eat much later than we do, between 9 p.m. and midnight, when the moon is already high in the sky and she's been asleep for hours. Later, I show her pictures of the mountains, and of Chilean children with their shiny, midnight-colored hair.

Keith, Ava, and I sit down to eat *pastel de choclo*. The chicken casserole is a minefield of sliced olives, raisins, and chunked hard-boiled egg—all tucked beneath an unassuming blanket of pureed sweet corn. I dig right in. The milky corn slides over my tongue, charming me. Then the mouthful suddenly explodes, turning at once briny and sulfurous. There's an aftershock of paprika, cumin, and cinnamon. As my lone fork clinks on my plate, I become aware of the stubborn silence around me.

Keith loathes olives and hard-boiled eggs. He stares at the casserole with a look of panic. I take a deep breath, put down my fork, and reach toward Ava's high chair, pointing at her plate. "The corn makes the chicken taste almost sweet!"

I pull a piece of chicken from beneath the squishy mass of corn and chopped egg and present it to Ava. Tentatively, she picks it up and slowly chews. A moment later, she goes back for more. Keith watches her, his plate still untouched.

"Eat it!" I mouth, catching his eye.

He extracts some of the chicken, avoiding the olives and eggs. Dutifully, and not without regret, he picks up a microscopic piece of egg, eats it, and downs a half glass of water.

For dessert we pour homemade *dulce de leche* all over heart-shaped *alfajores,* soft orange zest–infused cookies. I make them heart shaped on purpose, as a gesture toward the trapped miners. Keith spreads his alfajores with extra spoonfuls of dulce de leche. Ava licks her lips.

As I watch my little family finally eat with gusto, I feel solidarity with Chile—a friendship of sorts. Later I tuck Ava into bed and crack the office window, grateful for the fresh air.

Keith retires behind his laptop and I behind mine. I'm supposed to be transcribing the Chilean experience for my readers, but I'm distracted by the news. Never before has any civilization lived with as much connection to communities outside of their tribes, villages, or towns.

Yet I know nothing about my neighbors. I glance out the window through the darkness and see the frenzied flicker of television light through my neighbors' blinds. I realize that although I don't know the names of the people living next door, I do know Mario's, the Chilean miner made famous for "starring" in the video updates occasionally sent up to the surface.

I want to ask Keith if he thinks we know too much about the world and not enough about our neighbors. But I can see that his eyes are heavy.

Unlikely connections continue to be forged with each country I cook. The week I cook Egypt coincides with a key moment in the Arab Spring, when thousands of protesters gather in Cairo to demand the resignation of President Mubarak. So, too, Tulsa cracks open, revealing itself to be abuzz with a vibrant international community. The same morning I plan to cook Finland, a mother at Ava's library playgroup mentions she is half Finnish.

Though we'd never met before, she cancels her plans and comes over to help me prepare *pulla*, sweet cardamom bread seemingly made for coffee. When I buy my groceries for Iran, the checkout girl at Whole Foods is Iranian. As she hands me my receipt, she eagerly confirms the menu I selected.

I add up the coincidences, and can only bow my head in humble appreciation. Perhaps it's not fate. But it *is* strange to consider that in the almost five years I've lived in Tulsa, I never noticed the richness of the community all around me.

After a life in transition, embracing my community certainly hasn't been my strong suit. For once I feel like I'm driving a train; I don't know where it's headed, or what the voyage means. But there's no way I'm stopping now.

CHAPTER 26

21 Layers of Memory

IT'S AN EARLY SATURDAY MORNING IN MAY, still not quite dawn, and I'm finally making the German Tree Cake. I haven't made it since I was a little girl, though I've thought of the 21 almond paste layers many times since. Now, well into the second year of the adventure, I'm excited to surprise Ava and Keith with this childhood favorite. After so much foraging in unknown countries, this cake at least is certain.

Mom mailed me the recipe, an eight-page document from the era when photocopies came out more like smudges than duplicates. As I look over her notes, I realize her overly complex method will create a ghastly amount of dirty dishes: two pots for melting and stirring the chocolate glaze, five bowls for whipping, mixing, and folding eggs, marzipan, flour, cream, and sugar.

When I ask her about it, she laughs and says that was the point: "How else was I supposed to keep you kids busy? Everyone had to have a bowl and a job and something to wash when the cooking was done."

I scribble alongside her notes, crossing out, filling in, and combining steps where I can. When I get the method down to two bowls, I tie on my apron and whip the thick, stiff marzipan into the cream. As the beaters coax the tan lumps into a smooth, creamy mixture, they toss the scent of almond into the air. I fold in the whipped egg whites until the batter falls into velvet ribbons. I turn on the broiler and brush a layer of the puffy batter into my springform pan, place it two inches from the flame, and wait until the gloss gives way to matte, speckled cake.

I repeat this step again and again until, 45 minutes later, I have 21 paper-thin layers of cake separated by 7 glazings of apricot jam. I set the cake aside to cool and head to the bedroom to find Keith.

The shower is running. The water sounds like rapids against the vinyl walls. Keith's up early, I think. I tiptoe into the bathroom and pull back the curtain to give him a good morning kiss. He's naked, hunched on the shower floor, surrounded by steam and hot water.

He doesn't lift his head, and I ask, "Should I call an ambulance?"

He mouths "no." I grab him by the arm and help him up, then turn off the shower and wrap a towel around him. He leans on me while I help him step into a pair of sweats. His every movement is slow and brittle.

I ask him a dozen more times what's wrong, but all he can manage is "Take me to the emergency room."

My heart hammers so loudly, so high in my throat, I feel as if the force might choke me. "If you're having a heart attack, you need to tell me. I'll call an ambulance."

He doesn't say anything, but takes the phone out of my hand and slowly shakes his head. "You can drive," he whispers, "It's not like that."

At the hospital, Keith hunches over the paperwork. I cannot hear what he says to the nurse over the din of Ava's giddy chatter, but they wheel him to a room immediately. From his wheelchair, Keith asks me to call his son.

Suddenly I'm 12 years old again, standing in the hospital waiting room, wondering if Michael's OK. I stand in the laminate glow of the doorway and do as I'm told, too scared of what the answer might be.

The call doesn't go through; the walls in the hospital are too thick. As the doctors prepare Keith for an echocardiogram, I approach a window to try again. When Ryan doesn't pick up, I consider hanging up without leaving a message. I don't want to be the bearer of bad news. But when the phone beeps, I say, "Your dad is having . . . trouble with his heart. Give me a call. We're at the hospital. St John's."

Ryan calls back almost immediately.

"Is he OK?" I can hear the fear in his voice. I do my best to strangle my own for his sake.

"The doctors are monitoring his heart. Can you come?"

"I'm stuck at work." He works as a pizza deliverer for Papa John's. Saturday is one of the busiest days of the week.

"Ryan, I know he would really like you to be here."

Then I call Keith's mother, three hours away in Geronimo and about to head to church. She listens carefully and then asks me to let her know what the doctors determine. There are so many heart issues in the family, including her husband's four stents and her own pacemaker, that they don't exhaust themselves with worry until they absolutely have to. As she hangs up, she adds that she'll say an extra prayer for us in church today. She's the essence of calm.

I thumb through my contacts for someone else to call.

If I could just find someone to watch Ava, I could be there with Keith and listen to the doctors to get a grip on what's happening. Ava is nearly two years old, and I still haven't let anyone babysit.

I try Vanessa: No answer. I consider Leona briefly. Our motorcycle days seem like a lifetime ago. Connor, Grace, Mom, and Tim are an airplane ride away.

I don't know who else to call so I put my phone away. As I stare at my lap, I realize I still have my apron on. I tear it off, and then realize the hallway is too quiet.

I find Ava squatting in front of an electrical outlet down the hall, peering at it as though it were a work of art. I scoop her up and sprint back into Keith's room. The only doctor left is looking over Keith's ECG.

He explains that Keith is experiencing a severe case of atrial fibrillation. His heart was beating so slowly that he couldn't breathe, so even the smallest steps left him winded. The doctor keeps talking and talking.

Ava starts chanting, "Eat, eat, eat."

"So, it's not a heart attack?" I say over her.

"No, but we told your husband this sort of episode is a sign of bad electricity in the heart. We can go into his heart with a laser, essentially burning a small section of it to get it in order again. There's not much else we can do." He pauses. "An episode like this may never happen again. But if it does, each one puts a strain on his heart. And in the long run, it will put him at an increased risk of stroke and heart attack."

The doctor refers Keith to a physician who can give him a heart monitor. He'll have to wear it for a week to find out if he needs the surgery.

For the first time I notice the sanitized, plastic hospital smell—the stench of death. I bite my lip. The diagnosis isn't terrible, I tell myself. It's the rest that I don't know how to deal with.

I don't want to tell Keith that Ryan isn't coming. As I smooth over the stiff cotton sheets at the edge of his bed, I find myself desperate to run away, as far and as fast as my feet could take me from this sanitized room where even the doctors have no control.

When we get home, I coat the German Tree Cake in another sheathing of apricot jam and, finally, the chocolate glaze. I am on autopilot, unwilling to reveal my fear to Ava, unwilling to add to Keith's stress. As I work, I realize why Mom always had us make this cake, even though we weren't German, even though the ingredients were expensive. This cake was a walking meditation. Step-by-step, one foot in front of the other, it was a sheer exercise in willpower—an edible prayer.

Like Mom, I crush the almonds and press them into the sides. I can still see her small hands pressing them over the smooth chocolate and then slicing the cake into wedges, revealing the 21 layers beneath. Michael and I ate that cake with the kind of hunger that comes from waiting for a good thing a little longer than expected.

Later, when Keith and Ava eat it, I smile, knowing that I have not only fed them: I have kept going.

Within the month, Keith has worn the monitor and seen the specialist, who determines that he doesn't need surgery. In fact, the doctor doesn't detect any atrial fibrillation. He's lucky, she says: This episode might have been his last. She even cancels Keith's prescription for Lanoxin, a drug sometimes used to treat abnormal heart rhythms. Friends tell me I should have called, that I *could* have called. Even my family halfway across the country tells me I should have called. I want to believe them, but I find myself shaking my head: "Don't bother, I'll be fine." A veritable martyr in training.

But the hospital visit shows me the reality of living without a support system. In hindsight, my reluctance to bother other people feels foolish, and I wonder if it's the reason that in the six years since I moved to Tulsa, I've met a lot of people but not made many close friends or taken the time to meet my neighbors.

"I'm not going to hound someone with my problems," I tell Keith. "People get *tired* of problems." It's easier not to make friends than to risk rejection.

A couple months later, Keith and I are sitting in the living room, each on one end of the couch, facing each other. Ava is dancing around the coffee table. When she slips in the narrow alley between furniture, I declare that it's high time for us to move. I try to make my voice enthusiastic and controlled, the same way Pierre did years earlier when announcing each of our new destinations.

"This was my bachelorette pad," I tell Keith. "We need a *family* home now—some space."

I cite our swaybacked roof and crumbling driveway as further evidence. I point out that we cannot even open the front picture window and get a breeze. "The air feels *stuck* in this place."

Keith doesn't immediately shut me down. When he asks where we should go, he crosses his arms and tilts his head back, listening. I shrug as though I'm not sure. But I am.

Before he can object, I rattle off my ideas, starting with the East Coast: near my mom in Boston, or my sister in New Jersey. I even suggest Virginia, near my brother Connor, or Florida, near my brother Tim.

"I didn't realize you were homesick," he says, a sad look on his face.

"I'm not," I say, but the words feel like a lie. "We don't even know our neighbors and..." I clear my throat and start again. "What would I even be homesick for? Boston? Atlanta? France or Luxembourg? This isn't about clicking my heels three times to get back to some childhood home. I don't think the homesickness of a perpetual wanderer can ever be quenched."

"Well," Keith considers. "I'd have to find a new job."

"You'd do that?" I shift in my seat. It feels as though he's called my bluff. I cannot figure out why his willingness to move bothers me. Perhaps it's because I could never live near all of my family at the same time. We're too spread out. But—no, that's not it. Not entirely.

"If you're going to go to all that trouble," I say, changing tactics, "let's go somewhere exotic."

I walk over to the map and begin plucking names at random: a castle on the Italian Riviera, where Ava can play among grapevines; a tree house in Brazil so we can live in the clouds; a fale in Samoa where we can drink chocolate all day long.

"Thanks to the blog, we know we can eat well wherever we go," I laugh, but the sound is hollow.

Keith falters. He wouldn't know how to begin finding a job in Italy, he says, his reaction checked by equal parts realism and inexperience. He's never lived anywhere but Oklahoma. His first time in the ocean or out of the country was with me, in his late 30s, when we vacationed in Mexico.

I press forward, suggesting England, or maybe Ireland. "You'll know the language there," I say, "even if the accent needs translating."

"What's really going on here, Sash?" he asks.

"Maybe I'm just in a slump," I say, embarrassed to be craving something more when I literally have the world at my stove top.

But the truth is I'm exhausted. The end of the blog is still two forever years away. The list of recent and upcoming countries blurs and blends: When it comes to Guinea, Guinea-Bissau, and Guyana, I struggle to keep straight which of the "Guineas" and "Guyana" are in Africa and which is in South America.

In a few weeks I'll be combining Haiti and Honduras, just to get them done before Mom's next visit. It makes no sense from a culinary point of view.

Keith jumps up. "Hold that thought—I forgot to take my blood pressure medication."

Though nothing changes in the room, I get a whiff of something sterile—the hospital. I realize with horror that the scent has been trailing me since Keith's episode two months earlier.

I take a deep breath and slowly release it while glancing around the living room. A photo of Michael hugging me on the beach catches my eye. I must be two or three—he's maybe five years old. He's run behind me, leaped and wrapped his arms around my middle. Mine have flown up from the force. I'm laughing.

The scent grows stronger.

Just for a moment, I feel the police officer's shoulder as he lifts me from my castle bed to the foster house. And then I smell the courts: ink, paper, marble. I taste the pound-cake goodbye, caught up with the smash of strawberry against sweet whipped cream. I can almost hear Mom's footsteps crunching through the snow on her way to work on Michael's card after he died. I never want to be that alone. Even cooking the world cannot compete with this hard reality.

When Keith sits back down, I turn to face him completely.

"I–I just don't want you to get sick again and . . ." I bite my lip. "And ruin our happy ending." I don't look him in the eyes when I say the words. Instead, I rest my head on his chest.

"Oh, Sash." He doesn't say anything for a minute. Then he picks me off his shoulder and looks into my eyes. He opens his mouth to speak, but before he does, I blurt out, "Can't you just . . . live forever?"

He hugs me tight, and we rock slowly. "I'll do my best."

───

I put all my energy into renovating our faux Tuscan kitchen. We pay a friend to paint the dark wood cabinets antique white, lightening the windowless room. I donate three boxes of kitchen gadgets, and when the kitchen sparkles, I ask Keith to drill through the faux finish so we can hang the Afghan stirring pot on the wall.

I use it more than any other pot, and it's time it had a place of its own.

───

From our front stoop we can see our neighbors on their lawn. Though the three roommates have lived next to us for about a year, we've never spoken. They are in their mid-20s with beards of varying lengths. There's the short George Michael, the fuzzy Bob Ross, and the fiery Vincent van Gogh. Today, they've brought their dining chairs and table onto the front lawn. They're playing poker.

When they spot me, they wave with openmouthed grins. Instead of my typical cursory nod, I say "Hello!" It's just one word, but it feels like a leap.

When Bob Ross hears I'm about to cook food from Haiti, he says he was just there. I shake my head: "Of course you were!"

"Nice setup," Keith says of their lawn turned dining room.

"We're on a mission to bring back the front lawn," van Gogh laughs.

"Fences are the worst invention to plague Western society," George Michael chimes in.

For the next 20 minutes, we stand in the Beards' outdoor dining room, debating the finer points of our Haitian menu. Passersby eye us curiously.

At home, Ava asks, "Who that, Mama?"

I tell her, "They're our neighbors. A neighbor is someone you live next to."

Keith qualifies, "A neighbor is someone you can count on, should you ever need anything, like a cup of flour."

At his words, I feel my cheeks redden. When Keith asks me what's wrong, I just shake my head and go into the kitchen. As I stand there, staring absently at the stirring pot on the wall, I remember Greg's words all those years ago: No one could create peace for me. Yes, I did the tough work to heal on my own. But in the process, I'd missed the finer point.

An insular life is just another wall. The realization rushes over me: There can be no peace without community. Real community

—people to count on, and who could count on me. Beyond Keith. Beyond Ava.

I cannot help but think back to the conversation I had with my mom when the Bulgarian came to my door—the dream of a perfect, enormous global table. I wonder what it would be like to have the whole world as a neighbor.

CHAPTER 27

———

Burnt Chicken

Your problem is you're out here by yourself," Mom says the next time she visits. It's June. We haven't seen each other since I cooked Cambodia almost a year ago. This time she's planned her visit to coincide with Hungary. "You don't make time to visit anyone. You need to connect with your roots."

She's right. There's only so much I can cook the world and study other people's family traditions without feeling pulled toward my own past: So many of the recipes have reminded me of the early years. I find I want to teach Ava about what makes *her* heritage unique. She's almost two now, with long brown hair, almost as dark as mine, Keith's round face, and Mom's almond eyes.

She still hasn't tried a cannoli from the North End or one of Mom's famous Hungarian crepes. I haven't been up north in two years, since before I started the blog. The omission feels a little like avoidance.

"I just don't have that kind of time, Mom," I say, tossing my hands up in the air. "I don't know what the answer is."

"What are you cooking for Hungary?"

I tell her I want to make her recipe for chicken paprika, crepes, and chilled cherry soup.

Mom tells me, "I went vayghan earlier this year."

"You went what?"

"Vayghan."

"You mean vegan?"

"Yeah. Vayghan. Vegan. Whatever."

She insists I make the chicken as planned. "Don't mind me; vegan or not, that's your heritage."

From the edge of the kitchen, she coaches me: "Make sure you *burn* the chicken. I'm serious, Sash; it's not done until it's burned. Don't add the cream until the skin is *black*."

On tiptoe, she peers over my shoulder as I pour on the cream.

"You didn't burn it! What's wrong with you?" she gasps.

"I-I didn't want to wreck the chicken. I got it nice and golden brown."

"The burn is where the flay-vah is."

At the table, Mom slurps the cherry soup until her bowl is empty, and then takes a nibble of the chicken. Ava and I follow suit. Mom was right: The lightly browned chicken skin turned flabby in the cream sauce—no character.

Mom doesn't say a word, instead turning her attention to the crepes. She holds one up to the light, admiring the lump-free surface. "You let this rest overnight, didn't you?"

I nod.

"It's perfect," she says, and shows it to Ava. "See? No burn spots."

"Guess your people know when to burn their food and when to hold back," Keith remarks.

Mom laughs.

"Apparently, it's an art," I respond.

After dinner Mom pulls out her suitcase and removes a folder full of family photos, all photocopies. She says she's trying to create balance: There's a conflict in our heritage. Italians, like her mother's people, talk about everything—loud and proud, probably to a fault. Hungarians, like her father's, "are all buttoned up."

She points to the pile of black-and-white photos on the table. I glimpse an old man standing over a dead deer with his rifle, a lumpy woman with a basket of laundry on her hip, and a few too blurry to make out.

"I have no idea who they are," Mom says. "Whenever I asked grandpa about them, he'd say, 'What do you want to know about that for?' So I stopped asking."

"So they might not even be our family?"

She blinks, considering. "Right, but that's no reason to get rid of the photos. They *might* be family. You don't get rid of family."

"Why don't you feel that way about Phoenix, Mom? She's my sister."

"Because it's not the same!" she yells, and then softens. "Sash, we're *all* brothers and sisters when it comes down to it. So. What?" She spits out the last words, agitated, and begins to stack the photos into a neat pile again. "You're going to wear yourself out if you keep trying to make room for everyone. Not every family fits the same mold. I know you're trying to figure out where you belong, but it's about quality, not quantity. Now Patricia and Pierre, they cared about you."

I nod, as I always do. She's said the words a hundred times before, but now it occurs to me that there's something beyond the words. She *needs* to believe they cared, because if they didn't, it would be too much to bear.

"They did, Mom. They loved me and Michael." I'd never been able to say those words before. But I know it was true—and it was a gift she needed to hear.

"It's about time you realized that," she chides, but her face relaxes in relief. She runs to her room and returns a moment later with a hatbox. "Remember the dolls you played with as a little girl?"

"The ones we found on the curb, that you helped me sew clothes for?"

She slides the hatbox across the table. "I brought them for Ava to play with."

The dolls are tucked in a bed of tiny clothes, a rainbow from the fifties and sixties. They have faux fur collars and trim cocktail dresses; a nurse hat looks more like wings. I trace my fingers along the clothes, recalling the moment Mom pulled up to the curb where the box of dolls had been abandoned outside a mansion. I remember her triumphant whoop and how, at the sound, I'd shrunk into my seat to avoid being seen by the "rich people."

"You kept them all this time?"

She nods. "I washed and ironed the clothes—put some tissue in the sleeves and bodices. But the dolls are still wearing the last outfit you put on them when you were ten."

I stare at the one I named Tammy. For the last 25 years, she'd been wrapped in a cranberry-and-white peasant skirt I'd fashioned from an old lace doily at Mom's kitchen table. Her top was a knotted handkerchief, over which she wore a wedding veil backward as an apron.

"Pretty," Ava says, and dances the doll across the table, the plastic feet clacking on the wood.

As I watch Ava play with this old treasure, I realize that every time Mom has surprised me with something from the past, she was telling me, in her own way, that she loved me.

Perhaps it's time for me to tell Mom that I understand—and that I love her, too.

🍴 Chicken Paprika

....

Nestled in its pale, freckled sauce, chicken paprika is not much to look at (even when browned properly). A bit of parsley or pureeing the onions into the sauce helps, but I am always too hungry to bother. Still, the sauce marries well to buttered noodles in true Hungarian comfort. Leftovers are excellent rolled up in Overnight Crepes (page 21), then coated with the sauce, covered, and reheated in a warm oven.

2 pounds bone-in chicken legs and thighs, skin on
1 or 2 glugs of vegetable oil
1 large onion
2 tablespoons paprika (try half-sharp for kick)
1 cup chicken broth
Salt

Finishing touches:
1½ cups sour cream

In a large skillet over high heat, brown the chicken in oil, 5 to 10 minutes a side. Do not crowd, working in batches as necessary. Set the chicken on a plate, cover, and set aside. Pour off all but a tablespoon of the fat. Peel, chop, and cook the onions in this tablespoon of fat until completely soft and golden. Sprinkle on the paprika and cook a minute, until fragrant. Pour in the chicken stock, and return the chicken to the pan. Season with salt.

Let simmer, covered, for about 45 minutes, or until the chicken is falling off the bone. While it's cooking, imagine lying in a field of Hungarian poppies as clouds dance across the sky.

When 45 minutes are up, turn off the burner and remove the chicken to a serving platter or bowl. Whisk the sour cream into the cooking liquid to make a pale pink sauce. Check the seasonings, and add more salt if necessary. Pour the sauce over the chicken. Serve over buttered noodles.

Enough for 4

My brother Tim comes to visit for Ava's second birthday. Between his new job in Florida and the breakneck pace of the blog, we haven't seen each other in almost two years. The week coincides with cooking India.

I whip together three easy recipes: homemade chai, seasoned with cinnamon sticks, peppercorns, and coriander; *saag paneer,* a spinach curry served with homemade cheese; and *kulfi* pops, an ice cream of sorts flavored with pistachios and cardamom. My selections are a one-dimensional interpretation of India, but I have a second birthday party to plan, and these seem a fun way to integrate the two projects.

My readers are upset, and have no hesitations about telling me so. They think I cheated India. They tell me I should have made something more complex, something that more finely represents the great cuisine of this enormous country. Brian, who's been reading since Afghanistan, asks if I've considered recipes from the south, which are relatively unknown in the United States. "There is Chettinad-style food from Tamil Nadu, Kerala cuisine, which is itself incredibly diverse, and the fabled biryanis of Hyderabad," he writes.

He's not alone. My readers are well traveled and knowledgeable. Some, like Laura Kelley of *The Silk Road Gourmet,* have devoted their work to understanding the food of a specific region. Their intimate knowledge of the cuisine adds richness to the blog and reminds me that I really am just a mom—curious, yes, but no expert.

But no amount of curiosity matters if I'm too busy to enjoy my family. I proceed as planned.

On cooking day, Ava takes great delight in flipping on the blender, whipping the kulfi into a pale green froth that displays the pistachios and whipped cream inside. There's also condensed milk, evaporated milk, and two slices of bread (this last, I'm told, for chew).

The mixture glugs when divided between two bowls. To the first, Ava adds a few pinches of cardamom, and to the second, several dew drops of rose water and enough red food coloring to make it flush. Uncle Tim pours the kulfi into plastic shot glasses from the party supply store. A press of plastic wrap helps keep inserted Popsicle sticks upright. Tim makes a show of having giggly Ava "help" carry the tray to the freezer.

Then we make masala chai. It is a simple concoction: spices and tea simmered together, then strained. Even as I stir the pot, the spices unfurl, their warm bouquet hanging heavy in the kitchen. Eventually this garden of ginger, cardamom, cinnamon, and fennel overruns the house.

Later, at Ava's birthday party, I smile to see her and her friends run around with the miniature pops and tumblers of iced chai, stirred together with long cinnamon sticks. Even in the heat of midsummer, India keeps us cool.

The morning Tim leaves, we have breakfast at an outdoor café. I tell him what my readers are saying, and apologize for making such simple recipes. I explain that I'm trying to celebrate my daughter, give her a normal birthday party, and have time to smile along the way, have time to visit with him.

"Don't give it a second thought! I loved it. Anyway, you have to prioritize family. It can't always be go, go, go." He pauses. "You know,

I was supposed to visit you and Michael three weeks before he died. I should have been there when he was in the hospital. I didn't know it was going to be the end. Stupid."

He shakes his head, as though willing the image away. "Work never matters as much as family. I learned that the hard way."

"You could have never known. None of us knew," I said. "I've spent most of my adult life trying *not* to run away from the past. We've all coped the best we could in a no-win situation."

"But look at you now! You've got a great kid and husband . . ."

"But you want to hear the ugly truth?" I lower my voice. "Sometimes I wonder if I deserve them. Sometimes it doesn't feel real—like I could blink and it could all just disappear."

Neither of us speaks.

Finally, Tim clears his throat. "We can't let the past get in the way so much." He suggests we plan our next visit right then.

As we talk, we realize that we've never given Mom a surprise party, that popular ritual that's so common in big, warm families who celebrate with supermarket cake, hot dogs, and not enough salad. Her birthday is coming up in February, six months away.

We decide to throw Mom a surprise party at Tim's home in Florida. He will send her tickets for a Christmas present, inviting her to visit him that February for her birthday. As far as she knows, she's just coming to see Tim for a quiet, sun-drenched weekend.

🍴 Masala Chai

. . . .

With coffee shops on every corner, I sometimes forget how easy it is to make my own spiced tea. Although I greatly dislike the cloying sweetness of premixes, this recipe can be adjusted to personal tastes. In India, there are regional variations, but one thing is certain: "Chai" means "tea," making the expression "chai tea" redundant. "Masala Chai," which means "spiced tea," is the proper nomenclature. I took Mark Bittman's advice in The Best Recipes in the World *and kept this spice blend simple (this way the drink stays in regular rotation); for a change of pace, try adding nutmeg, clove, or star anise to the pot.*

6 cups prepared black tea, tea leaves removed

Spice blend:
10 cardamom pods, lightly cracked
1 teaspoon fennel seeds
10 black peppercorns
1 or 2 cinnamon sticks
1 large knuckle unpeeled fresh ginger, sliced in 3 or 4 coins

Finishing touches:
Up to ¼ cup sugar
Up to 1 cup milk

Tumble the prepared black tea and spices into a medium pot. Bring to a bubble, cover, and cook 10 to 15 minutes, or to desired strength. Remove from heat. Stream in some sugar and milk (my preference is a touch of sugar and *all* the milk). Strain. The spices have done their work—lay them to rest in the garden. Serve steaming hot in the winter or ice cold in the summer.

Makes a good 1½ quarts

In the months leading up to the trip, I spend days mulling what kind of gift to give Mom. One day I dig up an old wooden picture-frame box and decide to fill it with strips of paper—one for every year of her life—each listing a different reason why I love her—except that there'd have to be dozens upon dozens. It's a lot of love notes to think of on my own.

I decide that dividing the project up by four would be a lot easier. With Connor, Tim, and Grace, we'd each have just 17 and a half reasons to contribute.

Tim loves the idea and asks when "it's due." Connor, my brother of few words, asks how long the notes have to be, and says he'll enlist his kids' help. Grace has a harder time. Raised without a mother at her side in a house full of boys, she still feels uneasy about her relationship with Mom. But after a sincere heart-to-heart, she takes the most artistic approach of all, using photos and doodles to enhance her sentiments. We decide to put a picture of the four of us in the frame to commemorate the celebration.

"Mom! You'll never believe this." I squeal into the phone a few months later. I've finished all the I, J, and K countries—and now we're well into the L's. "I just got off the phone with Rick Steves, host of his own show on NPR. He interviewed me about my stove top travel concept—which he *loved*. They're going to air our conversation all over the country in January!"

Mom *oohs* and *aahs*, and I smile, grateful for the distraction. We're only a couple of months from her surprise party; it's getting harder to keep my mouth shut.

"He got really excited about the Guinness Chocolate Cake With Baileys Buttercream."

The cake had gone viral that summer. It isn't fussy, or prim. But the Irish stout and the Baileys give it a certain swagger, helped by the striking contrast between the dark chocolate crumb and pure white frosting. There's festivity to each bite, and although many might have reserved the cake for Saint Patrick's Day, I'd made it for Keith's birthday. Once our plates were clean, we almost felt like we'd had a swashbuckling time on the Emerald Isle.

"Sounds like the perfect celebration," Mom says.

"Who doesn't love a good party?" I ask, bursting to share our secret. Perhaps in anticipation of her surprise, I include *Global Table* desserts at all our family celebrations over the next months. When Keith's son Ryan starts his own budding family, we celebrate the new baby boy with Latvian "birthday cake," bread studded with plump raisins, bitter orange peel, and delicate saffron threads.

❙❙ Dark Chocolate Guinness Cake With Baileys Buttercream

Jet-black, ultra-moist cake topped with pure white frosting makes this Irish confection resemble a real pint of Guinness. Although beer and cake might sound like a bad night at a frat party, the Guinness actually works to deepen the chocolate flavor, much like espresso—even as the alcohol cooks off. It's a very easy batter, with no egg separating or careful folding. Sometimes an easy cake is just the thing.

For the cake:
12 tablespoons (1½ sticks) butter, plus more for cake pans
1 cup Guinness Extra Stout
1 tablespoon vanilla extract
¾ cup unsweetened cocoa
1½ cups sugar
1¼ cups all-purpose flour

1 teaspoon baking soda
2 large eggs

For the buttercream:
¾ pound (3 sticks) unsalted butter, softened
1 pound powdered sugar, sifted
2 to 4 tablespoons Baileys Irish Cream

For the cake:
Preheat the oven to 350°F. In a small saucepan, heat the butter until just melted, then whisk together with Guinness, vanilla extract, and cocoa. While the Guinness mixture is cooling, grease and line the bottoms of two 8-inch cake pans with rounds of parchment paper. Whisk together the sugar, flour, and baking soda in a large bowl. Pour the Guinness mixture onto the dry ingredients, and then whisk in the 2 eggs. When the batter is shiny and smooth, pour it into the two prepared cake pans. Lick the whisk when no one is looking. Bake for 30 to 35 minutes, or until a skewer comes out clean. Cool completely.

For the buttercream:
In a stand mixer, whip the softened butter until fluffy. Add the powdered sugar on low speed, then increase to medium-high, and drizzle in just enough Baileys to get the buttercream loose and fluffy. The key to making whiter frosting is to whip it 5 to 10 minutes, scraping occasionally.

To assemble the cake:
Run a knife around the edge of the cake pan to loosen and turn out cakes. Level the layers with a serrated knife, if needed. Spread about a third of the buttercream on the bottom cake layer. Top with the second layer. Wiggle them around until they line up just right.

Thinly spread another third of the frosting mixture over the top and sides of the cake to make a crumb coat. This will seal in the crumbs so chocolate flecks don't ruin the white frosting. Refrigerate to set—about 30 minutes or overnight if desired.

Once the crumb coat is firm to the touch, add the final third of the frosting to the cake—top first, then sides. Spread it around evenly. Slice and serve with an extra cold pint of Guinness.

Enough for 8 to 10

When the NPR interview airs, thousands of visitors flock to the website, crashing my server many times over. Some read to remember travels past; others come to dream about trips they'll never take.

Mom calls to check in.

"It's incredible," I say, "People from everywhere are finding the site."

"Oh, yeah?" Mom replies dryly.

"Aren't you the least bit excited? Where's the enthusiasm you had the other day?"

"I just don't want you to get hung up on all that . . . attention."

"It has nothing to do with that, Mom. People from tiny countries finding the site—Nauru, Tuvalu, the Ivory Coast—are just happy to have their recipes brought to light. And there's more!" I exclaim. "Right here in Tulsa, a woman who runs a program where kids garden and cook their harvests has asked me to speak."

Josie's Global Gardens classroom is literally a garden: 2-by-6s hammered together for raised beds, with an oven fashioned from straw and mud that cranks out perfect, brown-bottomed pizzas. I come prepared to teach the children about food in Japan. But the dozen eighth graders guide me under the wind-battered pergola and instruct me to take off my shoes because, as they proudly share, Japanese people don't wear shoes in the house.

"And which direction should our guest sit?" Josie prompts them from behind a sweep of short, blond hair.

"Facing the entrance," a bright-eyed girl tells me.

I am impressed with their preparedness, and on a whim ask them about their favorite foods from around the world. I expect the list of tacos, spaghetti, and pizza; what I don't expect is the sideswipe of raw emotion. One little boy's parents work two jobs, and he eats alone a lot. Another child tells me she used to eat more Mexican food when her grandmother was alive, but her mom doesn't have time to make Grandma's food anymore. But when *she* grows up, she plans to revive the family recipes.

They over-share with wide eyes, hoping I'll hear them. I do, for the better part of an hour. After the session, Josie and I talk while our daughters play together. I ask her about the children's stories, and her eyes sadden as she nods. "They just need someone to hear them. Thank you for listening."

An unexpected friendship forms.

In February, all of us—Keith, Ava, and I, plus Connor, Grace, and her kids—arrive at Tim's squat palm-shaded bungalow in Florida the day before Mom is due in. It's the start of the third year of the blog and our first reunion since it started. Come to think of it, it's the first time we siblings have been together, under one roof, for a week straight since I was ten—minus Michael, of course.

To keep busy until Mom's arrival, I buy the groceries for our next Global Table Adventure, this time from the Maldives, an island nation off the coast of India. I'm making curry-crusted fish and the island's popular honey, ginger, lime drink called *lomi lomi*. The fishmonger helps me select a giant red snapper. The eyes shine like glass marbles, so fresh I wonder if they might blink when I look away.

According to the recipe, the fish is supposed to be grilled, preferably on the beach. But I've always had terrible luck grilling fish; the sticky skin fuses to the grate, inevitably tearing the flesh into a jumble of unrecognizable flakes.

That night I find the Twitter handle of the Four Seasons in the Maldives and send them a request for advice about grilling the fish, adding that if they have a recipe for the *lomi lomi*, I'd be forever grateful.

Almost immediately I get a reply. The tweet reads: "250 g chopped ginger blend with 1 litre water, strain. Add 20 ml ginger juice, 30 ml lime & 60 ml honey, lots of ice, to taste." They send a second tweet: For the fish, I just need to preheat the grill on high for a long, long time and obsessively rub the grate with oil until it gleams.

The next day, Tim leaves to pick up Mom. When he escorts her into the house, we all pop out from behind the wall in the sunroom. She leaps back, squealing with fear, then delight, clasping her hand to her chest and laughing.

She hugs us all and keeps saying, over and over again, with a grin a mile wide, "Oh wow, you're all here, you're all here!" and a while later, "I never had a surprise like this before! *Never.*"

A lump forms in my throat as I watch her. I ask Tim if he thinks she ever felt this loved.

"Just wait until she gets all those notes after dinner," he grins, ear to ear.

That afternoon I ask the family to wait for me while I cook and photograph the recipes from the Maldives. No one complains, but while I chop the onion and grind it together with the curry leaves for the fish paste, I notice the heat for the first time. It must be 90 degrees in the shade. Everyone looks wilted. I regret keeping them from the beach just so I didn't have to cook alone.

I work as quickly as I can, passing out the lomi lomi drink while I finish up. Next, I ask Tim to preheat the grill, deciding, after all, to go for the true, authentic cooking method. I want to feel the freedom and taste the salt air on the crust. But we forget to oil the grates, and the fish fuses to the metal, shredding as I struggle to pry it loose. I rush to the store to pick up a second $45 snapper, unwilling to let the mangled fish serve as the picture-perfect specimen.

I notice that the family is becoming askance at my obsessive behavior, but I cannot seem to stop myself. I want everything to be exactly right.

I roast the second fish in the oven. In my fourth hour of cooking, it comes out perfectly browned, with no tears. When I pop the snapper, glass eyes and all, onto the table, there's a noticeable quiet. Everyone's stomach seems to be shifting in the fish's unblinking, charred gaze.

I talk about the culture in the Maldives, where no bits go uneaten and the eyes are prized by the most ardent of diners. (Not that I plan on eating them *myself*). After a fair amount of throat clearing and mock eyeball eating, everyone digs in. Eventually we work our way through the perfect fish. Still hungry, we start in on the mangled one and eat it all, too.

After we share a vegan birthday cake—from Whole Foods, not the Maldives—we present Mom with the box. I watch her face as she opens the lid. When she realizes what the notes are, she shuts the box with a click: "I'll enjoy reading these later. Thank you."

We all urge her on, telling her to read them now, but she shakes her head, puts the box back in the gift bag, and offers everyone a second slice of cake.

But the surprises aren't over. Tim tells us to leave the dirty dishes: We're taking a sunset trip to the beach to commemorate Michael's passing. It's the 20th anniversary of his death. I am dumbfounded that so much time has passed. Tim brought red balloons. We release just one into the blue—for Michael.

As I watch the balloon float away, I wonder what Michael would think of the last 20 years—if he would feel I've spent them well. I wonder what notes he might have put in the box. Quicker than expected, the balloon becomes little more than a dot, then a pinprick, until the vivid red disappears into the transparent ether.

I wish we could be together like this more often. But at the end of the day, we all have to go home to our separate lives and responsibilities.

That night, Keith and I whisper while Ava sleeps.

"Did you see your mom reading the notes?"

"Wait—what? She actually read them?"

"Yeah, when you all were doing the dishes, she sat off by herself and went through every one of them. After a while she even read a few out loud. She *loved* them."

"Of course she has to do it when I'm not watching," I sigh, not attempting to hide my irritation. "I don't get why she always has to hide like that."

"Maybe she didn't want to have all eyes on her while she read through the notes. Receiving all that . . . love . . . it's got to be pretty overwhelming, don't you think?"

He studies me a moment, then links his pinkie around mine. "You seem really tense, Sash. Are you OK?"

"What do you mean?"

"All day you tried to control everything. I think you're making everyone nervous."

I roll over without responding. He thinks I'm pouting, that I'm mad at him, but what I'm really thinking is: *I know. That's exactly what I'm doing. And I don't know how to stop.*

🍴 Fire-Roasted Fish | Fihunu Mas

....

Spice-encrusted whole fish is often cooked beachside in the Maldives, over live flame. The deep brown crust can be quite the scorcher depending how many chilies are used. The spice paste I offer draws from the best local recipes, using garlic, cumin, curry leaves (available in Indian grocers), black peppercorns, and hot chili peppers (I use habaneros, instead of more traditional dried red chilies). Although Maldivians might grind the paste by hand, I make quick work of it with a food processor.

Any large, meaty fish holds up well to this spice paste. Locals like a bright-eyed, whole red snapper, grouper, or tuna. When cooked with the skin on, bones in, the end result is impossibly moist. Whatever the choice, I save time by having the fishmonger prep the fish for cooking. They can remove the scales, guts, and gills.

The traditional way to cook a whole fish is to thread a rod through it and grill over an open fire. For home cooks, I suggest roasting the fish in an oven. For those who prefer to grill: As I learned the hard way, the skin can easily stick. To avoid this, preheat the grill on high and carefully rub the grill grates five times with a folded paper towel dipped in vegetable oil. Then pop on the fish, shut the lid, and reduce the temperature to medium, flipping only once.

Makes enough spice paste to cover one large whole fish, or several small. Allow one pound a person. Tip: If no whole fish are available, try the paste on a side of salmon. Though not traditional, the flavor is divine.

A large, whole fish like snapper, grouper, or tuna, ready to cook—about 5 pounds—or a couple small whole fish (1½ to 2 pounds each), ready to cook

Spice paste (makes about ⅔ cup):
Half a medium onion, quartered

4 cloves garlic

5 curry leaves

2 teaspoons black peppercorns, lightly cracked

2 teaspoons ground cumin

2 teaspoons salt

2 teaspoons chili powder (or to taste)

Habanero pepper (to taste)

A touch of vegetable oil

Finishing touches:
1 lime, sliced in half-moons

Add the onion, garlic, cumin, curry leaves, black peppercorns, and salt to the food processor. Spoon in the chili powder and hunks of habanero to taste (for a less incendiary rub, omit the habanero). Puree into a thick paste, scraping the sides once or twice with a spatula.

To prepare the fish, rinse and dry it. Cut diagonal slits along both sides of the body—about every 2 inches—to ensure even cooking. Wearing gloves to protect the hands from the spice, spread the paste all over, being sure to rub it into the crevices and belly cavity. Let rest this way for a good half hour.

Preheat the oven to 375°F.

Roast the whole fish on a lightly oiled rack over a foil-lined baking sheet until the crust is deeply browned, the flesh flakes easily, and a food thermometer placed into the thickest part of the fish reaches 135° to 140°F.

Cooking times will depend on the size and type of fish used; the general guideline for a whole fish is 8 to 12 minutes per inch thickness of fish (take measurements from the girthy middle). The weight and number of fish will also impact things: A 5-pound snapper might take 45 to 55 minutes, whereas two 1½-pound fish might take 35 to 40 minutes.

When in doubt, insert a knife and gently try to flake the flesh at its thickest section, down near the bone.

Finishing touches: Serve the whole fish at the dinner table. Lift the upper fillet off of the bone by cutting along the backbone and sides, then slide a spatula between the fillet and the rib cage to lift the top fillet off. For the bottom fillet, do not flip the fish; simply lift off the backbone from the tail end to reveal the fillet below. Be mindful of any bones, but enjoy the spicy skin. Serve with rice and a squeeze of lime.

CHAPTER 28

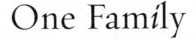

One Family

O NCE BACK IN TULSA, I miss my family more than ever. But in the summer I find unexpected solace in Mongolia. It is impossible to feel sorry for myself after reading about Mongolian nomads.

Between the constant moving (about five times a year with the changing seasons) and the Gobi's brutal winters (especially in the mountainous north and on the dry, grassy steppes, where temperatures can plummet to minus 40°F), Mongolians have to be tough. Even their homes—tents made of wood and felt called *gers* or yurts—are portable. Since little can grow in their country's harsh conditions, they rely on meat—30 percent of the population breeds livestock. With a lifestyle constantly on the go, the food has to fit in when it can.

But the nomads are never truly *homeless. Never alone.* For starters, the hospitality is extensive; anyone who turns up at a nomad's tent will be invited for a meal and even an overnight stay. When something happens, good or bad, other nomads show up to help. They come out of nowhere, from miles away, from over bleak hills through the vast emptiness. And they chip in however they can. Although it can seem like each family unit is isolated in nothing but a giant expanse of blue sky and crusty grass, nothing could be further than the truth. These are *real* neighbors. Friends. Family.

I realize with astonishment that there is a way to have a family, even from afar. But it involves reaching out continually, and communicating. In the meanwhile, even our neighbors have a role to play.

We need each other, near and far.

That's when the packages from Mom start arriving. Each one contains several three-inch binders—17 total, with thousands upon thousands of pages comprising every single post and reader comment of my blog since day one.

"Mom!" I exclaim when I call her. "What is all this?!"

"I thought you should have a backup of the website. You've worked so hard."

I laugh. "Oh, Mom, Keith *does* back it up—on two different . . ." I stop myself before I get too technical. I explain that Keith knows what he's doing. In fact, he'd recently been offered a double promotion to senior technical engineer responsible for 911 design and structure on a national scale for AT&T.

"Don't worry, Mom—he can handle this blog. It's safe."

"What if the Internet disappears someday, Sash? You can't take any chances."

Ava helps me line up the binders that span half the office wall. I tell her what they contain and she repeats the words, stringing them together for the first time: "Gwobal Twable Abenture."

Mom isn't the only one waxing nostalgic.

The international meals now pepper our whole week. I realize that we've already tried more than 500 recipes: We've made our own sushi, preserved peppers from our garden, and learned to make chicken 32 ways, with versions from every continent.

On any given day, we might eat a Greek salad with green bean soup from Luxembourg and naan from Afghanistan. Dessert just as well might be Ireland's famed Dark Chocolate Guinness Cake With Baileys Buttercream, as a tropical fruit salad inspired by Rwanda, heavy with banana and avocado. Even Grace cooks the food from her New Jersey home, every so often sharing photos of her renditions with me. It makes me feel a little closer to her somehow, almost as though we're sharing a kitchen.

That fall, winter won't come. Summer lingers in the air, hot and humid, well into October. There's only about a year left to the adventure; Ava is three and a half. As I'm deciding whether or not I should bother putting a pumpkin on our hot stoop for fear it'll rot in the sun, I get a Facebook message from Toni.

I haven't heard from her in a couple of years. She says she wants to visit in November. "Yes," I type, without hesitation, "Please come."

The week we cook Samoa, Toni arrives from Boston with her laugh still full of ripples. I am transported to another era, even though we're both grown women; she now uses her neuroscience degree to research alternative medicine. She brings small gifts: a Wonder Woman apron for me, a Superman mug for Keith, and Superman pajamas for Ava.

I don't have gifts, I tell Toni, but I do have Samoa. I warn her she might not like the food; it's going to be a big pot of spinach and canned meat cooked in coconut milk. I wince as I describe it, but she nods enthusiastically.

I rinse the spinach and add it to the stirring pot, along with the meat and coconut milk. As the mixture simmers down into a swampy stew, I explain that I got the recipe idea from my mom, who once stayed in Samoa when she was pregnant with me.

"I didn't know that," Toni says. I realize how little she knows about my childhood—my *first* childhood.

"I don't know why I never asked you about it," she adds.

"We were just kids," I say, shrugging it off. But there's a twinge of pain in my eyes I can only hide by looking away.

For dessert, we head to the kitchen to make *koko Samoa*—Samoan rice pudding. First, I steam the rice. In another pot, I plunk a few chocolate squares into coconut milk. As the two slump together, I zest in a heavy orange. The citrus oil mists my hand and glistens on the brown surface before my spoon folds it deeper into the pot. I draw a breath. Bitter zest might not sweeten the mix, but it does deliver a gust from the rambling orchard in which it once grew.

Toni helps me tip the tender rice into the chocolate and coconut milk. I whip with tight circles. But something is wrong. The mixture doesn't thicken.

Toni leans over the mixture and suggests cooking the rice *with* the coconut milk. She speaks with the confidence of experience; rice pudding is one of her favorite desserts. She adds that when the dry rice plumps with liquid, the outer starches slough off like the scarf and hat of a hot traveler. These swirl about and thicken the coconut milk.

But I don't have any more coconut milk to try the recipe a second time.

"I don't mind," she says as she ladles herself a bowl of the too-thin pudding. It's chocolate, after all.

While we spoon the thin dessert, I ask Toni about her parents. She smooths her napkin, "Good. They're . . . good."

"I stopped reaching out after my wedding. I thought it best to honor their wishes. But I can start again, if you think they . . ."

She nods, and then slowly shakes her head. "I would just leave it alone."

She sighs. "They've never really talked about your stay with us. I don't think they know how. Maybe that comes from their childhoods; both of them lost a relative in sudden, tragic deaths—Papa's brother, Mama's mother."

For the first time, I tell her about how Patricia blamed me for Michael's death. Her face falls.

"Oh, Sasha..." She swallows hard, looking down. "That might be my doing. I told them his death was their fault. I was so angry—at them, at myself, at God. I didn't know how to deal with the feelings. I didn't think my outburst would affect you. I'm sorry." She brings her tear-filled eyes back to mine. "Communication isn't our family's strongest suit. It wasn't until just recently that I learned how to name *my* feelings about *anything.*"

"There's nothing to forgive," I say quickly, seeing her flounder. "We were all young and struggling—unsure what to do with our emotions. It's not like I handled it well. And later, I wasn't banging down their door. I just . . . disappeared."

She leans forward, "Maybe they were afraid to make you their daughter. We could all see how much you missed your family."

I think about how exhausting it must have been to pour so much energy into me when I wouldn't even let myself *be* their daughter.

"But I still want to be your sister," she quickly assures. "If I ever get married, I'm going to invite you to the wedding."

I shake my head quickly. "No, I—the sentiment is nice, but I wouldn't want to fill your special day with that kind of stress. You don't need it. And if I'm being honest, I don't think I can take another rejection. I'll always be open if they want to reconnect, but at some point I just have to say *enough is enough.*"

She shakes her head, tears falling down her cheeks. I put my hand on hers.

"This is enough," I tell her, gesturing between us, softening. "This is good."

⁓

There's a Samoan proverb that says, *"O le fogava'a e tasi"*: We are one family. I cannot help but wonder if Mom knew the quote when she sent us to live with the Dumonts.

After Toni leaves, I call Mom and ask her.

"Of course!" she chides, "Those people help each other—they know you can't raise a child alone. Look—if a teen gets in trouble, the whole village has a meeting. Family, friends, neighbors. That's what Margaret Mead's research was all about—that was the main point of my trip. I wanted to see firsthand what I'd studied in psychology class."

Understanding came like a thunderclap. Mom had used the wisdom of the islands to circumnavigate her tough parental choices.

That night, I write a post about Samoa and talk about Mom's time there: how she was a free spirit, dropping everything and exploring in an era when few women would have dreamed of traveling single, pregnant, and with a toddler.

Grace sends me a message, asking how I can always paint such a rosy picture of Mom.

"We were the ones she escaped from when she went halfway around the world," she said. "We were her 'drop everything.' Sometimes you seem to forget about *all* her children when talking about her."

But even as I read her words, I do the math: The divorce was years before Mom's trip to Samoa. For the first time, I wonder if Grace grew up feeling like I took her mother away from her. Horrified, I want to apologize, tell her I was insensitive—not just about the blog post, but for never realizing how hard it must have been for her to see me living with Mom, even for those ten short years.

I read on.

"I don't know if you understand how important you and Michael were to me, Tim, and Connor . . . we loved you and yearned for a relationship with you. We never ever forgot about you . . . ever! We did what we could to stay connected. I constantly missed you both, I sooooo wanted my sister!"

In her words, I see my own heart reflected.

Slowly and carefully, I write: "I couldn't have made it without you—truly! About Mom—I'm so sorry. We have different experiences, different memories, so of course we see her—and Samoa—differently. I might paint a rosy picture—too rosy at times—but when it comes to parents, she's all I have, Grace."

"I only had my dad," she replies, and I can feel her pain through the letters on my glowing screen.

"I never had that choice," I type back. "Sure, sometimes I wonder about Mom's choices. I used to try to make her the parent I needed her to be, but she is who she is. She's all I have.

"It hurts too much to be angry at anyone, let alone my own mother. And she is there for me now. Under it all, I know she operates out of love. I have to love her back, Grace. It's not even a choice any more. It just *is*."

¶| Samoan Chocolate & Orange Coconut Rice Pudding

....

There's nothing like chocolate for breakfast. This Samoan pudding uses koko Samoa (the tower of cocoa nibs and chocolate for which this dessert is named), a few orange leaves from the canopy, and fresh-squeezed coconut milk. For those of us on the mainland, dark chocolate chips and grated orange peel get across the spirit of things. As rich as this is, I find a small bowl does the trick.

1 cup white rice (preferably medium-grain)
4 cups water
15 ounces coconut milk, fresh or canned
Zest of 1 orange (or 2 to 3 orange leaves)
¾ cup (4 ounces) dark chocolate chips
½ cup sugar, or to taste

Finishing touches:
A small pitcher of coconut milk (optional)

Add the rice, water, coconut milk, and orange zest to a medium pot. Bring to a simmer over high heat. Reduce heat, and maintain a gentle bubble (uncovered) for 20 to 25 minutes, or until very thick. Stir occasionally. Remove from heat, and stir in the chocolate and as much sugar as you can stand. At first the chocolate will melt unevenly. Give it a few minutes—it'll smooth out. Serve warm, with a drizzle of extra coconut milk if desired.

Enough for 8 to 10

PART SIX

Feast of Nations

— ▬ —

"A ripened fruit does not cling to the vine."
—Zimbabwean proverb

CHAPTER 29

—●

A True Global Table

S ORRY, IT'S TOO COLD to eat on the front lawn," I tease.

Our neighbors shake their heads regretfully. We've invited the Beards and their girlfriends over for a San Marino potluck. There was much laughter when we realized we'd unwittingly made the same recipe for this tiny country nestled inside the mountains of Italy: swallows' nests, called *nidi di rondine*.

Given the choice, I'd do it again. Swallows' nests are like a cross between white lasagna and cinnamon buns. A drop cloth of pasta dough is smeared with béchamel sauce, layered with ham and Emmentaler cheese, rolled into a log, and sliced. A second dose of béchamel is spooned into a casserole. The coils nestle in this white bed, insulated from the dry oven heat.

A second quick-fix version uses puff pastry and tomato sauce. This is what the Beards made. There's no sweating over béchamel, there's no rolling of homemade pasta dough. But the buttery rosettes are equally decadent.

The Beards have inhaled both casseroles; there's not a drop of tomato or béchamel sauce on the pans.

"That was incredible," van Gogh says.

"The best moment of my life," adds George Michael.

"It seems a shame," I muse, "that not everyone can experience what we experienced over these last years—to taste the world's beauty. All of it."

I'm not certain if I'm feeling nostalgic because it's the week after Toni left, or if it's because there's only one year left to the adventure. The list of remaining countries, less than 50, feels truncated. Though I know it is the last country we'll cook, I find myself looking past Zimbabwe into the gutters of the page, as though I might find a forgotten country there.

"Your mom must be proud," Bob Ross says.

I nod, smiling. "Yeah, I guess she is." I tell them about the Bulgarian man who came by two years earlier, and how Mom and I talked about inviting the whole world to come together around a single table.

"I just can't seem to get the idea out of my head. I'd love to do something like that." I look at Ava. She's trying to use her small knife to cut her pasta in pieces. She's three, speaking in full sentences. I feel both insanely proud, and also at a loss, somehow.

"Kids grow up knowing there's a big world out there. If they could just see all that food, from every country in the world in one place, they'd realize that we're all connected. Since the beginning of this project, and since I arrived here, I've felt that Tulsa has offered up the best of its markets and produce. Now I guess I want to pay it forward."

The Beards nod in pendulous enthusiasm.

"That's a great idea," one of them says. "A spectacle like that could really change people's perspectives. But how are you going to cook all that food in one day?"

Keith suggests a citywide potluck, but the question of food safety makes us all squirm.

I think about the movie *Babette's Feast*, my inspiration for going to culinary school years earlier. The heroine created a French feast, food from just one country, fed to a small group. But the effort took her days. I imagine multiplying her feast by 195. It would be a tremendous amount of food—too much for one person.

That night I ask Mom what she thinks.

"When I don't know what to do about something," she tells me, "I just leave the idea alone for a while. A good idea will feed itself and grow. A bad one will disappear—as it should."

She laughs. "What's that expression? Set it free. If it's meant to be, it'll come to you. Things will start happening. Two years later you're still thinking about it. That's a good sign."

So I keep talking about the idea to anyone who will listen. Where I expect to be met with cynicism, again and again I find excitement and affirmation.

When I bump into Griffin, a social media visionary at the local art museum, things really start moving. "You must do it at Philbrook," he says of the Tulsan landmark. The diverse art collection is curated within a 72-room mansion built in the 1920s. It costs thousands of dollars to rent even a corner of their immaculate grounds for a brief wedding reception. I study his unblinking face. He's serious.

Three months later, he sends me an email. "We're a go. Pick your date."

The museum will donate the space on one condition: I keep the entire event free and open to the public. I couldn't have asked for a better condition, and add that if people want to "pay," they can provide a donation to the Community Food Bank of Eastern Oklahoma.

Now that I have a location, there are no excuses. I write out a list of things that need to be done. Beyond the food, I need a volunteer sign-up form for each of the 195 recipes so I can track who's making what. I need a website to promote it; a brochure; recipe identification cards, so people know what they are eating; decor; people to set up, serve, and clean up.

Keith tells me I simply have to ask. I don't know how, so I just keep talking about the idea wherever I go until the right people hear me.

Over the next month, the Tulsa community throws itself into the idea so forcefully that I nearly get whiplash. One company wants to donate rentals; another wants to donate flowers. One woman offers event-planning services, while another offers to help with PR. My friend Josie helps me find chefs, and after two hours of emails and cold calls, we have about 50 countries claimed.

"Not bad," Josie says.

"I'll be happy if we can get 90," I say.

"That's not even half," she says. "We can do better than that. We're going to get them all."

Josie won't let the idea rest until we fill all the slots. We keep calling, asking. Chefs sign up, taking ten or more countries. The Culinary Institute of Platt College takes 20. Chefs for local nonprofits get involved. We get up to 120, then 140, then 160 countries claimed—85 percent of the world.

A women's recovery group joins the list, making it 175 countries claimed, about 90 percent of the world. We only need to find two more chefs to cook 21 more recipes, and we'll have everything covered.

There's just one problem: Turns out that food from every country in the world requires a tremendous amount of space—200 feet of table to be precise. If we can hold the event outside, Philbrook's immaculate gardens will provide the perfect backdrop, with ample room. But if it rains, we'll have to fit the entire world in one tight hall, precariously poised between a Rodin statue and the temporary exhibit space.

Months of planning go by in a blur of phone calls and meetings. All the while I continue cooking the world. But now it's different. I cook fewer recipes and ratchet back the pace so I can enjoy the process more. In this marathon of food, I find the right stride, savoring the process, not the destination.

We partake in South Sudan, the newest country in the world, with our most devoted reader, Brian. After spending six years traveling across Asia and Africa, he now resides a mile from my house. We tuck into a feast of peanut-laced tomato salad, sorghum crepes called *kisra,* and a spinach peanut butter stew called *combo.* This deep-voiced, bespectacled man has contributed so many comments to the blog, as lengthy as they are historical. I am honored to have him share our table.

Through the summer we mop up Syrian lentils—a bossy blast of garlic and pomegranate syrup—with pita bread. Then there's Swedish princess cake, and meatballs. Each jockeys for attention, the meatballs winning ultimate favor for their simplicity and ability to dance between caramelized crust and lingonberry cream.

When I cook Togo, my old friend Annie from Luxembourg visits with her two children, ages six and eight. Her husband is on tour in Afghanistan. I haven't seen Annie in at least a decade.

"Can you believe we're all grown up with our own families?" I ask her. She nods, and then shakes her head.

"Can I tell you something?" I lean forward.

"Sure!"

"Sometimes I feel like a fraud as a mother—like I'm playing dress up. Do you ever feel that way?"

"All the time."

We laugh, and I relax. Maybe some of this motherly anxiety has nothing to do with my past. Maybe it's simply . . . normal.

The month before the big feast, I cook the Vatican City, the celebrated walled enclave inside Rome, Italy. The Vatican City is 0.17 square mile of gilded glory—0.53 mile by 0.65 mile. To walk across the country is like taking *two laps around a standard jogging track*—that's why there's no country smaller.

I decide to make a gallon of Cousin Alfred's Meat Sauce. There is plenty. I think of the Mongolians.

We pop over to the Beards.

"We were just planning a front lawn brunch!" van Gogh proclaims. "Why don't you bring it over?"

A few minutes later, sun hot on our necks, we sit on the overgrown lawn around two plastic tables strung together and covered with mismatched tablecloths. In the center are two pounds of spaghetti, topped with twice as much sauce. There are no walls. No fences. Finally.

The Beards raise their forks, and we begin, twirling the pasta in our spoons. I glance over at Ava and see noodles hanging off her arm. "But the question is, how do you keep the pasta out of your beards?"

"Magic," they laugh.

Mom arrives the week before the big event to help with Ava. On the radio, the weatherman predicts thunderstorms. The decision no one wants to make must be made: The food will have to be set up indoors.

As the weekend approaches, erratic weather patterns increase and interfere with flights. Tim gets in without incident, but my friend Katya's flight is delayed. Grace's flight, set to land the night before the event, is canceled. She won't arrive in Tulsa until midday on Saturday, just before the buffet opens.

I try to keep track of all the missed connections, but there's too much out of my control. I expand my anxiety to include the people who won't be able to make it: my brother Connor, Toni—even Michael crosses my mind. On Friday night, Mom eyes me as I pour my second glass of port.

"You can't fix it, Sash, any of it. You just have to let this thing happen however it's going to happen."

She pulls out two outfits, one from Pakistan and one from India, and asks me what she should wear.

But I can't decide. I can't even decide what Ava should wear. I fall asleep to the crack of thunder and the sound of rain pummeling the roof.

In the morning the clouds are gone. In their place: blue skies, 65 degrees in the shade. Still, the ground is wet and shows no signs of drying. When I get to Philbrook, the team of volunteers is already helping the 16 chefs and their assistants bring food into the museum. There's a colossal amount of bowls, platters, and chafers, but no one falters. The line of chefs moves in and out smoothly, building a world of food.

The dozens of tables stretch on and on, like chatty postcards, flavor memories smiling back at me from the years of our cooking adventure. Even the tablecloths glow like jewels: ruby for South America, turquoise for Oceania, peridot for Europe, lapis for Africa, amethyst for Asia, fire opal for North America. The floral arrangements correspond with the continents, from the North American wildflower to the red puff of the African protea, Europe's roses, South America's large-stemmed anthurium, Asia's lilies, and Oceania's enormous sea sponges and birds of paradise.

And the food, so much of it: a chafer of kabeli palau, a platter of beef-filled empanadas, a bowl of chilled cherry soup, and then the German Tree Cake beyond a dispenser of rosewater lemonade. With 90 percent of the world on display, each platter with a recipe card that reads like an encyclopedia, there's hardly room for all the globes. It's hard to believe we've cooked and eaten all this food over the last four years—so much of it foreign to us, but so much dug up from my past as well.

Even with all this, I wonder if anyone will come. There are, after all, no tickets. I look at my watch: It's already 10:30, but Grace's flight has yet to land. Katya soothes, "She's going to come—they're all going to come."

Until noon the hall is empty save a few curious onlookers. Then, beyond the stanchions, they start to arrive in flurries: a few, then a few more. Soon they pile up, hundreds at a time, filling every inch of the museum. And still more are arriving.

And there, finally, is Grace, suitcase in hand, her goldenrod hair shining. We hug and I realize, as I always do, how much I miss her. "I hope you're hungry," I smile. She hugs me tight and swoops Ava into her arms. Tim leads the girls back to where the rest of the family has gathered.

I step out into the rotunda and the waiting crowd. Beside me, a drummer dressed in traditional West African garb pounds out a heartbeat. Children dance around him. When I lock eyes with him, he smiles as he plays, his shoulders dipping up and down in waves.

"I can't believe all these people," I say.

He smiles bigger. "You're the one who did this?" he asks. Even as he speaks, he fills the room with his music, never pausing, never stopping. The beat feels like a lifeline.

I look behind me at the teams of volunteers, the 16 chefs, and the food bank, now buried in canned food donations. In the mix I see the Beards, friends from my motorcycle days, old co-workers, and other mothers—all helping, helping. Behind them, silently waiting in the wings, I see my family and Keith's, too. I can just catch the top of Mom's hair in the farthest corner. I notice that she opted for the black-and-red dress from Pakistan. She has a list of foods to try—on a stack of oversized paper, and I can see her writing, circling, crossing out, erasing. Her brows are knit, every once in a while she exclaims, "Oh! That's going to be *so* good."

I look back at the drummer from Africa.

"It was just an idea, a little dream," I tell him. "All these people, they did this. *They* made it happen."

He nods, and I notice the rhythm of his drum change, the sound softening like the first drop of water melting from a frozen roof.

The farther into the crowd I go, the smaller I feel. I call Keith to my side. "I can't do this alone," I say. "I need you."

We welcome families of all kinds. I hear accents: a woman from Australia, a man from Nigeria. We meet children from Ethiopia, China, France, and the United States. Old faces, new faces: I open my arms to all of them.

Finally the line stirs, and the people move inside the stanchions. Families pile food on their plates, moving slowly, reading the signs, learning about the dishes and their country of origin. Many sample something from every continent. Children show their parents what they've found.

Keith and I help Ava build her plate. After all these tastings, she chooses pasta salad and cookies. But even these aren't ordinary: The buckwheat noodles from Montenegro are tossed with feta and cracked black pepper. The Maltese cookies are filled with marzipan.

Tim, a video camera strapped to his forehead, has piled mounds of food from as many countries as he can manage. "I'm going to catch every moment!" he calls, weaving around the professional film crew.

I look over at Mom, and see she's made a plate, too, with *saag paneer*, the famous spinach and cheese dish from India. I realize that she's changed out of the Pakistani dress into a beryl-and-gold silk skirt from India.

She tests a spoonful. "Oh WOW, this is so good." The exclamation turns a few heads, but I laugh. This is my *mother*. Like her, I burst out enthusiastically when I bite into something delicious.

"I'm proud of you," Keith says, squeezing my shoulder as he looks over the tables. "You must be so happy."

Even as I nod, I know it's not that simple. Happiness is not a destination: Being happy takes constant weeding, a tending of emotions and circumstances as they arise. There's no happily ever after, or any one person or place that can bring happiness. It takes work to be calm in the midst of turmoil. But releasing the need to control it—well, that's a start.

"Let's just say I feel a . . . settling," I say as I lean on Keith's shoulder.

My thoughts drift to Michael. I wonder what he'd think about this feast. I picture him running through the crowd, grabbing his fill. So many years after his death, my mind plays tricks on me. He's now my *little* brother—my lost, little 14-year-old brother, awkward with braces and bursting with too-big feelings. I cannot quite see his eyes or face anymore. The details have faded. And yet, like a shooting star, he seems brighter somehow, more memorable than the billion others that blink at me from the sky night after night.

This is his gift, this feast. Unexpected as it was, his bequest led me to question what I wanted from life. But this place, this moment, is unlike *Babette's Feast*. There are no chairs, no formal plates, no quail or turtle. Instead—a thawing of a crowd, mountains of simple, easy food, from a world of people.

This feast is alive.

One woman has scavenged a lunch tray—from where, I don't know. She's balanced three heaped plates, two bowls, and a few cups onto it. Her small children surround her, also carrying plates.

How hungry they seem. It's against the rules, taking so much. I wonder what their story is.

I glance over at Mom, head bowed over her plate. I know what she'd say if she saw them: "Good for them!" And if I protested, she'd say, "There'll be enough. One way or another, there's always enough. They wouldn't be taking it if they didn't need it."

And perhaps that's been Mom's secret all along: her brutal common sense that slices through any and all notions of what "should" be. From our living room kitchen back in Jamaica Plain to this global table, it's been about getting our fill. Not just of food, but of the intangible things we all need: acceptance, love, and understanding.

This is not the time to turn people away, but to pile them in, in greater heaps than ever—the way we did in Mom's living room kitchen. Perhaps this feast is my own living room kitchen, where everyone lives and breathes in one jumbled space. Where we bump elbows as we cook, laugh even as we chew, track the dirt in and clean it up later. Where there is enough room, enough space.

Even without enough chairs, we can stand, all of us—even those who might come later. We'll make room. Take our fill. Though I'd always be wandering, I can always create a living room kitchen, wherever I am.

I smile, hoping they get their fill.

~⚬

After the feast, the adventure staggers on for another month and then ends quietly with just Keith, Ava, and me around our small table with the oven door open, blowing warmth into the kitchen. On the wall, the stirring pot gleams with a dull luster.

My global table adventure ends with roasted squash three ways, and mini Zimbabwe candy cakes called *chikenduza*, found in big-city bakeries. The dense, yeast-risen balls of dough balloon in the oven to become equal parts cake, muffin, and bread. One fills my palm perfectly.

The texture is chewy and tight, but my Zimbabwean readers assure me that this is correct. Ava, now four, helps me drape the craggy domes with the traditional bubblegum-pink icing. Mouths watering, we relinquish the perky chikenduza to the spot by our plates where our water glasses might go.

I'd mistakenly thought we ought to have someone over when we cooked our last meal for Zimbabwe. From the beginning of the blog, I'd imagined a crowd for this meal, to celebrate with us. But we'd already had the big feast. As important as it is to free-fall into the jumble and chaos of community, there must be quiet moments, too, in the intimacy of family.

The blushing tops of our chikenduza dry to a matte luster, tempting us even as we eat our squash. A whole meal of squash seems a curious thing, but there's winter in the air, and their sugared warmth promises comfort.

We start with pumpkin dusted with cinnamon—a twist of my mother's, too. Then there's "gem," squash stuffed with corn and cheese then roasted until crackling brown. I use more readily available acorn squash, split and seeded. After the flesh roasts for the better part of an hour, it takes on the flavor of roasted chestnuts—striking when paired with the sweet corn and salt of cheese.

Finally, we spoon butternut squash smashed with peanut butter, called *nhopi:* a salty-sweet side dish, the peanut more whisper than shout, especially if coaxed smooth with an immersion blender—then it is velvet.

When the last of the too-sweet icing is licked from our fingers, I hold Ava on my hip and we look at the world map, now covered with gemstones. They twinkle like 200 jeweled bindis, the South Asian mark of the sixth chakra, seat of concealed wisdom, balance.

"Can we start cooking the world all over again, Mama?" Ava asks.

She knows no time before this adventure, no feast before eating the world. A rush of sentimentality overcomes me. I blink and when I open my eyes, I half-expect to find a seven-month-old baby nestled in my arms again.

But time waits for no one. I look at her face and see the unrecognizable future—hers and mine, too. Even as I cooked my way around this uncharted world, there were constant bridges to the past, beginning with the apricots of Afghanistan and ending with Mom's beloved cinnamon on pumpkin. Now I know my food is inextricably tied to the past. It always will be.

Though I may not have secured a new future, I'd secured something much better by filling those empty spice jars nearly four years ago. Cooking the world has opened my eyes to other ways of being, loving, and mothering. Most importantly, it has taught me to savor the present moment, sinking into the ephemeral like the ripe fruit that it is. There's an ease about not knowing what will come next—an ease I never could have felt before.

Each bite is a flash of the past and the present.

After Ava goes to bed and Keith retires for the night, I walk through the kitchen and pluck a crumb from the hard tile. I feel the sharp, dry edge against my scarred fingertips and an immense, immeasurable love washes over me.

Zimbabwe Peanut Butter & Butternut Mash | Nhopi

The punch of salty peanut butter with sweet squash is a celebration of opposing forces—one I wish I might have encountered years ago. Though a spoon of this puree might not have altered the rough-and-tumble course of my life, it surely helps confirm my long-held suspicions: There is much delight to be had in a spoon of the unconventional.

1 hefty butternut squash
A good ¼ cup natural creamy peanut butter
Salt or sugar

Finishing touches:
A handful of crushed peanuts

Peel, cube, and steam butternut squash for about 30 minutes or until a fork sinks easily into the flesh. Next, mash the peanut butter into the squash with a little salt or sugar. To get a silky smooth texture, use an immersion blender. If the mash remains stiff, thin with a little water.

Sprinkle with crushed peanuts and serve hot. Smile.

Enough for 2 to 4 as a side dish

Acknowledgments

I T IS ONE THING TO GIVE, but another thing entirely to give exactly what is needed. I have been blessed by such generosity my entire life, and this book would have never been written without the loving, purposeful support of my family, friends, editors, and agent. They led me through the memoir writing process, helping me share a story that I hope will show others that peace can come, even after turmoil.

Thanks to my husband, Keith, and daughter, Ava, for being my champions. Not only did they endure my four-year marathon of cooking the world, but they supported me as old grief resurfaced and during frequent absences at hotels, cafés, and bakeries as I immersed myself into the world of my past. Thanks to Mom—not only for being my friend, but also for waiting patiently for me to realize that she *is* my friend. Thanks to my loving siblings for their trust; without their support I may never have had the nerve to share my story. Thanks to Keith's son and family for bringing me into the fold so readily—their unquestioning acceptance is a gift. And thanks to the families who have cared for me through the years. Without their support, who knows where I would be.

Thanks to my agent and cheerleader, Lisa DiMona, who enthusiastically pushed me to share my story, along with Caitlin Ellis, Jean Garnett, Henry Ginna, and Julie Trelstad. Without Lisa's fearless optimism, I may never have sought out a contract in the first place.

I'm incredibly grateful to National Geographic for taking the leap with me. Thanks especially to my editor Hilary Black, who never let me tell the easy truth but pushed me to dig deeper every step of the way. She taught me that not all stories have to be dark, but every story needs depth. Thanks also to Janet Goldstein and Anne Smyth for many wise insights along the way, to Jonathan Halling for his artistic grace, and to Heidi Vincent, Heidi Egloff, Ann Day Saperstein, and Lauren Hodapp for their impressive marketing and publicity contributions. Warm gratitude to Patricia Mulcahy for her wisdom and humor as she helped me rein in my meandering prose. In the process she taught me not only to trust the reader, but also to trust myself. Cheers and chuckles go to my copy editor, Heather McElwain. Because of her I now know that the possessive form of Paris is in fact Paris's—a detail that escaped me not only during the three years I lived in the city but for decades afterward.

As I wrote this book, I relied on so many fellow writers, whose warmth and humor refueled me as I worked. Kelly Crow's pep talks went beyond technical advice to teach me about the contract between writer and reader. Because of her, "Carry the reader through to the end" became a catchphrase through many late-night writing sessions. When my writing got muddled with emotion Marina Teper and Rebekah Shannon steadied me with calming logic. Tina Nettles always asked the right questions to get me back on track. Much appreciation goes to my other devoted readers, many from

Write Process and Harwelden Writers' Group: Terry Collins, Steve Chalmers, Jamie Naifeh, Barry Parks, and Gina Conroy. Thanks also to those writers whose work has provided endless inspiration—in particular, the mouthwatering brilliance of Nigel Slater and Jeanette Walls's uncanny ability to convey the fourth dimension of love.

So many friends and colleagues took the time to test recipes, help with research, or otherwise cheer me on: Judy Allen, Heather Anderson, Tony Ash, Alexandra Bergman, Julie Bielza, Bodean Seafood Market, Danielle Carlotti-Smith, Karen Coates, Gina Conroy, Ken Downey, Malorie Farrington, Raquel Fagan, Annie Ferris, Chris Guillebeau, Sophie Herbert, Laura Kelley, Robert Johnson, Morgan M. Kuhn with PBS, Anitra Lavanhar, Carla Lechner, Ruby Libertus, Shane Maak, Jamie Magurno, Janine Maraviglia, Andee Marksamer, Jill Meredith, Becky Morales, Tina Nettles, Dan Noll, Marianne Oliver, Dr. Mary Parker, Elke Säubert, Brian Schwartz, Audrey Scott, Rebekah Shannon, Brigid Santiago, Amanda Simcoe, Janine Smith, Homa Sabet Tavangar, Marina Teper, Steven Wooley, and Jonathan Wooley. Their kindness will always be remembered with a smile.

I cannot begin to explain how much I appreciate the efforts of all those who helped make the Global Table Experience come true: Philbrook Museum, for donating their grounds—especially Jeff Martin, for unequivocally embracing and supporting my idea for the Global Table Experience, and Meghan Hurley of Concepts PR for bringing it to life along with ABCO Rents, Angela Evans, Argie Lewis Flowers, Eisenhower School, J. Traczyk Creative, Restaurant Equipment & Supply, Amanda Waller, Jason Burks, Retrospec Films, Rebekah Shannon, Andrea Leitch, and countless other volunteers. Thanks, too, to all the cooking schools and caterers who came together to create recipes from 176 countries in the world with no expectations of payment or compensation: Chef Howard and all of Culinary Institute of Platt College, Mike Mitchell of Blue Label Bartending,

Kenny Wagoner of Cancer Treatment Centers of America, Rob Stuart of Chimera, Jonathan Haring of Deco Restaurant Group, Gary Copper of Euro-Mart, Annie Ferris and all of Global Gardens, Hale High School Culinary Program, Justin Thompson (of Juniper, PRHYME, and Tavolo), Miranda Kaiser of Laffa, Libby Auld of Elote and The Vault, Candace Conley of The Girl Can Cook!, Tuck Curren of Biga Italian Restaurant, Michael Yip and all of Tulsa Technology Center, Whole Foods Market of Tulsa, and Family and Children's Services, especially Dianne Hughes and the Women In Recovery Culinary Creations Program.

Thank you to the readers of GlobalTableAdventure.com, who unwaveringly supported my mission of creating peace and understanding through food.

And finally, thanks to those who have been in my life now or in the past, who have shown me love unconditionally or conditionally, who have given me support when I couldn't appreciate it, and who have lifted me up when it seemed like I could only fall down. I love you.

Recipe Index

Hungry for More?

If you'd like to try even more recipes from around the world, you can access the 650+ recipes Keith, Ava, and I tried for free at www .GlobalTableAdventure.com. Several are listed from each country. New subscribers will receive a free copy of our Global Table Adventure Starter Kit—an invaluable tool for anyone looking to cook their way around the world. Special recipes, discussion guides, and other resources are also available for your book club.

Follow my latest adventures:

 Global Table Adventure

 @GlobalTable

 @globaltable

 Global Table

#LifeFromScratch